AFTER UNITY

Modern German Studies

A Series of the German Studies Association

This series offers books on modern and contemporary Germany, concentrating on themes in history, political science, literature and German culture. Publications will include original works in English and English translations of significant works in other languages.

Volume 1:

Germany's New Politics
Parties and Issues in the 1990s
Edited by David Conradt, Gerald R. Kleinfeld, George K. Romoser and Christian Søe

Volume 2:

After Unity
Reconfiguring German Identities
Edited by Konrad Jarausch

Volume 3:

Beyond 1989
Re-reading German Literary History since 1945
Edited by Keith Bullivant

AFTER UNITY

Reconfiguring German Identities

Edited by

Konrad H. Jarausch

Berghahn Books
Providence • Oxford

First published in 1997 by

Berghahn Books

© Konrad H. Jarausch 1997

Library of Congress Cataloging-in-Publication Data

```
After unity : reconfiguring German identities / edited by Konrad H.
  Jarausch.
      p.   cm. -- (Modern German studies ; 2)
   Includes bibliographical references and index.
   ISBN 1-57181-040-4 (alk. paper). -- ISBN 1-57181-041-2 (alk.
paper)
   1. Germany--Politics and government--1990-  2. Political culture-
-Germany.  3. Germany--Ethnic relations.   I. Jarausch, Konrad H.
II. Series: Modern German studies (Providence, R.I.) ; vol. 2.
DD290.29.A36  1997
320.943--dc21                                              97-2040
                                                              CIP
```

British Library Cataloguing in Publication Data

A catalogue record for this book is available from the
British Library.

Printed in the United States on acid-free paper.

CONTENTS

PREFACE

Lack of information on current German developments makes it difficult to follow, let alone understand them in the U.S. Except for spectacular incidents, the media tend to cover controversies over the Holocaust, such as the Goldhagen debate, in greater detail than the present transformation of the center of Europe. While it is important "never to forget," preoccupation with the past reinforces old images of Germany as the dark "other," the counterpoint to Western democracy. Since such stereotyping blinds even perceptive commentators like Jane Kramer ("The Politics of Memory" *The New Yorker*, August 14, 1995), American intellectuals often know more about the nagging failures than the impressive successes of the Federal Republic in the half-century since 1945. This discrepancy between prior conceptions and present realities would not matter, were the Germans not becoming the pivotal force in the European Union on the continent.

For over two decades concerned scholars have tried to remedy this deficit by combining their efforts in a German Studies that ranges across the humanities and social sciences. On the organizational level these initiatives have created a burgeoning association, well-attended annual meetings, and a flourishing journal, the *German Studies Review*. In pedagogical terms, this attempt has produced useful curricular guidelines and enriched materials for highschool and college teaching. But intellectually the results have proven rather disappointing so far, since the high-flown rhetoric of trans-disciplinary cooperation is all too often ignored in actual research. Entrenched opposition to building bridges between the fields with methodologies such as poststructuralist linguistics or cultural studies suggests that only an effort to wrestle with the same intellectual problem can break down the walls between the different disciplines.

This volume is an experiment in practicing cross-disciplinary collaboration through the writing of co-authored texts. Representing diverse ages, genders, ethnic backgrounds, and institutional affiliations, its contributors constitute a cross-section of North American scholarship on modern Germany in political science, history, and German literature. They came together as experts in a particular subject who were willing to engage in an interdisciplinary adventure without fixed rules and with an uncertain outcome. In order to structure their broad-ranging interaction, they agreed to address five flashpoints of public debates: the politics of memory, the question of multiculturalism, the issue of Eastern integration, the gender struggle over abortion, and the role of Germany within

Europe. The purpose of this exemplary effort is the presentation of a multi-vocal, and yet focused examination of major areas of current controversy in German society, culture, and politics.

Achieving a constructive cooperation proved, however, more difficult than imagined. Getting such varied academics to speak with rather than past each other was complicated by the invisible boundaries of the respective disciplines, which made for numerous tensions. Distinctive agendas lead to clashes over the framing of the questions, methodological approaches to the material, and modes of interpretation. Different ideological positions also produced contention over the representation and evaluation of controversial German points of view. Because of the wide range of intellectual styles the production of joint texts that address common questions while yet providing distinctive answers required more extensive editing than expected. In order to reflect on these experiences, a postscript addresses the methodological, political and practical difficulties of interdisciplinarity in German Studies.

By harnessing some of the excitement of intellectual border-crossing this thematic collaboration has nonetheless yielded remarkable insights that transcend the constraints of a single ideology or discipline. The contending political orientations, ranging from Marxism or feminism to liberalism as well as conservatism made for creative tensions which forced contributors to re-examine their unspoken assumptions. The contrasting methodologies that rely on positional readings of literary texts, hermeneutic examination of historical documents, or theoretical generalization from statistical evidence helped to illuminate different dimensions of the respective questions. The combination of distinctive intellectual styles into a single essay created multi-layered texts which provide a more comprehensive exploration of the issues. By being alive to a greater range of problematics than a single approach, this interdisciplinary interaction offers an extraordinarily rich reading of recent German debates.

The success of this undertaking owes special thanks to a number of institutions and individuals. The German Academic Exchange Service (Heidrun Suhr) and the College of Arts and Sciences of the University of North Carolina at Chapel Hill generously funded a preliminary conference in April 1994. The coordinator of the UNC/Duke Center for European Studies, Ruth Mitchell-Pitts, tirelessly facilitated the interaction of the participants with technical assistance. As commentators Claudia Koonz, Stefan Immerfall, Siegfried Mews, and Julia Hell helped direct the revisions of the papers with incisive suggestions. When Antonia Grunenberg proved unable to participate in the symposium, Christiane Lemke generously offered to extend her comments into a substantive contribution. As participant-observer, the Canadian-German political economist Andreas Pickel agreed to provide a concluding reflection on strategies of interdisciplinary cooperation in German Studies.

The purpose of this volume is to share the debates of well-informed experts in German Studies with interested readers. A general introduction into the problem, thorough annotations to the individual chapters and a concluding postscript hope to make the content, interpretation and methodology more accessible. To give proper credit for authorship, the name of the contributor who took the lead in drafting the joint essay is always listed first, with the others following according to the sequence of their sections. As paradigmatic examples of intellectual collaboration, these contributions seek to demonstrate the potential gains of a closer cooperation in German Studies that progresses from a loose multidisciplinarity to a more systematic interdisciplinarity. By providing some fresh evidence, these reflections on post-unification changes also hope to stimulate a more informed debate about the problems and prospects of the new Germany.

Konrad H. Jarausch, Berlin and Chapel Hill, October 1996

RESHAPING GERMAN IDENTITIES

Reflections on the Post-Unification Debate

Konrad H. Jarausch

uring the last two centuries German identities have been more unsettled than the self-conceptions of most European countries. In contrast to the established nation-states of England and France, the political organization of Central Europe has been unstable, with states, boundaries, and constitutions changing virtually every generation. The religious, class, and ethnic divisions among German speakers have been so profound as to override common allegiances and to push many people who did not fit the dominant pattern into emigration. Belated industrialization transformed the tranquil countryside with greater speed than among neighboring countries, creating a deep chasm between rural roots and urban society.[1] Is it any wonder that in such a turbulent place loyalties grew confused and the collective sense of self remained uncertain?

The rapid changes of the modern era have left both insiders and outsiders at a loss about the precise meaning of Germanness. Self-descriptions and foreign characterizations developed contradictory stereotypes that range, for instance, from thinkers and poets to ruthless industrialists, from bumbling pacifists to swaggering imperialists, from

---

1. As problematic introductions, cf. Harold James, *A German Identity, 1770-1990* (New York, 1990) and the special issue of the *German Studies Review* on "German Identity," (Winter 1992).

earnest republicans to racist Nazis, from inventive engineers to anti-technological ecologists.[2] Because of the frequent transformations, attempts to distill the essence of German identity into national character traits have been largely doomed to failure. Nonetheless, Germans keep searching for a collective sense of themselves, while outside commentators continue trying to define what these perplexing people might really be like.

Just when the postwar division seemed to be on the way to providing some definitive answers, the collapse of communism once again upset all certainties. In both West and East, the excesses of nationalism in the Third Reich had led to a series of flights from Germanness into such disparate directions as cultural Americanization, political Sovietization, or normative Europeanization, just to mention a few. Due to the burden of guilt, many intellectuals had redefined Germanness as denying being German at all, even if this revulsion implied an inverted identity of shame. But the unforeseen return of the nation-state through unification blocked these escape routes and forced Germans once again to confront themselves as a people.[3] The subsequent crisis of ideological beliefs has initiated another round of redefinitions of what it could or should mean to be German at the end of the twentieth century.

In the wake of unity, talk about the emergence of a new German identity has become the rage in the media as well as in academe. On both sides of the Atlantic symposia have been convened under this heading, perhaps aspiring through the combination of two murky topics to achieve a profounder kind of clarity.[4] As many as one-tenth of all panels at the 1995 German Studies Association Meeting referred to identity in some fashion, with about half stressing individual development and the others emphasizing national self-conceptions.[5] In recent books such diverse subjects as the construction of the human body, the memory of the holocaust, and new literary trends were somehow covered by the

2. Konrad H. Jarausch, "Huns, Krauts or Good Germans? The German Image in America, 1800-1980," in James F. Harris, ed., *German-American Interrelations: Heritage and Challenge* (Tübingen, 1985), 145-159.

3. Konrad H. Jarausch, *Die unverhoffte Einheit 1989-1990* (Frankfurt, 1995), 323ff.; and "Die postnationale Nation. Zum Identitätswandel der Deutschen 1945-1995," *Historicum* (Spring 1995): 30-35.

4. For example, Peter Eisenmann and Gerhard Hirscher, eds., *Die deutsche Identität und Europa* (Munich, 1991); Eduard J. M. Kroker und Bruno Deschamps, eds., *Die Deutschen auf der Suche nach ihrer neuen Identität?* (Frankfurt, 1993); and Claudia Mayer-Iswandy, ed., *Zwischen Traum und Trauma: Die Nation. Transatlantische Perspektiven zur Geschichte eines Problems* (Tübingen, 1994).

5. German Studies Association, *Program of the Nineteenth Annual Conference* (Tempe, AZ, 1995), 8-13.

same label of identity.[6] This inflation of the term to mean everything and nothing would be enough to make it suspect for analysis, if the Germans were not themselves framing their discussion about their future with the notion of *Identität*.

In spite of the current popularity of the catchword, scholarly treatment of German identity has remained disappointing in depth and scope. During the past decades, literary analysts have primarily looked at pronouncements of intellectual figures and commented on attempts to construct a national literature from an aesthetic or a critical perspective.[7] Historians have probed the ideological seductiveness of nationalism, explored the social carriers of its program, sometimes even pursued their economic interests and, above all, denounced the disastrous consequences of its implementation.[8] Searching for a broader theory, political scientists have favored empirical opinion surveys in order to construct national stereotypes or to probe conflicts in political culture.[9] Because identity is often used as an empty label or as a foil for speculative commentary, the question has rarely been posed systematically.

The limitations of such approaches to national self-conceptions might be overcome by a more interdisciplinary perspective. Diatribes against the recurrence of nationalism, surveys of normative pronouncements or symposia on political behavior have yielded unconvincing results, because most investigate only one aspect of their topic, employ simplistic methodology, and argue from the vantage point of a single discipline.[10] Otherwise informative balance sheets, drawn up five years after unification also remain somewhat inconclusive, as they

6. Barbara Heimannsberg and Christoph J. Schmidt, eds., *The Collective Silence: German Identity and the Legacy of Shame* (San Francisco, 1993); Leslie A. Adelson, *Making Bodies, Making History: Feminism and German Identity* (Lincoln, NE, 1993); and Arthur Williams, Stuart Parkes, and Roland Smith, eds., *German Literature at a Time of Change, 1989-90: German Unity and German Identity in Literary Perspective* (Bern, 1991).

7. Hinrich C. Seeba, "'Einigkeit und Recht und Freiheit': The German Quest for National Identity in the Nineteenth Century," in Peter Börner, ed., *Concepts of National Identity: An Interdisciplinary Dialogue* (Baden-Baden, 1986): 153-166 as well as "Germany – a Literary Concept? The Myth of National Literature," *German Studies Review* 17 (1994): 353-369.

8. Otto Dann, *Nation und Nationalismus in Deutschland 1770-1990* (Munich, 1994), 2nd ed.; and Hagen Schulze, *Staat und Nation in der europäischen Geschichte* (Munich, 1994).

9. Werner Weidenfeld, ed., *Die Identität der Deutschen* (Bonn, 1983); and Elisabeth Noelle-Neumann with Renate Köcher, *Die verletzte Nation. Über den Versuch der Deutschen, ihren Charakter zu ändern* (Stuttgart, 1987).

10. See, for instance, Eric J. Hobsbawm, *Nationen und Nationalismus. Mythos und Realität seit 1780* (Frankfurt, 1991); Studienzentrum Weickersheim, ed., *Deutsche Identität heute* (Stuttgart, 1983); and Rudolf Wildenmann, ed., *Nation und Demokratie. Politisch-strukturelle Gestaltungsprobleme im neuen Deutschland* (Baden-Baden, 1991).

break the subject down into unrelated sectors.[11] Since identity is an elusive, multilayered, and contradictory feeling, any attempt to map its properties requires a more comprehensive view, self-reflective proce-dures, and interdisciplinary cooperation. Only a complex blending of cultural, historical, and political perspectives has a chance to capture the confusing shifts in the intellectual, psychological and political definitions of Germanness.

1. Approaches to National Identity

Perhaps some methodological reflections on the concept of identity can help set the stage for a more focused debate. Skeptics wonder whether one should even bother to analyze something that may prove unfathomable and that may make little difference in understanding actual events. But such defeatism is misplaced for several reasons. First, self-conceptions serve to impart meaning to the world and offer important clues to the core beliefs of a subject. Second, identities define attitudes towards one's surroundings that operate as important constraints for political decisions by facilitating some and excluding others. And finally, such self-definitions also powerfully influence actual behavior, especially in crisis situations that require existential choices based as much on emotion as on reason.[12] Instead of giving up on this vexing concept, scholars therefore ought to try clarifying its essential properties.

Identity is one of those "common sense" terms that prove quite difficult to define analytically. Following popular usage, the historian Christian Meier suggests that it is an "answer to the question of who somebody is," a sense of self as distinct from others that provides conti-nuity through the many changes of a lifetime. However, a quick look at the semantic history of the concept indicates that it is by no means a self-evident category but rather an elaborate academic construct. Proposed by Erik H. Erikson, it was initially a psychotherapeutic perspective that focused primarily on the inner development of a personality during the

11. For instance, Ralf Altenhof and Eckhard Jesse, eds., *Das wiedervereinigte Deutsch-land. Zwischenbilanz und Perspektiven* (Düsseldorf, 1995); Martin Diewald and Karl-Ulrich Mayer, eds., *Zwischenbilanz der Wiedervereinigung. Struturwandel und Mobilität im Trans-formationsprozess* (Opladen, 1996); Robert Hettlage and Karl Lenz, eds., *Deutschland nach der Wende. Eine Bilanz* (Munich, 1995); and Peter H. Merkl, ed., *The Federal Republic of Germany at Forty-Five: Union without Unity* (New York, 1995).

12. Comments by Mitchell Ash at the 1995 GSA meeting. Cf. also Werner Weiden-feld, "Identität," *Handwörterbuch zur deutschen Einheit* (Frankfurt, 1992), 376-383.

life-cycle and its attendant "identity crises".[13] Only after the end of World War II was this individual psychological notion extended to groups and even nations in order to explain the puzzling behavior of America's totalitarian enemies.

Instead of stressing singularity, role and reference group theory emphasizes that identities develop in interaction with others. Every "I" belongs to numerous plural "we's" as part of a family, town, profession and the like. People may be born into some of these categories such as gender and race without individual option, but they have considerably more freedom in choosing other associations in their leisure activities, careers, mates, etc. Both involuntary and voluntary associations exert loyalty claims which often clash, such as the demands of being German and Jewish in the Third Reich. As personalities, human beings represent a series of individual selections from among competing potential identifications which overlap and blend in a particular way that makes up a self. Unlike the inherited sense of community in traditional society, individual self-conception in a modern setting tends to be the result of conscious self-reflection.[14]

As a more flexible alternative to an essentialist view of national character, the identity perspective suggests that nations can also construct a certain sense of their own self.[15] Transposed to a metaphorical level, the notion of a collective personality describes a feeling of belonging to a larger community by sharing its language, history, and purpose, which are justified and held together by a store of cultural myths and symbols. But its precise contours are difficult to determine, since they are fiercely contested among rival parties, ideologies, and interests, which advocate their own national vision in prescriptive prose in order to make it prevail over others. Instead of residing in a single unified definition, a nation's self-conception is therefore more likely to be found in the competing discourses about what it ought to be. Whatever version achieves a measure of cultural hegemony at any given time is generally assumed to express the common identification of a polity.[16]

13. Christian Meier, *Die Nation, die keine sein will* (Munich, 1991); and Philip Gleason, "Identifying Identity: A Semantic History," *Journal of American History*, 69 (1983): 910-931.

14. Jürgen Habermas, "Können komplexe Gesellschaften eine vernünftige Identität ausbilden?" in Jürgen Habermas and Dieter Henrich, *Zwei Reden* (Frankfurt, 1974), 57-59; and Georg Weber, "Identität als Problem der Moderne," *Die Deutschen auf der Suche nach ihrer neuen Identität?*, 15-34.

15. Hagen Schulze, ed., *Nation-Building in Central Europe* (Oxford, 1987); and Benedict Anderson, *Die Erfindung der Nation. Zur Karriere eines erfolgreichen Konzepts* (Frankfurt, 1988).

16. For such a culturalist perspective see Geoff Eley and Ronald G. Suny, eds., *Becoming National: A Reader* (Oxford, 1996).

On the nation-state level, identity does not consist merely of symbolic visions but also involves actual political practices. As the development of modern nationalism demonstrates, there is a fundamental difference between the West European pattern of creating a common citizenry within pre-existing patrimonial states and Central or East European nation-building that begins with a cultural reawakening, fosters a national movement and only subsequently leads to state creation.[17] Depending upon the circumstances of its origin, the existence of a shared state with a settled constitution and clear borders can either be a precondition or a distant goal for the development of a national identity. Moreover, the construction of collective identifications requires distinctions from rival groups who are often reduced to enemies and invested with negative stereotypes so as to justify one's own separate sense of destiny.

In historical perspective, national identities such as the German sense of self therefore tend to be changing ascriptions rather than fixed properties. While a social sense of solidarity may exist through time, the overriding identification with nation rather than town, region, or supranational entity is a product of that political movement that created the modern nation-state. As Ralf Dahrendorf pointed out nearly three decades ago, the very compulsiveness of nationalism in Central Europe can be interpreted as a desperate attempt to overcome the many forms of fragmentation in that area.[18] As a result of many political, social and economic upheavals, changes in the definition of Germanness during the last centuries were so rapid and fundamental as to make it difficult to distill a stable essence that could be contrasted with a more malleable content.[19] Since any agreement on a given version like the Wilhelmian Empire turned out to be merely provisional, the only thing fixed about Germany seems to have been the continual dispute about what being German might mean.

As a complex and contested process, the construction of national identities involves both intentional and unintentional elements. The propagation of Bavarian loyalties by the Wittelsbach dynasty after the Napoleonic wars indicates that allegiance to a state can be successfully

17. Rogers Brubaker, *Citizenship and Nationhood in France and Germany* (Cambridge, 1992); and M. Rainer Lepsius, *Demokratie in Deutschland. Soziologisch-historische Konstellationsanalysen* (Göttingen, 1993).

18. Thomas M. Gauly, *Die Last der Geschichte. Kontroversen zur deutschen Identität* (Cologne, 1988); and Ralf Dahrendorf, *Society and Democracy in Germany* (Garden City, N.J., 1967).

19. Hans-Ulrich Wehler, "Nationalismus und Nation in der deutschen Geschichte," in Helmut Berding, ed., *Nationales Bewußtsein und kollektive Identität* (Frankfurt, 1994), in contrast to Gregory Flynn, ed., *Remaking the Hexagon: The New France in the New Europe* (Boulder, CO, 1995).

fostered from above by the conscious creation of new symbols. But the resistance of national minorities to the Germanizing efforts of the Second Empire also illustrates the potential for popular rejection of imposed conceptions in the name of alternative attachments.[20] In their imaginative debates, intellectuals might develop complex rationalizations for collective self-definitions; but only when the media simplify and translate their proposals into emotional appeals do they begin to sway mass sentiment. Seen in this light, national identities consist of layers of symbolic residues that serve, by rejecting competing claims, to mobilize popular feeling in favor of allegiance to their own state.

Analyzing such a perplexing phenomenon therefore requires a combination of linguistic, social science, and historical perspectives. Postmodern approaches are particularly useful, because they seek to identify the discourses that promote certain self-images. The deconstruction of texts can uncover the politics of identity claims and guard against conflating description with prescription. But more traditional social science methods also continue to be useful for measuring public opinion over time in order to get at its frequent transformations. In regard to demographic or economic issues, the establishment of a firm database allows generalizations beyond fleeting impressions which reduce the numinous quality of the subject. Finally, historical sensibility is essential for understanding the importance of changes in memory and representation for self-conception. A temporal perspective might expose the dangers of perpetuating one's own national prejudice in the guise of scholarship about another country.[21] Since identity rests on perception, its analysis demands a special effort at self-reflexiveness.

These conceptual preconsiderations raise a series of questions about the nature of the renewed debate on German identity. First, the importance of context suggests a need to reflect on the impact of the caesura of 1989-90 which, by upsetting prior certainties, triggered the most recent round of soul-searching. Second, viewing identity as contested implies the necessity of identifying the key issues, speakers, and interests that dominate the public discussion. Third, the centrality of unifying discourses requires an exploration of the pattern of controversy

20. Norbert A. Mayr, *Particularism in Bavarian State Policy and Public Sentiment, 1806-1906* (Ph.D. diss. University of North Carolina at Chapel Hill, 1988); and William Hagen, *Germans, Poles and Jews. The Nationality Conflict in the Prussian East, 1772-1914* (Chicago, 1980). Cf. also Celia Applegate, *A Nation of Provincials* (Berkeley, 1991).

21. Michael Geyer and Konrad H. Jarausch, "Great Men and Postmodern Ruptures: Overcoming the 'Belatedness' of German Historiography," *German Studies Review* 18 (1995): 253ff., and the subsequent debate on H-German net.

across specific topics to distinguish competing visions of self-conception for the enlarged FRG. And finally, the politicization of national self-conceptions makes it imperative to ponder the most recent choices between these alternatives in order to understand the direction of the puzzling changes that will make up the new Germany.

2. The Unification Shock

The importance of the rupture of 1989-90 has more often been asserted in general than demonstrated in detail. The endless debates of prior decades about division as punishment for Nazi crimes, ways of reuniting the German states, or measures to maintain human and cultural ties have suddenly ceased.[22] Instead, public rhetoric has shifted to proclamations of the end of the Second World War, the Cold War, and the postwar era, without yet being able to clarify the precise implications of these developments for German self-consciousness. Opinion surveys have begun to chart shifts in collective attitudes towards key policy issues that were triggered by the process of unification in East and West Germany.[23] While their initial results suggest both major changes and astounding continuities, any evaluation of their meaning must remain tentative, because the process of reorientation is still underway and the outcome not yet definitive.

Before unification, Germans were, in spite of some remaining similarities, well on their way to developing separate identities in their competing states. Because of a surprisingly high level of European and international orientation, surveys revealed little overt pride in being German in the West. But at the same time, there was much sense of economic accomplishment, considerable trust in the social safety net, and a certain attachment to the Basic Law *(Verfassungspatriotismus)*. In the East, the SED's effort to create a separate consciousness of a socialist nation was less successful, but people shared some social solidarity and a certain satisfaction in coping with difficult circumstances.[24] In Austria the claim to have been Hitler's first victim and the adoption of neutral-

22. Lest one forget, Konrad Adenauer Stiftung, ed., *Heimat und Nation. Zur Geschichte und Identität der Deutschen* (Mainz, 1984).

23. "Stolz aufs eigene Leben," *Der Spiegel* 27 (1995): 40-52. Cf. Elisabeth Noelle-Neumann, *Demoskopische Geschichtsstunden. Vom Wartesaal der Geschichte zur Deutschen Einheit* (Zürich, 1991).

24. Bernhard Schweigler, *Nationalbewußtsein in der BRD und der DDR* (Düsseldorf, 1973); and Volker Gransow, "National Identity and Non-Identity as Problems of the Two German Societies," *Studies in GDR Culture and Society* 3 (Boston, 1983): 13-26.

ity reinforced the turn to a distinct nationality.[25] Though Westerners were closer to developing a new patriotism than their Eastern counterparts, a sense of cultural community lingered and there was an underlying feeling that the national issue had not yet been resolved.

The democratic awakening during the fall of 1989 revealed many postwar loyalties to be precarious, especially in the GDR. The whole elaborate structure of two separate states, linked by rivalry and cooperation in *Ostpolitik*, crumbled when the Eastern population could vocalize its desire for a more democratic political system and an improved living standard without fear of reprisals. Living in the smaller and less fortunate part of the country, the East Germans had always looked more to Bonn than West Germans had to East Berlin. It should not have been surprising that the silent majority in the GDR demanded help from the West and the FRG leadership responded to their appeal on grounds of national solidarity, even if that notion was no longer accepted by the younger generation. During the upheaval of 1989-90 an older set of identities resurfaced with elemental strength and eventually superseded many of the newer postwar identifications.[26]

This historic rupture was bound to have a profound effect on German identities. In the East the disappearance of the separate state and its ruling party threatened to devalue a considerable part of individual lives that were tied to them and required the construction of substitute identifications through pride in the new states. The price of the immense readjustment from a planned economy to a market system and from a tutelary state to a democracy was personal anguish and political confusion, which is fueling the *(N)ostalgie* of the PDS. Due to the euphoria of winning the Cold War, Westerners only gradually realized that the old FRG had also disappeared and that their previously comfortable existence was threatened not just by massive transfer payments but by new political responsibilities.[27] Ironically, the accomplishment of the rhetorical aim of reunification has left German politics with a curious void of purpose beyond the completion of internal unity.

The result of these dramatic changes has been a widespread sense of uncertainty in the old and new states of the FRG. While Easterners

25. Lepsius, *Demokratie in Deutschland*, 246ff.; and Gerhard Botz and Gerald Sprengnagel, eds., *Krisen um Österreichs Zeitgeschichte. Verdrängte Vergangenheit, Österreich-Identität, Waldheim und die Historiker* (Frankfurt, 1994).

26. Elizabeth Pond, *Beyond the Wall: Germany's Road to Unification* (New York, 1993); and Peter Merkl, *German Unification in a European Context* (University Park, 1993).

27. Jochen Maaz, *Gefühlsstau. Ein Psychogramm der DDR* (Berlin, 1990); and *Das gestürzte Volk oder die verunglückte Einheit* (Berlin, 1991). Cf. also Konrad H. Jarausch and Volker Gransow, eds., *Uniting Germany: Documents and Debates* (Providence, RI, 1994), 185ff.

know all too well that they have to learn a whole new set of regulations and behaviors, Westerners are only slowly becoming aware that they might have to rethink their previous rules and values as well in order to develop some new common patterns. This insecurity has been aggravated by a concurrent redistribution of spoils in which Eastern dissidents or Western carpet-baggers have displaced the old Communist elite, ending many a compromised business or research career prematurely.[28] This personnel turnover has added a practical edge to otherwise abstract quarrels about the involvement of literary figures in the regime, the collaboration of leading cadres with the secret service, the use of asylum in place of an immigration policy, or the greater German responsibilities in the international arena.

The unforeseen unification therefore triggered a new conflict for intellectual hegemony in the enlarged Germany. The defeat of communism has fundamentally transformed the conditions for the old ideological confrontation between Left and Right by discrediting the former and bolstering the latter. Newly confident due to their triumph over the East, various economic, moral, and national conservatives are trying to reclaim the ground they had largely lost to the new social movements after the cultural revolution of 1968. At the same time, a motley group of feminists, environmentalists, pacifists, moderate social democrats, and ex-communists is attempting to stamp its own progressive agenda on the reunited state.[29] Because it overthrew many pragmatically accepted postwar certainties, the return of national unity necessarily unleashed another round of reconfiguring of identities.

The early 1990s represent yet another redefining moment in German history. After every collapse, in 1918, 1933, and 1945, the new regime viciously criticized what had previously gone wrong in order to set itself off from its predecessor. The victorious party saw its ascendancy as a chance to implement its ideological blueprint, which sought to transform not only the form of government but also the political beliefs of its citizens. At the same time the disruption of the implosion demanded solutions to practical problems that often ran counter to the high-flown ideological aims.[30] The 1989-90 caesura has reenacted that pattern with

28. Jürgen Kocka, *Die Vereinigungskrise. Zur Geschichte der Gegenwart* (Göttingen, 1995), 64ff.

29. Konrad H. Jarausch, "Normalisierung oder Re-Nationalisierung? Zur Umdeutung der deutschen Vergangenheit," *Geschichte und Gesellschaft* 21 (1995): 559-572.

30. Carola Stern and Heinrich August Winkler, eds., *Wendepunkte deutscher Geschichte 1848-1990* (Frankfurt, 1994); and Konrad H. Jarausch, "Zwischen Niederlage und Befreiung. Das Jahr 1945 und die Kontinuitäten deutscher Geschichte," *Gewerkschaftliche Monatshefte*, May 1995.

a crucial difference: this time only one of two states collapsed and the other in effect took over the former's territory, imposing its own system on the loser. By being generally limited to the East, the latest rupture has created more asymmetrical conditions for redefining self-perceptions than did the broader upheavals of the past.

3. Flash-points of Public Debate

To foreign observers of the German media, many discussions of the 1990s seem disjointed and opaque. The newspapers and talk shows are replete with acrimonious exchanges over sensitive topics which serve as rallying points for particular reference groups. Some issues such as the economic prospects for the East or the financial sacrifices of the West are framed largely in pragmatic terms and seem therefore amenable to political compromise, such as a gradual reduction of the solidarity tax-surcharge for the new states. But other questions, such as revision of the Basic Law or the politics of memory are seen more in an ideological light, which endows them with much emotion and makes communication difficult.[31] Ironically, the latter issues are precisely the ones that seem to define collective identities. Since self-conceptions are rarely debated in global abstractions but rather argued out in concrete controversies, it might be useful to examine a handful of such exemplary cases.

Not surprisingly, one of the most pervasive themes is the debate about the double burden of the German past. The fiftieth anniversaries of the Second World War, commemorating aggression, holocaust, resistance, and defeat were a stark reminder of the excesses of Nazi definitions of racial identity. The inglorious end of the GDR has added another layer of historical questions about legal accountability for the shootings at the Wall and moral responsibility for collaboration with the hated *Stasi*. As the toppling of Lenin statues, the changing of street names, and the quarrel over a holocaust museum illustrate, these controversies are both symbolic contests over public memory and real-life struggles over property ownership, pension rights, and the like.[32] Due to the discrediting of Left anti-fascism as tool of communist repression, one trajectory of refashioning identity is (as the rededication of the Neue Wache as a

31. Cordt Schnibben, "Das deutsche Wesen," *Der Spiegel* (1995) Nr. 50, 118ff.; and Jane Kramer, "The Politics of Memory," *New Yorker*, August 14, 1995.

32. Eberhard Jäckel, "Die doppelte Vergangenheit," *Der Spiegel* 52 (1991): 39ff.; Klaus Sühl, ed., *Vergangenheitsbewältigung 1945-1989. Ein unmöglicher Vergleich?* (Berlin, 1994).

memorial to all "victims of war and repression" shows) the effort to establish anti-totalitarianism as the consensus of united Germany.[33]

Another post-unification debate, much publicized abroad, revolves around the psychological and legal definitions of natives and foreigners. Until they were slowed by demonstrations for tolerance and sharper punishments, incidents of xenophobic violence revealed a shocking extent of popular resentment against Turkish strangers within and asylum seekers without. Attracted by one of the most liberal policies in the world, hundreds of thousands of political and economic refugees had crowded into Germany, overtaxing the municipal welfare system. At the same time the remigration of ethnic Germans from Eastern Europe and the former Soviet Union further strained the tolerance of the working population. When bilingual children of established "guest workers" encountered new Russian-speaking resettlers, questions of who was more "German" and deserved citizenship rights became muddled.[34] Since the Left demands open immigration while the Right seeks to maintain exclusivity, another conflict revolves around the role of multiculturalism in German identity.

Predictably, the difference between East and West that replicates a traditional cultural divide is also a focus of public controversy. On the one hand the Bonn government issues success bulletins that praise the increase of growth rates, the reconstruction of the legal system, the renewal of education, and the like. On the other hand the new states point to the collapse of their industry, high unemployment levels, and public resentment. The ideological polarization of election campaigns has aggravated the clash between these celebratory and catastrophic discourses that exaggerate real aspects into unreal representations. Continuing their self-definition as losers, disappointed Easterners take refuge in a GDR nostalgia that has not only revived some of their products and rock-bands but also fueled the electoral rise of the PDS.[35] By both hindering and helping integration, the transformation of political separation into a defiant regionalism that led Brandenburg to reject a merger with Berlin in May 1996 is yet another problem for self-perception.[36]

33. Christoph Stölzl, ed., *Die Neue Wache unter den Linden. Ein deutsches Denkmal im Wandel der Geschichte* (Berlin, 1993).

34. Hajo Funke, *"Jetzt sind wir dran." Nationalismus im geeinten Deutschland* (Berlin, 1991); and Klaus J. Bade, ed., *Das Manifest der 60. Deutschland und die Einwanderung* (Munich, 1994).

35. "Vor den Kopf geschlagen," *Der Spiegel* 21 (1995): 50ff.; Klaus von Dohnanyi, "Die Lage ist dramatisch," ibid., 75ff.; and Herbert Raisch, "Zur Innovation raumbezogener Identität in Deutschland nach der Vereinigung – Schwerpunkt Ostdeutschland," in Herbert Raisch ed., *Auf dem Weg zur Einheit. Aspekte einer neuen Identität* (Idstein, 1994), 177-197.

36. "Jetzt kommt's drauf an!" *Berliner Rundschau*, May 4, 1996; Senatskanzlei Berlin, *Volksabstimmung zur Länderfusion am 5. Mai '96* (Berlin, 1996). Cf. also Detlef Pollack,

Flaring up with new intensity, gender issues are symbolically and practically involved in the reshaping of national identity. The difference between both systems has inspired constant comparisons between the legal equality and social service of the East and the feminist consciousness and consumer-friendliness of the West. Critics often argue that women were the actual losers of unity, since they suffered higher unemployment levels and lost such supports as universal child- and health-care. Because of the clash between maternalist and pro-choice views, much of the discussion has focused on abortion, which had been routinely available in the East, but was more restricted in the West. While the victorious Right saw unification as a chance to extend compulsory counselling to the new states, the Left wanted to adopt the more liberal GDR practice for the entire FRG.[37] Though both sides worked out a tenuous compromise during the summer of 1995, the recent Bavarian attempt to reinterpret it in a pro-life fashion continues to worry not only feminists.

Finally, Germans are debating their appropriate role in Europe and the world with new intensity. The postwar distancing from nationalism and retreat from *Machtpolitik* no longer seem adequate for the largest and most powerful country on the continent. As protests against the Gulf War showed, inside Germany the accession of the new states initially reinforced pacifist tendencies, based on the suffering of World War Two and the Cold War. But at the same time outside expectations rose for a stronger leadership role in such instances as the admission of the East Central European states into NATO and the EU. Though the majority of the population is loath to give up the hallowed DM in favor of a foreign-sounding European currency, the political elites and parties support the Maastricht process. It still remains to be seen whether the Germans will be able to add a European layer to their regional and national identities or whether they will insist on refocusing their loyalties on the revival of a more traditional national state.[38]

This recapitulation of some of the main areas of controversy yields contradictory impressions about the reshaping of German self-concep-

---

"Alles wandelt sich, nur der Ossi bleibt stets der gleiche?" *Frankfurter Rundschau*, 29. June 29, 1996.

37. See the articles on abortion in the special issue on "Germany and Gender: The Effects of Unification on German Women in the East and the West," *German Politics and Society* 24-25 (Winter 1991-92): 111-141.

38. Arnulf Baring, *Deutschland, was nun?* (Berlin, 1991); and Hans-Peter Schwarz, *Die Zentralmacht Europas. Deutschlands Rückkehr auf die Weltbühne* (Berlin, 1994) versus Hans-Ulrich Wehler, "Angst for der Macht? Die Machtlust der Neuen Rechten" (Bonn, 1995), Nr. 8. of the *Gesprächskreis Geschichte* of the Friedrich-Ebert-Stiftung.

tions. No doubt, unification has eroded many of the postwar assumptions which had, especially in the East, aided in dealing with past guilt and in coping with present problems. Yet despite the altered circumstances the ideological camps show an extraordinary tenacity in attempting to provide coherent readings of past and present in order to maintain their followers' loyalties. In some of the disputed areas such as asylum or abortion, political dealing is gradually producing pragmatic compromises, which has reduced public controversy over these topics. But the underlying self-images seem to be changing more slowly, indicating that it will take considerable time until the intellectual and psychological adaptation to the altered circumstances yields a coherent set of new identities.[39]

4. Patterns of Reconfiguration

Perhaps a switch in perspective, from specific issues to the question of whether the arguments form a more general pattern might help clarify the identity debate. When the various controversies are seen together, it becomes apparent that the speakers often are the same, their presentation styles similar and their ideological arguments repetitive. Even if there is some disagreement within each side, most confrontations therefore take place between the ideological camps. But current discussions are complicated by the confusion of labels after the collapse of communism, evident in the article series sponsored by the *Frankfurter Allgemeine Zeitung* on what is Left and what is Right.[40] In spite of the immobility of ideologies, the boundaries of the respective camps have blurred enough to allow members to reposition themselves in order to cope with the new realities.

At the same time, the East versus West dichotomy is beginning to erode somewhat as a reference point. The media are still full of confrontations between *Ossis* and *Wessis* over the closing of the Stasi files, the danger of foreign criminals, the problem of unemployment, the dearth of child-care, and the legitimacy of military force. But due to greater resources and self-confidence, Western voices tend to sound louder and to drown out Eastern comments in the public sphere. Moreover, crossovers are becoming more frequent, since the great majority of the

39. Heinrich August Winkler, "Rebuilding of a Nation: The Germans Before and After Unification," *Daedalus*, 123 (Winter 1994): 107ff.

40. Essay series in the *Frankfurter Allgemeine Zeitung* on "What's Left" (Summer 1992) and debate on "What's Right" (Summer 1994). Cf. the summary of Henning Ritter in *Deutschland* 6 (1994): 44-49.

Easterners votes for Western parties and is gradually moving towards their ideas, even if a significant minority endorses the leftist protests of the PDS.[41] Since the East/West polarity is no longer identical with the Left/Right split, the result of the overlay of these two dimensions is a confusing set of new contradictions, cutting across older identities.

Some unresolved issues, such as the double burden of the past, involve particularly German themes. The ambivalent reception of the book by Harvard political scientist Daniel J. Goldhagen on *Hitler's Willing Executioners* in the German media is a case in point. Most professional historians welcomed its questions about the role of ordinary people in the holocaust, but rejected the charge of an "eliminationist anti-Semitism," inherent in German culture, as somewhat oversimplified. In the general public Leftist insistence on further penitence surprisingly seemed to drown out a Rightist desire for amenesia. A similar conflict between amnesty or retribution also informs the discussions about dealing with the troubling legacy of Communism. The postwar reluctance to accept responsibility for the holocaust helps a relatively small group of SED victims to insist on a more thorough house-cleaning of communist remnants, which is now creating precisely the opposite problems of excess zeal.[42]

The memory of Third Reich atrocities also complicates the debate about asylum, immigration, and citizenship. The peculiar conjunction of the most liberal asylum policy in Europe and an ethnic definition of citizenship that offers a law of return led to an influx of hundreds of thousands of strangers in the early 1990s, which overtaxed local resources and triggered massive resentment. The tortuous recasting of the asylum process during the summer of 1993 that classified certain states of origin as safe and allowed the automatic return of those who had travelled through a potential host country to Germany reduced the number of asylum seekers by over half. But with the slogan "Germany is not an immigration counry," the conservative government refuses to draft an immigration law and to ease naturalization procedures. Promoted by liberal opinion, the redefinition of Germanness in an open, multicultural fashion, based on citizenship rights instead of ethnicity, still remains incomplete.[43]

41. Martin und Sylvia Greiffenhagen, *Ein schwieriges Vaterland. Zur politischen Kultur im vereinigten Deutschland* (Munich, 1993), 369ff.; and Richard Schröder, *Deutschland schwierig Vaterland. Für eine neue politische Kultur* (Freiburg, 1993).

42. Antonia Grunenberg, ed., *Welche Geschichte wählen wir?* (Hamburg, 1992); Peter Steinbach, "Vergangenheitsbewältigung in vergleichender Perspektive: Politische Säuberung, Wiedergutmachung, Integration," in Klaus Schröder and Jochen Staadt, eds., *Geschichte und Transformation des SED-Staates* (Berlin, 1994).

43. Daniel Cohn-Bendit, *Heimat Babylon. Das Wagnis der multikulturellen Demokratie* (Frankfurt, 1992); Klaus J. Bade, "Immigration and Social Peace in United Germany,"

In some problems that are also shared with other countries, the German dimension is less clearly visible, but still important. For instance, all of Eastern Europe is facing the post-communist transition, but only Germans have the chance of being able to incorporate a bankrupt region into a functioning Western state. Also the gender issues that excite public opinion in many advanced industrial societies have a particular edge in Central Europe, due to paternalist traditions and recollections of the excesses of Nazi biopolitics. Similarly the questions of appropriate participation in international efforts to establish a post-Cold War system that all leading countries confront evoke special fears in Germany, due to the legacy of the World Wars. Because historical overtones make these broader policy debates more complicated in Central Europe than elsewhere, their resolution is often seen less in pragmatic than in ideological terms.[44]

The identity debate is further muddled by a fundamental change in the connotation of Germanness during the last half-century. Both within and outside of the country opinion surveys find remnants of traditional national stereotypes of such secondary civic virtues as hard work, honesty, obedience to authority, etc. But in the West the generational shift to post-material values after the cultural revolution of the late 1960s produced more hedonistic and individualistic preferences that have undercut some of the traits previously apostrophized as most "German."[45] Similarly in the East, decades of indoctrination in the "new socialist man" have left traces of class consciousness and higher expectations for social services that deviate from older national patterns.[46] Some of the conflicts are therefore the result of efforts to reinvent a coherent self-conception under altered circumstances.

At the same time definitions of the "other" have modified so much that they are less able to serve as a negative foil. Especially among the young and the socially marginal, traces of older racial and ethnic prejudice against foreigners still erupt in violence. But in the West consumer

Daedalus (Winter 1994): 85-106. Cf. Christiane Lemke, "Crossing Borders and Building Bridges: Migration, Citizenship and State-Building in Germany," in Louise A. Tilly and Jytte Klausen, eds., *Paths to European Integration: Migration, State and Citizenship in the Nineteenth and Twentieth Centuries* (Forthcoming 1997).

44. Sidney Tarrow, "'Aiming at a Moving Target': Social Science and the Recent Rebellions in Eastern Europe," *PS: Political Science and Politics* (March 1991): 12ff.; and Mary Fulbrook, "Aspects of Society and Identity in the New Germany," *Daedalus* (Winter 1994): 211-234.

45. Gerd Langguth, *Suche nach Sicherheiten. Ein Psychogramm der Deutschen* (Stuttgart, 1995), 21ff.

46. Christiane Lemke, *Die Ursachen des Umbruchs 1989. Politische Sozialisation in der ehemaligen DDR* (Opladen, 1991), 84ff.

capitalism and international travel have led to an easy cosmopolitanism in behavior and attitudes, in which foreign goods and holidays abroad are a status symbol. Moreover, decades of living together with mostly Southern European immigrants in the big cities has also produced a blending of styles that is quite evident in the multiethnic restaurants and stores as well as the feel-good tolerance of the "techno-love parade." Though East Germans still have much catching up to do in this area, so many foreign aspects have been implanted in the new living patterns that it is becoming more difficult to distinguish specifically German from wider European traits.[47]

The current controversy over "normalization" is to a large extent a debate over which sense of self should animate the reunified country. While the conservative political scientist Hans-Peter Schwarz claims that Germany has at last become a regular nation-state, the progressive critic Jürgen Habermas calls this assertion the new basic lie *(Lebenslüge)* of unification.[48] At stake in this clash are different conceptions of the implications of the terrible past for the present: while the Right sees the end of division as a chance to escape from the burden of German exceptionalism, the Left emphasizes the argument of historical guilt in order to maintain a special responsibility. The point of the vague notion of "normalcy" is not so much which side has the better argument (in a sense, both are partially correct), but rather the shift of intellectual initiative from a now defensive Left to a suddenly attacking Right.[49]

These ideological alternatives are attempting to stamp contradictory imprints on the political culture of united Germany. Rainer Zitelmann's neo-conservative appeal for a re-nationalization, an intellectual return to a national tradition, has received much play in the media, but the membership of the self-appointed generation of 1989 seems to be a small group at best. On the other extreme, Peter Glotz's emphatic advocacy of post-nationalism and of European integration still arouses much favorable response among intellectuals, although many nonetheless suspect that an unchanged commitment to pre-1989 values no longer quite

---

47. The blurring of borders between Germans and others has yet to be analyzed systematically, since most commentators are preoccupied with tracing nationalism. Cf. Leslie Adelson, "Opposing Oppositions: Turkish-German Questions in Contemporary German Studies," *German Studies Review* 17 (May 1994): 305-330.

48. Hans-Peter Schwarz, "Das Ende der Identitätsneurose," *Rheinischer Merkur*, September 7, 1990 versus Jürgen Habermas, "Wir sind wieder 'normal' geworden," *Die Zeit*, December 18, 1992. Cf. Jarausch, "Normalisierung oder Renationalisierung," 559ff.

49. Stefan Berger, "Der Dogmatismus des Normalen," *Frankfurter Rundschau*, April 26, 1996; and "Historians and Nation-Building in Germany after Reunification," *Past and Present*, (1995): 187-222. For a less alarmist view see Gerhard A. Ritter, *Der Umbruch von 1989/91 und die Geschichtswissenschaft* (Munich, 1995).

meets the needs of the altered circumstances. Christian Meier's intermediate position, which proposes the development of a Western-style democratic patriotism, seems slowly to be gathering strength, remains less visible than the more extreme views, but precisely due to its moderation may become the majority opinion in the long run.[50]

Taken together, many seemingly disparate debates over particular topics are part of a broader process of redefining German national identity. The Right generally seeks to use unification in order to escape the burden of past guilt, reduce the influx of foreigners, serve Western·business interests, safeguard the existence of male privileges and promote greater international assertiveness. Conversely the Left tries to cling to a sense of historical shame, create a multicultural society, support Eastern redistribution claims, advance affirmative action, and argue for circumspection abroad. Ironically, both sides represent different forms of traditionalism, since the former hopes to revive older national legacies, while the latter attempts to preserve the progressive heritage of the FRG. So far, the neo-conservatives have regained some intellectual ground, because the end of exceptionalism due to division made some readjustment necessary.[51] But since the Left still controls a good part of the media and younger generations often favor leftist views, the contest is far from over at this point.

5. Conceptions of a New Germany

How will German identities develop in the future? This question not only dominates intellectual discussions within the country, but also troubles observers abroad, since its answers will decide how the FRG uses its newfound power. Though the creation of a democratic national state with accepted borders has solved many aspects of the old German problem, the very process of unification has created a new set of peculiarities, such as a sharper internal East-West gradient, and made the protected junior status of the Federal Republic obsolete. Because of these new challenges, the unification euphoria has long given way to a depression, characterized by a paradoxical disparity between private optimism and a public pessimism. By upsetting the physical and

50. Rainer Zitelmann, *Wohin treibt unsere Republik?* (Frankfurt, 1994); Peter Glotz, *Die falsche Normalisierung. Die unmerkliche Verwandlung der Deutschen* (Frankfurt, 1994); and Christian Meier, "Wir brauchen Vertrauen," *Der Spiegel* 5 (1995): 149-154.

51. Lothar Probst, "Das Dilemma der Intellektuellen mit der Nation. Ein Plädoyer gegen die Kontinuitätslogik," *Deutschland Archiv* 27 (1994): 1287-1291; Jarausch, "Normalisierung oder Renationalisierung," 559ff.

psychological certainties of the postwar division, the reintegration of the East has posed the question of German identity in new and different ways.[52]

Although it may take another generation for definitive answers to be found, some outlines of likely developments are already beginning to emerge. Due to the disappearance of the GDR as a separate state, the abrupt changes threaten many Easterners with a loss of identity. By rushing to join the successful FRG instead of creating a hybrid confederation, Easterners forced themselves to adopt the Western model without much chance to preserve their own ways. Initially the common national identification as Germans and the familiarity with the virtual reality of Western media helped the transition. Also regional pride, expressed in the founding of the new states, cushioned the shock, since it aided the survival of some previous peculiarities. But eventually the enormity of the transformation, coupled with a devaluation of life experiences, sparked a nostalgic memory of the old GDR that magnified its achievements while forgetting its repressions. As they are beginning to master the new demands, some Easterners are becoming more insistent on inserting their own views, based upon different memories, into the national debate.[53]

Vindicated by the accession of the Eastern *Länder*, the old Federal Republic has continued to set the tone for the united German state. Although some perceptive analysts predicted that with unification the character of the Bonn Republic would also have to change, the West German establishment and population have proven amazingly reluctant to adopt new ways. Much of this response is understandable, since the West holds all the advantages in population size, economic clout, political power, and ideological success. Due to media dominance, the post-unity debates therefore often look like West German affairs that continue pre-1989 conflicts under different auspices, with the Center-Right attempting to regain the opinion leadership from a dispirited Left.[54] But the size

52. Anne-Marie Le Gloannec, "On German Identity," *Daedalus* (Winter 1994): 129-148. Cf. also Matthias Kepplinger, "Wie sehen sich die Deutschen?" in *Die Deutschen auf der Suche nach ihrer neuen Identität*, 45-59.

53. As an example of Eastern self-reflection, Jens Reich, *Rückkehr nach Europa. Zur neuen Lage der deutschen Nation* (Munich, 1991); and *Abschied von den Lebenslügen. Die Intelligenz und die Macht* (Berlin, 1992). See also Daniela Dahn, *Westwärts und nicht vergessen. Vom Unbehagen in der Einheit* (Berlin, 1996); and Hans Misselwitz, *Nicht länger mit dem Gesicht nach Westen. Das neue Selbstbewußtsein der Ostdeutschen* (Berlin, 1996).

54. Michael Mertes, "Germany's Social and Political Culture: Change Through Consensus?" *Daedalus* (Winter 1994): 1-32. Cf. also Eckhart Fuchs, "'Mehr als ein Koffer bleibt.' Gedanken zu den gegenwärtigen Geschichtskulturen in Deutschland," *Z. Zeitschrift für Marxistische Erneuerung*, 5 (1994), 110-124.

of the material task of rebuilding and the vocal expression of Eastern sentiment by the displaced elite are slowly forcing a realization that some of the touted Western conceptions might have to change as well.

This redefinition of roles is complicated by the context of continuing European integration. The reconstitution of German national identity is taking place simultaneously with the intensification of the Maastricht project of creating a unified currency and advancing political union, the price for French approval of German unity. Though the political elite of the FRG treats both processes as complementary, they may conflict as future self-conceptions, since renationalization sets other priorities than Europeanization. Resentment against abandoning the DM, a substitute for identity as the symbol of postwar economic success, is growing and closer union is hampered by the problem of the Eastern extension of the EU.[55] Ultimately the success of the European identification is not entirely in German hands, since it also depends upon the willingness of their partners, especially the French, to undertake further integration steps.

The protraction of the capital's move to Berlin is also slowing down the emergence of a new national identity. In the confusing debate over the location of the government, Bonn came to represent the Westernization of the Federal Republic while Berlin stood for national traditions as well as Eastern sensibility. The eventual compromise, which left a substantial presence on the Rhine but called for the transfer of most power to the Spree, has apparently settled the issue politically. But the halting implementation of the decision and the massive construction projects are creating almost a decade of uncertainty in which Bonn continues to function as usual while Berlin gradually prepares for its new tasks. Understandable from a logistic point of view, this lengthy transition has created a state of suspension, a kind of Indian Summer for the old FRG. Whether the "Berlin Republic" will be as harmonious as the popular pilgrimage to the "wrapped Reichstag" will only become apparent when politics has moved to the metropolitan setting and begins thinking in larger terms.[56]

In spite of the dislocation of unity, the internal redefinition of identity has hardly begun to express itself politically. Though surveys show

55. Hilmar Hoffmann and Dieter Kramer, eds., *Der Umbau Europas. Deutsche Einheit und europäische Integration* (Frankfurt, 1991); Hans Buchheim, "Die europäische Zukunft als Element der deutschen Identität," in *Deutschland auf der Suche*, 35-44; and Jürgen Kocka, "Die Ambivalenz des Nationalstaats und die Perspektive der Einheit Europas," *Vereinigungskrise*, 151-169.

56. Deutscher Bundestag, ed., *Berlin – Bonn. Die Debatte* (Cologne, 1991). Cf. also Jürgen Habermas, *Die Normalität einer Berliner Republik* (Frankfurt, 1995).

some Eastern disappointment in unity, a retrospective appreciation for the GDR, and a growing awareness of difference from the West, less than one-sixth of the new citizens wants the SED back.[57] Also the reelection of the Kohl government signals continuity and the CDU/CSU/FDP coalition has so far held up despite its slim Bundestag majority, since the FDP has managed to reverse its decline. The advance of the ecologist Greens and the success of the post-communist PDS as Eastern protest party in some state elections do herald potential transformations of the political landscape, but they are slowed by the disarray of the SPD. The Red-Green coalition in North-Rhine Westfalia has therefore proven difficult to assemble, PDS toleration of a left cabinet has been limited to Saxony-Anhalt, and a Black-Green coalition has only been a talking point. Despite the strains of the unification crisis, the inner stability of the enlarged FRG has been remarkable so far.[58]

The external search for a new German role has not yet produced any startling results either. While some rightist commentators demand greater assertiveness, FRG foreign policy has, with the exception of aspiring to a permanent seat in the UN Security Council and the Croatian *faux pas*, been quite circumspect. Bonn continues to adhere to its proven postwar axioms of transatlantic cooperation, friendship with France, advocacy of European integration, and NATO membership, even if it has become more vocal within these constraints. After the troop deployment issue was decided by the courts, the Germans have, for historical reasons, hesitated to go much beyond providing logistical support for the SFOR mission in the Balkans. The only new elements are an improved relationship with post-Soviet Russia and an advocacy of military and economic integration of the East Central European states in Western structures. Quite in contrast to the turn-of-the-century clamor for *Weltpolitik*, current practices continue to adhere to incrementalism, multilateralism, and economic diplomacy.[59] Internationally the united Germany has used its increased power only reluctantly.

Yet new realities are slowly forcing the modification of some sacrosanct doctrines. Regarding the double burden of the past, ideological

57. Erik Natter, "Wie sehen sich die Deutschen selbst? Empirisches Material aus West- und Ostdeutschland," in A. Knoblich, ed., *Auf dem Weg zu einer gesamtdeutschen Identität* (Cologne, 1993), 19ff.; as well as youth survey in *Der Spiegel*, September 19, 1994 and the poll, ibid., July 3, 1995.

58. Stephan Eisel, "The Politics of a United Germany," *Daedalus*, (Winter 1994): 149-171.

59. Philip Zelikow and Condoleezza Rice, *Germany Unified and Europe Transformed* (Cambridge, 1995); and Timothy Garton Ash, "Germany's Choice," *Foreign Affairs, Agenda 1995* (New York, 1995), 68-84. The media flurry, caused by the pro-Serbian travelogue of the Austrian writer Peter Handtke, had little if any effect upon policy.

lines have blurred, since many PDS supporters and conservatives call for an amnesty while most civic movement members, Social Democrats and moderates oppose amnesia. Prodded by the left wing of the CDU and the FDP, parts of the Right are edging towards a reform of naturalization procedures that will make obtaining citizenship easier for members of other ethnic groups living in the Federal Republic. Regardless of party affiliation, the governors of East German states are creating alliances to safeguard financial transfers and to maintain sufficient economic incentives for their region. After years of ideological wrangling, both sides of the abortion debate also compromised in a mandatory counselling but open access bill that recently passed the Bundestag. Finally, the Left, led by Joschka Fischer and Jürgen Habermas, is beginning to shed some of its pacifist illusions and to work out a more realistic international stance.[60]

The most unexpected problem five years after unification has been a crisis of public finances that challenges established self-conceptions. Tight limits on borrowing, set by the Maastricht criteria, have made it harder to restart the stalled and overregulated economy. Hidden by the post-unity boom, the structural problem of eroding competitiveness in the global economy is now confronting an overpriced system with the necessity of reducing labor costs as well as benefits. Against fierce union opposition the government did push through a modest increase in shopping hours, but the corporatist style of decision-making renders gains in flexibility of work-time or in deregulation excruciatingly difficult. The push for a reduction of public expenditures via a lowering of services requires a fundamental redefinition of the German model away from pride in prosperity and an unequalled social safety net. Though claims of the end of the welfare state are exaggerated, government inaction in the face of rising unemployment suggests that the adjustments demanded by competitiveness will be painful.[61]

Coming to terms with the pressures of a global age will require a further recasting of notions of Germanness. Since the functional erosion of the nation-state undercuts the traditional conception of an ethnic homogeneity, it makes the adoption of a different, looser sense of political

60. See the other chapters in this volume, the interview with Joschka Fischer, and statement by Jürgen Habermas, *Der Spiegel*, August 7, 1995; as well as Robert Leicht, "Aus Knechten Bürger machen," *Die Zeit*, June 28, 1996.

61. Gunter Hofmann, "Alles Standort, oder was?" *Die Zeit*, July 5, 1996. Cf. also Friedrich Fürstenberg, "Deutschlands Wirtschaft nach der Wende," in *Nach der Wende:* 93-118; as well as Hartmut Tofaute, "Kosten der Einheit – Refinanzierung der öffentlichen Haushalte," in Dirk Nolte, Ralf Sitte, and Alexandra Wagner, eds., *Wirtschaftliche und Soziale Einheit Deutschlands. Eine Bilanz*, Cologne, 1996), 161-194.

community necessary. Responding domestically to this change might mean the elaboration of an open-ended self-conception that tolerates, even celebrates differences in age, region, gender, religion, ethnic background, and the like. Internationally, a rethinking of the German role could imply the endorsement of a multi-centered, variable-speed Europe, built upon and at the same time transcending national states. Should they insist on returning to a single and exclusive concept of national destiny, the Germans will provoke fierce internal and external conflicts. But if they accept the challenge of living with their differences, they might at last manage to construct a more plural sense of post-national identities that could serve as an example to others.[62]

62. Heinrich August Winkler, "Nationalismus, Nationalstaat und nationale Frage in Deutschland seit 1945," in Andreas Huyssen, *Twilight Memories: Marking Time in a Culture of Amnesia* (New York, 1995), 67-84; August Winkler and Hartmut Kaelble, eds., *Nationalismus – Nationalitäten – Supranationalität* (Stuttgart, 1992); and Jarausch, "Postnationale Nation," passim.

Chapter I

THE PRESENCE OF THE PAST
Culture, Opinion, and Identity in Germany

Konrad H. Jarausch, Hinrich C. Seeba,
and *David P. Conradt*

History plays a central role in the creation of national identity. According to one prominent definition, a nation's sense of self is the result of appropriated experiences, "the sum of remembrances of its own political behavior."[1] In practice, groups represent their fate in stories which create a feeling of community by recounting their trials and tribulations. Often dramatic incidents like the storming of the Bastille function as political founding myths that are told and retold, not to remember certain facts, but to establish a bond between past and present that might unite speakers and listeners. In the construction of such national identities actual events matter less than their careful arrangement in a master narrative that presents a highly selective but all the more compelling account of common destiny.[2]

A classic case of such an invented tradition is the Prussian conception of history that emerged in mid-nineteenth century. A group of national and liberal historians and publicists appropriated certain aspects of the Central European past in order to justify Berlin's conquests, which led to the unification of Germany. Though they differed

---

1. Gerhard Schmittchen, *Was den Deutschen heilig ist* (Munich, 1979).
2. Benedict Anderson, *Imagined Communities: Reflections on the Origin and Spread of Nationalism* (London, 1983). Cf. also Lloyd S. Kramer, "Nations as Texts: Literary Theory and the History of Nationalism," *The Maryland Historian*, 24 (1993): 71-82.

on the need for a constitution, both Heinrich von Sybel and Heinrich von Treitschke agreed on a master plot that departed from the glory of the Holy Roman Empire and deplored German decline due to religious quarrels, territorial splits, and foreign interference, only to celebrate redemption through the national movement and Bismarck's unification wars. By selecting some strands and ignoring others, these Borussian historians sought to legitimize the Protestant and *kleindeutsch* reign of the Hohenzollerns over the Second Empire at the expense of the Catholic and *großdeutsch* rest.[3]

In contrast to this success story, events of the twentieth century proved deeply problematic due to German responsibility for the two World Wars. In some ways, the nationalist invention of the stab-in-the-back-legend tried to repeat the plot structure of earlier prominence in the Empire and present decline in the Weimar Republic so as to call for German recovery in a revived Third Reich. After the failure of neo-conservative alternatives, this hope materialized as Hitler's dictatorship, surpassing all expectations, first in restoring national pride and then ending in renewed disaster. Only the collapse of 1945 broke this cyclical pattern by revealing to the survivors the full extent of the "German catastrophe," which seemed beyond hope of redemption the second time around.[4] To explain the inexplicable, critics simply inverted the old master plot and constructed a negative teleology towards an inevitable defeat of the Prusso-German state through its Nazi exaggeration, apparently ending the story forever.

In this narrative, the postwar period functioned largely as a postscript, an ahistorical space of prolonged penitence for previous transgressions. In light of the unprecedented horror of the crimes committed in its name, German identity could only continue to exist as a thorough renunciation of earlier affirmations of Germanness. The East therefore embraced anti-fascism, partly in genuine revulsion and partly as a prop for the SED regime, while the West struggled to cope with the past through a curious mixture of repression and restitution.[5] This endless task of *Vergangenheitsbewältigung* strangely linked both rival offsprings of the Third Reich and continued to embarrass their leaders during various anniversaries. Though the population wanted to forget what might not

3. Georg G. Iggers, *The German Conception of History* (Middletown, CT, 1968).

4. Friedrich Meinecke, *Die deutsche Katastrophe. Betrachtungen und Erinnerungen* (Wiesbaden, 1946). Michael Geyer and Konrad H. Jarausch, "Great Men and Postmodern Ruptures: Overcoming the 'Belatedness of German Historiography'," *German Studies Review*, 18 (1995): 253-273.

5. Konrad H. Jarausch, "The Failure of East German Antifascism: Ironies of History as Politics," *German Studies Review*, 14 (1991): 84-102; and Alf Lüdtke, "'Coming to Terms with the Past': Illusions of Remembering, Ways of Forgetting Nazism in West Germany," *Journal of Modern History* 65 (1993): 542-572.

be forgiven, critical intellectuals on both sides of the Wall became preoccupied with guilt that negatively defined them as Germans through
the imperative of atonement.[6]

The unification of 1989-90 has offered an unexpected continuation
of the erstwhile master narrative by providing a new redemption. While
the Left now worries about the doubling of the burden of the past, the
Right sees the return of unity as a chance to undo the effects of the cultural revolution of the 1960s and to restore a positive sense of identity.
Many of the current debates on the Stasi legacy, the collaboration of
writers, the morality of *Ostpolitik*, etc. can be understood as clumsy
attempts to rewrite history in order to renationalize Germany.[7] This
open-ended contest for cultural hegemony poses several important questions: Which symbolic traditions originally shaped German self-consciousness and may continue to color the larger FRG? What historical
learning processes transformed public opinion after the war and are
likely to determine the political behavior of united Germany? And
which current appropriations of the past will inform its national self-
conceptions in the future?

1. The Cultural Construction of Germanness

Due to the lack of a national state, the creation of a German identity
was, above all, a cultural project. Frustrated with the particularism of
petty principalities after the Seven Years' War, the educated sought to
reinvent a common polity, based upon the bond of language, literature,
and tradition, shared among the peoples of Central Europe. Since the
real history of German speakers was pre- and transnational, an imagined
past had to be created that could serve as symbolic representation of a
national unity that was to be restored.[8] In the construction of a sense of
self, several strains of arguments about German traditions emerged that
came to vie with each other: an aesthetic view that was content to stress
the bonds of common culture, a liberal view that put a premium on constitutional freedom, and an ethnic view that emphasized national unity.

6. Ulrich Battis et al., eds., *Vergangenheitsbewältigung durch das Recht* (Berlin, 1992);
Manfred Kittel, *Die Legende von der 'zweiten Schuld'. Vergangenheitsbewältingung in der
Ära Adenauer* (Berlin, 1993).

7. Konrad H. Jarausch, *Die Unverhoffte Einheit* (Frankfurt, 1995); and "Normalisierung oder Renationalisierung," *Geschichte und Gesellschaft*, 21 (1995): 559-572.

8. Benedict Anderson, *Imagined Communities*, 13: "My point of departure is that
nationality, or, as one might prefer to put it in view of the word's multiple significations,
nation-ness, as well as nationalism, are cultural artefacts of a particular kind."

In some fashion or other, these relatively set visions would structure the debate on German self-conceptions over the space of two centuries.

As a precondition of a political revival, Germany had to be conceived of as a cultural community. In the second half of the eighteenth century some intellectuals began to complain that the Holy Roman Empire provided but a weak link among over three hundred sovereign territorial states, imperial cities and knightly possessions. Friedrich Carl von Moser was among the first who, in his book *Von dem deutschen Nationalgeist* (1765), lamented an alarming degree of collective alienation among the diverse German provinces: "We no longer know ourselves; / We have become estranged from one another, / Our spirit has left us." In promoting governmental reform, Moser argued for "a German interest" as a rallying point for better integration of what appeared to be a rather heterogeneous, localized culture.[9] As a struggle against parochialism, the inception of nationalism was linked to a project of political modernization.

The formation of a German identity, therefore, began with an aesthetic campaign for establishing a "cultural nation." In 1766 Gotthold Ephraim Lessing still ridiculed "the bright idea of creating a national theater for the Germans as long as we Germans are not yet a nation."[10] But when the hopes for a political revival of the Holy Roman Empire began to fade, Friedrich Schiller chose the opposite direction, recommending the creation of a German theater as the best path to political unity: "If we were to have a national stage, we would also become a nation."[11] Leading to the comforting notion of a cultural nation, this aesthetic perspective became the dominant outlook of the *Bildungsbürgertum* in the nineteenth century. In accordance with Schiller's distych of 1795 "Germany? But where is it? I don't know how to find that country. / Where the learned one begins, the political one ends,"[12] the gradual disappearance of the political Germany would be balanced by the emergence of a symbolic Germany represented culturally.

In the search for a common denominator, educated promoters of the national revival could appeal to a common language. In his *Wörterbuch der Deutschen Sprache* (1807), Johann Heinrich Campe argued that in view of the political misery following the Prussian defeat at Jena and Auerstedt nothing would be "more necessary, pressing and valuable" than to strengthen the German sense of linguistic cohesion. After the

---

9. Friedrich Carl von Moser, *Von dem deutschen Nationalgeist*, (Frankfurt, 1766), 7, 23.

10. Gotthold Ephraim Lessing, "Hamburgische Dramaturgie" (1766), in Herbert G. Göpfert, ed., *Werke* (Munich, 1973), 8: 698.

11. Friedrich Schiller, "Was kann eine gute stehende Schaubühne eigentlich wirken?" (1785), in *dtv Gesamtausgabe* (Munich, 1966), 20: 24.

12. Schiller, "Das Deutsche Reich" (1795), in *dtv Gesamtausgabe*, 2: 30.

break-up of the Holy Roman Empire in 1806, their language, the last string to hold together the German people, was believed to be the only hope for "the possibility of future reunification into an independent nation."[13] Thus *Wiedervereinigung*, a key word of the political debates in postwar Germany, was used already 150 years earlier to champion a predominantly philological venture. From the beginning, much of the discourse on "cultural nation" was cast in a rhetoric of regaining a mythical political unity which had been lost.

Historiographers of national literature such as Ludwig Wachler (1818) and August Koberstein (1827) sought to create an ethnic master narrative.[14] Often fabricating, like A. F. C. Vilmar in his popular work of 1844,[15] a mythological origin of ethnic Germans, this tale of national development tried to construct a plot that departed from a golden age, declined to the present and hoped for future redemption. Tracing the Germans' tribal identity back to Arminius (a renegade officer who had beaten the Romans in 9 A.D., thus bolstering Germanic pride forever) and to Siegfried (a mythical figure who would kill any enemy disguised as a ghastly dragon, thus becoming the quintessential Germanic hero) turned into the favorite (and richly rewarded) pastime of mythologizers. It was mainly to honor his popular edition of the *Nibelungenlied* that a minor philologist, Friedrich Heinrich von der Hagen, was appointed the first professor of German literature at the newly founded University of Berlin in 1810.

Other intellectuals attempted to advance a constitutional nation-state through creating a literary canon and promoting linguistic standardization. In his pivotal *Geschichte der poetischen National-Literatur der Deutschen* (1835-42) the historian Georg Gottfried Gervinus set out to strengthen German identity through the construction of a literary pantheon. Especially after Weimar classicism had ended with Goethe's death in 1832, literature seemed to present the most significant, if not the only, point of reference on which all Germans, however divided they were, could agree.[16] "What do we have in common beyond our language

13. Johann Heinrich Campe, *Wörterbuch der Deutschen Sprache* (Braunschweig, 1807), I: 23.

14. Jürgen Fohrmann, *Das Projekt der deutschen Literaturgeschichte* (Stuttgart, 1989) and Hinrich C. Seeba, "Germany – a Literary Concept? The Myth of National Literature," *German Studies Review* 17 (1994): 353-369.

15. A. F. C. Vilmar, *Geschichte der Deutschen National-Litteratur* (1844). 25th edition (Marburg, 1901).

16. Georg Gottfried Gervinus, *Geschichte der poetischen National-Literatur der Deutschen* (Leipzig, 1846), I: 9f.: "I would like to see that artful historian who could leave us consoled after portraying the present political condition of Germany. In contrast, the history of German poetry seemed as interesting in its inner constitution as it is attractive due to its value and our contemporary needs."

and literature?" similarly asked Jacob Grimm in 1854 when he set out to collect Germany's linguistic memory in his *Deutsches Wörterbuch*.[17] Through documenting the richness of the common language, the founder of the academic study of *Germanistik* hoped to speed the establishment of a common state.

A second major strand in the cultural formation of German identity was the liberal rhetoric of individual freedom. With the celebrated drama of Swiss liberation from Habsburg control, *Wilhelm Tell* (1804), Friedrich Schiller issued a stirring call for liberty in the Rütli oath: "We want to be as free as our fathers were!" Forced to shoot an apple from his son's head and taking revenge on his torturer, the protagonist William Tell became a powerful symbol of the desire for political freedom and stirred the popular imagination. Censors, still afraid that "freedom" meant "revolution," and ever-cautious stage directors insisted on changing the text of the drama, and eliminated the subversive fifth act, or banned the celebrated liberation drama altogether. If staged at all, the play was at least barred from repeat performances (e.g., 1832 in Frankfurt, 1846 in Mainz) after the audience had ostentatiously applauded lines that could be seen as directed against the German authorities of the day.[18]

The easy accessibility of Schiller's message made the poet immensely popular as a spokesman for German liberation. The famous lines from *Don Carlos*, "Give freedom of thought, sire!" could be interpreted as support for cultural quietism or, in connection with other plays like *Die Räuber*, seen as a demand for actual political freedom. Popular fervor culminated in the "Schiller year" 1859 when nation-wide commemorations of Schiller's one-hundredth birthday reiterated the call of the 1848 revolution for liberalization and unification. "The spiritual celebration of unity," writes the editor of a two-volume anthology of speeches on that occasion "was a firm foundation for the great edifice which we will yet labor for centuries to build."[19] No wonder that more monuments were dedicated to the "poet of freedom" than to any other German figure and that the national foundation for supporting indigent writers bore his name.

During much of the nineteenth century Liberals promoted their cause by producing their own historical iconography. As an alternative to the black-and-white Prussian flag, supporters of constitutionalism embraced

17. Jacob Grimm, *Deutsches Wörterbuch*, vol. 1 (Leipzig, 1854).

18. H. H. Houben, *Verbotene Literatur von der klassischen Zeit bis zur Gegenwart* (Berlin, 1924), 563-567.

19. Karl Tropus, Nach dem 10. November 1859, in *Schiller-Denkmal* (Berlin, 1860), 1: 7. Cf. Hinrich C. Seeba, "Auferstehung des Geistes. Zur religiösen Rhetorik nationaler Einheit," in Gert Ueding, ed., *"Nicht allein mit den Worten." Festschrift für Joachim Dyck zum 60. Geburtstag* (Stuttgart, 1995), 206-221.

the black-red-gold tricolor of the *Burschenschaft*, the liberal and national student movement that arose after the War of Liberation and was repeatedly persecuted by restoration authorities.[20] During the Hambach festival (1832) and the 1848 Revolution, radicals tried to introduce French symbols of Republicanism such as phrygian caps and American-style propaganda, such as songs and broadsides. The middle-class effort to build a statue to "Hermann the German" in the Teutoburg Forest was also a national-liberal attempt to celebrate "liberation" from foreign domination. Inspired by solidarity with the Commune, the Socialist movement adopted the red banner of revolt so as to suggest that it followed a powerful revolutionary tradition, in tune with the march of history.[21]

The effect of liberal appeals was, however, blunted by the unsolved question of national unity. In Schiller's play *Wilhelm Tell* the first line of the oath of the Swiss confederation, "We want to be a united folk of brethren,"[22] served as the fictional battle cry for national unity by turning the internal demand for freedom into an external cry for liberation from oppression. This vow was frantically applauded in August 1870, when during the Franco-Prussian War the theater season in Berlin was opened with *Wilhelm Tell*.[23] It was applauded again at the end of World War I, when the call for unity was used to balance military defeat and economic misery.[24] It was applauded during the Third Reich when the Nazi movement claimed to be the true heir of all national traditions.[25] Finally, it was applauded in 1951, when following the Berlin blockade the newly built Schillertheater was opened with this play and Berliners rallied to withstand the Cold War.[26]

20. This strain has largely been forgotton. Cf. Konrad H. Jarausch, "The Sources of German Student Unrest, 1815-1848," in Lawrence Stone, ed., *The University in Society* (Princeton, 1974), 2: 533ff.

21. John L. Snell, *The Democratic Movement in Germany, 1789-1914* (Chapel Hill, 1976); Vernon L. Lidtke, *The Alternative Culture: Socialist Labor in Imperial Germany* (New York, 1985).

22. Friedrich Schiller, "Wilhelm Tell," in *dtv Gesamtausgabe* (Munich, 1966), 8: 138.

23. It was Fontane who in his very first theater review commented on the nationalist fervor of this premiere on August 17, 1870; "Schiller - Wilhelm Tell," in Walter Keitel, ed., *Sämtliche Werke* series III (Munich, 1969) 2: 5f.

24. Günther Rühle, *Theater für die Republik 1917-1933 im Spiegel der Kritik* (Frankfurt, 1967), 190.

25. For example, the *Zeitschrift für Deutschkunde* proclaimed in 1934 that every German teacher should interpret the famous Rütli line as "the meaning of *our* national uprising" (quoted in program notes for Hansgünther Heyme's production of *Wilhelm Tell* in Stuttgart, season 1984-85).

26. Friedrich Luft, "Die erste Premiere der Berliner Festspiele" in Ferdinand Piedmont, ed., *Schiller spielen. Stimmen der Theaterkritik 1946-1985. Eine Dokumentation* (Darmstadt, 1990), 252f.

As inspiration for resistance against Napoleon's occupation, national-ist intellectuals demanded moving towards actual politics. In his *Reden an die deutsche Nation* (1808) the philosopher Johann Gottlieb Fichte lectured the Germans to act politically rather than retreat into the realm of intellect: "Long before recent events we have had to hear so to speak in advance what has been repeated frequently since, that even if our political independence were lost, we would nonetheless keep our lan-guage and literature and would always remain a nation in these respects and could easily console ourselves about everything else."[27] In Fichte's view such cultural solace, later called "inner emigration," would amount to defeatism, because internalizing the site of identity in imagination would mean the end of political resistance. Echoed by Friedrich Ludwig Jahn and Ernst Moritz Arndt, this philosophical call to arms inspired an exclusive, ethnic definition of German identity.

In conjuring up times of paradise, golden age, and holy empire, other intellectuals invoked the triadic myth of restored unity, associated with the heroic "Emperor Barbarossa."[28] This figment of national imagina-tion was constructed from two historical figures, Frederick I, who reigned between 1155 and 1190, and his grandson Frederick II, who reigned from 1212 to 1250. Barbarossa was believed to be condemned to wait in the Kyffhäuser mountain for hundreds of years until his time would come to wake up and rid Germany of the divisive regional princes and restore the unified "Reich" in its medieval, imperial, i.e., centralized grandeur. This late medieval myth took on new significance, when after the collapse of the Holy Roman Empire in 1806, only one generation before its one-thousandth anniversary, the nostalgic dream of the empire lost turned into the drive for a national state to be regained.

Ironically, this vision was revived by a single poem by Friedrich Rück-ert, "Kaiser Friedrich im Kyffhäuser" (1817). In addition to all the ele-ments of the popular tale – the emperor dozing for another hundred years deep down in the mountain, with his red beard grown through the marble table and the ravens keeping watch – this evocation suggests an identity that conflates the old Empire with a hoped-for nation-state: "He has taken away / the Reich's glorious shine, / and shall return one day / With it, in his own time."[29] As it was a "holy" empire – named for

27. Johann Gottlieb Fichte, *Reden an die deutsche Nation* (1808), in Fritz Medicus, ed., *Ausgewählte Werke in sechs Bänden* (Darmstadt, 1962), 5: 562.

28. Hinrich C. Seeba, "Fabelhafte Einheit: Von deutschen Mythen und nationaler Identität," in Claudia Mayer-Iswandy, ed., *Zwischen Traum und Trauma: Die Nation. Transatlantische Perspektiven zur Geschichte eines Problems* (Tübingen, 1994), 59-74.

29. Friedrich Rückert, "Kaiser Friedrich im Kyffhäuser" (1817), in Conrad Beyer, ed., *Werke in sechs Bänden*, vol. 1, part 1: *Lyrik* (Leipzig, n.d.), 50.

the fact that the medieval emperor had to be crowned by the pope – the image easily took on, in the triadic scheme of history, a quasi-religious quality of paradise lost and regained, with the cyclical nature of events to come expressed in the prefix *Wieder-*. As a restoration of past bliss in a timeless millenium, the dream of *re*-unification would lift the old curse of fragmentation and dispel the recent nightmare of defeat, which signified the end of former "unity" as the dawning of modernity.

Due to the mythical character of such cultural constructions, the transition from *Kulturnation* to *Nationalstaat* would exact a heavy price. The liberal Karl Biedermann insisted in his entry on "nation, nationality" to Rotteck/Welcker's famed *Staats-Lexikon* that "the culture of a common language and literature does not suffice in order to create a fully developed nation and a generally capable national character."[30] But in going from culture to politics the goal of personal freedom often lost out to the connected but distinct aim of national unity when the two were in conflict. In Hoffmann von Fallersleben's 1841 text for what was to become Germany's national anthem in 1922 and again in 1952,[31] the call for "unity" soon proved more popular than appeals for "right and freedom." While the liberal Biedermann argued for civil liberty at the *domestic* level, national critics turned the language of freedom into a call for unification by demanding liberation from *foreign* oppression.

In the struggle for a separate identity, definitions of what ought to be considered German narrowed decisively. Based on the cosmopolitan project of enlightenment, the eighteenth century was marked by a certain pride in cultural heterogeneity, with Justus Möser, among others, praising the aesthetics of local diversity to counter Frederick II's contempt for German provincialism.[32] After Napoleon's defeat the homogenizing forces in German identity formation grew stronger, since the negative foil of an external enemy was replaced by the problem of defining standards of Germanness internally. The emphatic criteria of what Ludwig Wachler preached in 1818 as "return to a German spirit"[33] increasingly became the yardstick of de-selection, excluding everybody

30. Karl Biedermann, "Nation, Nationalität," in Karl von Rotteck and Karl Welcker, eds., *Das Staats-Lexikon* (Leipzig, 1864), 10: 317.

31. Hinrich C. Seeba, "'Einigkeit und Recht und Freiheit': The German Quest for National Identity in the Nineteenth Century," in Peter Börner, ed., *Concepts of National Identity: An Interdisciplinary Dialogue. Interdisziplinäre Betrachtungen zur Frage der nationalen Identität* (Baden-Baden, 1986), 153-166.

32. Justus Möser, "Über die deutsche Sprache und Literatur. Schreiben an einen Freund" (1781), in *Anwalt des Vaterlands. Wochenschriften, Patriotische Phantasien, Aufsätze, Fragmente* (Leipzig, 1978), 409.

33. Ludwig Wachler, *Vorlesungen über die Geschichte der teutschen Nationallitteratur* (Frankfurt, 1818-19), 1: 3.

who could be identified outside "Germandom," such as members of linguistic minorities. This redefinition of what it meant to be German from a cultural into a racial pattern was the milieu in which anti-Semitism, the most hostile exclusion of the "other," could eventually thrive.[34]

Unpersuaded by such efforts, perceptive critics tried to expose the anachronistic fictionality of German claims to unity. Although even Heinrich Heine liked to play with a liberal version of the Barbarossa myth,[35] he realized in more sober moments that the Germans, like the Jews, were still waiting in vain for their "secular Messiah."[36] During the *Vormärz* the exiled poet, therefore, considered the hope for any "reunification" of the Germans to be a nostalgic and anti-modern return to a kind of totality which, if it ever existed, was assigned to a mythological past. If the world had ever been united before, it was preserved, Heine argued, if not created, by "whole poets" who were restricted to antiquity and the middle ages. They should be respected but not be emulated; for "every imitation of their wholeness is a lie, a lie which any clear eye can see and which cannot escape ridicule."[37]

In the first three-quarters of the nineteenth century the cultural and political struggle over German identity remained undecided. On the one hand, the building of roads and canals, the growth of railroads,and the construction of telegraphs began to link the Central European states more closely. Also the Prussian-led effort to forge a customs union freed trade across petty frontiers while newspapers and book publishers started to cater to a national opinion market. But on the other hand, the efforts of countless civic associations, either directed towards pursuits like singing and gymnastics or openly political only slowly succeeded in wresting some constitutional concessions from the various crowns. The failure of the 1848 revolution doomed dynastic Prussian and Austrian efforts to create a nation-state, so that the question of political unity in Central Europe remained an intellectual project rather than practical reality.[38]

---

34. Wilhelm Marr, *Der Sieg des Judentums über das Germanentum* (Berlin, 1879). Cf. also Mosche Zimmermann, *Wilhelm Marr, the Patriarch of Anti-Semitism* (New York, 1986).

35. Heinrich Heine, "Elementargeister" [1835], in Klaus Briegleb, ed., *Sämtliche Schriften* (Munich, 1971) 3: 1020.

36. Heinrich Heine, "Ludwig Börne. Eine Denkschrift" [1840], in *Sämtliche Schriften*, 4: 119.

37. Heinrich Heine, "Die Bäder von Lucca" [1829], in *Sämtliche Schriften*, 2: 406. For Goethe's similar skepticism about the mythical nature of Germany, see his letter to Karl Friedrich Zelter, July 27,1807, in Karl Robert Mandelkow, ed., *Briefe* (Hamburg, 1966) 3: 47.

38. Theodore S. Hamerow, *The Social Foundations of German Unification, 1858-1871* (Princeton, 1969-1972), 2 vols.

Only the founding of the Second Reich in 1871 seemed to settle the issue of Germanness once and for all. Bismarck's military triumphs strengthened the ethnic conception of identity and national fervor pushed advocates of diversity, tarred as *Reichsfeinde,* onto the sidelines. In order to instill a uniform civic consciousness, the new Reich combatted political Catholicism in the *Kulturkampf,* reneged on Jewish emancipation by fostering racial anti-Semitism, and persecuted socialism and trade-unionism. Bismarck ended the confrontation with Catholics when he needed the support of the Center Party and eventually shifted to social policy so as to wean workers away from Marxism.[39] But once raised by the historian Heinrich von Treitschke, the Jewish question[40] would not go away, since many believed, like Julius Langbehn in 1890, that it called for a solution "in a hostile sense."[41] Instead of increasing liberality, the creation of the Second Empire reinforced the intolerant aspects of German identity.

As support of the fragile new state, the Barbarossa myth could suggest a seemingly solid historical justification. In 1881 a group of nationalist and anti-Semitic students gathered on the Kyffhäuser mountain to pledge eternal loyalty to "the resurrected Barbarossa, their beloved Emperor William."[42] A decade later, construction began on a colossal monument which iconically juxtaposed Barbarossa's awakening and William I's triumph: "On the Kyffhäuser, where according to myth Emperor Frederick the Redbeard waited for the renewal of the Reich, Emperor William the Whitebeard shall arise, who has fulfilled the legend."[43] The Kyffhäuser manifests a series of correspondences in which *Rotbart* is replaced by *Weißbart* so as to prove that the newly founded Deutsches Reich was taking the place of the medieval empire. Typically, the dedication in 1896 took place on June 18, a date that marked the anniversaries of Barbarossa's crowning, the Prussian victory over the Swedes at Fehrbellin, the defeat of Napoleon at Waterloo, and the victory celebration in Berlin in 1871.[44]

39. See Otto Pflanze, *Bismarck and the Development of Germany* (Princeton, 1963-1990), 3 vols; Lothar Gall, *Bismarck, the White Revolutionary* (London, 1986); and Ernst Engelberg, *Bismarck* (Berlin, 1985-1990), 2 vols.

40. Heinrich von Treitschke, "Unsere Aussichten" (November 1879), in Walter Boehlich, ed., *Der Berliner Antisemitismusstreit* (Frankfurt, 1988), 13.

41. Julius Langbehn, *Rembrandt als Erzieher. Von einem Deutschen,* 42nd edition (Leipzig, 1893), 349.

42. Albrecht Timm, *Der Kyffhäuser im deutschen Geschichtsbild* (Göttingen, 1961), 24.

43. Quoted from Thomas Nipperdey, "Nationalidee und Nationaldenkmal in Deutschland im 19. Jahrhundert," *Historische Zeitschrift* 206 (1968): 545.

44. All speeches at the ceremony were printed in *Deutscher Reichsanzeiger und Königlich Preußischer Staatsanzeiger* 144, (June 18, 1896).

To strengthen its political legitimacy, the Second Reich created a patriotic version of history to "nationalize the masses." The government sponsored national holidays such as the Emperor's birthday or Sedan's day (commemorating the victory over France), celebrated with military parades, patriotic speeches, and liberal consumption of alcohol. The Hohenzollern dynasty seized on occasions such as the opening of schools, hospitals, or railway stations, built in neo-medieval style, to represent itself as a legitimate heir of the imperial tradition by affecting a chivalric pose. The educated and propertied burghers sponsored a series of Bismarck columns to memorialize the founder of the Second Reich and constructed a series of national monuments, such as the Porta Westfalica, the Leipzig tower to the War of Liberation, and the Rüdesheim Germania.[45] Amplified in schools, churches, and barracks, this invented tradition of German glory spread the nationalist gospel to the lower class.

Unification fundamentally transformed the outlook of the educated middle class from a liberal to a nationalist stance. Before there had been a German state, the national movement had to advocate political change in order to overthrow the particularist princes. But after 1871, national agitation became defensive, intent on maintaining the newly gained state by making reliable German citizens out of a welter of different loyalties. Not content with internal consolidation, ethnic radicals directed their agitation outward towards a pan-German gathering of German-speaking minorities in Europe that had not been unified. Invoking a transition to *Weltpolitik*, nationalists also advocated imperialism, the creation of a world-wide empire for the German latecomers. Based upon a mythological reading of the imperial past, the volkish fringe and the Fatherland Party became ever more radical during World War I, advocating racist and linguistic suppression at home and military expansion abroad.[46]

After the defeat and collapse of the Second Reich, the different conceptions of German identity once again clashed. Democratic and socialist attempts to infuse the Weimar Republic with the counter-tradition of liberty foundered on circumstances, incompetence, and hostility.[47] When the Nazi Party succeeded in creating the neo-Conservative dream

45. Georg Lachmann Mosse, *The Nationalization of the Masses: Political Symbolism and Mass Movements in Germany* (New York, 1975).
46. Friedrich Paulsen, *Geschichte des gelehrten Unterrichts*, 3rd ed., Rudolf Lehmann (Berlin, 1921), 2: 686 f. Cf. also Roger Chickering, *We Men Who Feel Most German: A Cultural Study of the Pan-German League, 1884-1914* (Boston, 1984).
47. In contrast to the vast literature on nationalism, the symbolic efforts at rooting democracy in Germany have been studied too little. Cf. Heinrich August Winkler, *Weimar, 1918-1933. Die Geschichte der ersten deutschen Demokratie* (Munich, 1993).

of a Third Reich, it used specious logic in claiming to be the culmination of all prior national dreams, a synthesis which would finally end internal strife and bring external might. At home, the SS and its collaborators attempted to homogenize ethnic conceptions of Germandom in a radical biopolitical fashion that culminated in concentration camps and the Holocaust. Even if he was motivated by the association with "red" in "redbeard," it was no accident that Hitler once again invoked the imperial myth by giving the attack on the Soviet Union, which would eventually bring him down, the code-name "operation Barbarossa."[48]

By its shameless exaggeration of exceptionalism, the Third Reich made a travesty out of the tradition of a German *Sonderweg*.[49] Domestically, Nazi chauvinism deeply discredited national definitions of Germanness by involving not just victims but also collaborators and perpetrators in suffering bombing raids and mass expulsions. Internationally, Hitler's expansion of Germany far beyond its historical or linguistical borders abused the notion of self-determination as a flimsy cover for racial imperialism. Since the Wehrmacht and the SS committed their atrocities in the name of the German people, they tarnished all claims connected to that concept for decades to come. The resistance effort of the previous elites or communist workers was too little and too late to save older, more moderate definitions of national traditions.[50] By destroying the national state and ruining the conception of a special identity, the Nazis also brought the German master-narrative to an inglorious end.

2. The Reshaping of National Identity After 1945

On the "allied reservation" in 1945 the question of German national identity was not a priority item on the cultural or political agenda. Viewed from the perspective of the 1990s it could indeed be argued that between 1945 and 1989 the identity question, like Barbarossa, had once again entered a long hibernation. Though the issue of self-definition after the historical catastrophe of the Third Reich continued to haunt German dreams, bedevil academic discussions and inspire turgid trea-

48. Gerhard L. Weinberg, *A World at War: A Global History of World War Two* (Cambridge, 1994).

49. Institut für Zeitgeschichte, ed., *Deutscher Sonderweg. Mythos oder Realität?* (Munich, 1982); and Helga Grebing, *Der "deutsche Sonderweg" in Europa, 1806-1945. Eine Kritik* (Stuttgart, 1986).

50. Peter Hoffmann, *The German Resistance to Hitler* (Cambridge, 1988); and Michael Geyer, ed., *Resistance Against the Third Reich, 1933-1990* (Chicago, 1994).

tises, it seemed at the same time curiously remote from the practical tasks of postwar survival and reconstruction.

At the war's end, most Germans did not have the leisure to worry about how they felt about themselves. When asked in surveys conducted in the American zone from October, 1945 to February, 1949 what their "greatest cares and worries at the present time" were, the great majority mentioned food, clothing, shoes, POWs, and missing persons. After the June, 1948 currency reform, "money troubles in general" replaced food and clothing at the top of the list.[51] By early 1947 most Germans in the American zone considered it unlikely that the Allies would leave behind a united Germany at the end of the occupation and by August, 1948, nine months before the creation of the two German states, 70 percent favored the creation of a provisional government, with only 12 percent opposed to the idea. In supporting a separate West German government, the respondents were well aware that it would mean the continued, if not permanent division of the country.[52]

Division was also on the agenda of Germany's occupiers. By the late 1940s it was clear that neither the United States nor the Soviet Union were prepared to allow "their" Germans to pursue policies that they could not control and that could possibly be directed against their interests. Each superpower wanted a single German state only on its own terms: a liberal, pluralistic democratic state for the United States; a communist, worker, and peasant state for the Soviet Union. Unable to achieve such a unified state without military conflict, the two superpowers reluctantly settled for two states each having the social, economic, and political characteristics of its respective protector. Ironically, the division of Germany enabled both states within a relatively short time to achieve a status within their respective power bloc that a single German state could never have attained. Yet, as Ralf Dahrendorf has remarked, both German states in the 1950s thus lacked an integrating core; their respective political centers were Washington and Moscow; they were both "floating in the air."[53] They were not integrated social entities; they lacked cohesion and an identity that would differentiate them from others. Perhaps unification might provide that integrating substance in the future; the process of regaining unity itself could become an integrating force.

Most Germans were indifferent to these fateful decisions of the Allies. In the immediate postwar period, for understandable reasons, many wanted to forget about being German at all. After 1945 an emotional

---

51. Military government surveys cited in Anna J. and Richard L. Merritt, eds., *Public Opinion in Occupied Germany* (Urbana, 1970), 16-17.

52. Ibid., 24-25.

53. Ralf Dahrendorf, *Gesellschaft und Freiheit* (Munich, 1962), 318.

vacuum took the place of the affective and integrative ties which previously had linked the national community with political culture. This was in large part the consequence of the Nazi perversion of national sentiments and symbols. To fill the vacuum some Germans enthusiastically embraced the "European idea," a politically united Europe with no national borders, or gladly submitted to the "Americanization" so apparent in popular culture. Most simply reduced their scope of allegiance to the self, the family, and perhaps the local community. This mass withdrawal to the primary sphere, or *privatization*, as some social scientists have termed it, gave German leaders considerable freedom of action but also imposed limits on the intensity of commitment or identification they could require from their citizens.[54]

Privatization was a reaction to the intense politicization of the Nazi period and to the dislocations caused by World War II. Political leaders and critical intellectuals therefore made little headway with *Vergangenheitsbewältigung* in the first postwar years. The vast majority of Germans had other, more basic concerns such as how to put their lives back together, raise fatherless children, forage for food, or simply try to replace the pots, pans, dishes, linen, and other necessities of everyday life lost in air raids. Though it initially made Germany an anomic society, this widespread withdrawal from any form of political engagement was also a reaction to being burned politically in the Nazi era. The American historian Leonard Krieger describes this mood perceptively: For the mass of Germans

> apathy was the rule, an outer lethargy and inner emptiness so pervasive as to indicate not simply a state of shock in the face of catastrophe and the deadening routine of daily exercise in the face of a crushing struggle for survival, but a political withdrawal so profound as to mark the Nazi experience off from any traditional authoritarian analogy.[55]

The postwar elites did not have the option of privatization. They had to govern. The republics proclaimed in 1949 were, like their predeces-

54. This privatization was analyzed in an excellent study by the late German sociologist Friedrich Tenbruck, "Alltagsnormen und Lebensgefühle in der Bundesrepublik," in Richard Löwenthal and Hans-Peter Schwarz, eds., *Die Zweite Republik* (Stuttgart, 1974), 289-310. Public opinion polls at that time also registered this indifference through the high proportion of "no opinion" and "don't know" responses. In one study, only 15 percent of a national sample, for example, had an opinion on the Basic Law being drafted at the time in Bonn.

55. Ralf Dahrendorf, *Gesellschaft und Freiheit* (Munich, 1961), 304. See also the insightful essay by Leonard Krieger, "The Potential for Democratization in Occupied Germany: A Problem in Historical Projection," *Public Policy*, 17 (1968): 27-58. The very depth of this *Umbruch* also brought to German society new possibilities for democratization.

sors, faced with the problem of creating and fusing a commitment to a particular political form with an already existent, albeit muted, national identity. This sense of belonging to a particular national community, usually sharing a common physical territory, language, history, and cultural values, had been present among Germans at least as long as it has among many other European nations. Such a general national identification had not been linked, however, with a stable unified state and political system. Thus, to ensure its own stability, each succeeding political regime unsuccessfully sought to broaden the scope of national identification to include a commitment to the given state. The absence of a shared attachment to a particular state and political system has thus been the missing component in the German sense of national identity.

The presence of a competing German state (the GDR) within the same prewar territory, and having its capital in the communist part of the historic center of the Reich, complicated the task. West German leadership compounded the problem at first by officially encouraging support for the values of the liberal democratic constitution but not for the specific West German state. Thus in effect West German leadership, at least until the 1960s, was urging citizens to become democrats but not to develop too strong an attachment to the Federal Republic because it was only "provisional" until all Germans were reunited within a single democratic state with Berlin as its capital. Until that time, however, this provisional West German state also claimed to be the only legitimate representative for all members of the German nation within or outside its borders. This viewpoint was not shared by the leaders of communist East Germany, but apparently it had widespread support among East German citizens.[56]

After the establishment of the two German states in 1949, most West Germans gradually accepted the country's division as part of a stable status quo and prerequisite for peace. Between 1951 and 1976 the proportion of the adult population who believed that the Federal Republic and East Germany would never be united increased from 28 percent to 65 percent.[57] Popular acceptance of the Oder-Neisse line (the then de facto boundary between Poland and East Germany) increased from only 8 percent in 1951 to 61 percent by 1972.[58] By the early 1970s about two-

56. Walter Friedrich, "Mentalitätswandlungen der Jugend in der DDR," *Aus Politik und Zeitgeschichte*, 16-17 (April 13, 1990): 25-37.

57. EMNID surveys cited in David P. Conradt, "Changing German Political Culture," in Gabriel Almond and Sidney Verba, eds., *The Civic Culture Revisited* (Boston, 1980), 227-228.

58. Elisabeth Noelle-Neumann, *Jahrbuch der öffentlichen Meinung*, (Allensbach, 1968-1973) 5: 525. The most comprehensive record of public opinion polls for the post-

thirds of West Germans had come to consider European integration "more urgent" than German unification. Responses to these questions were strongly related to age, with younger Germans being far less interested in unification than older respondents.

Public opinion throughout most of the immediate postwar period was also indifferent to questions of national identity and their symbolic representation. Even in the mid-1950s most Germans reported little interest, much less "joy" over the constitution, national flag or anthem (the *Deutschlandlied*) than other democratic societies.[59] The level of national pride remained well below that found in other Western societies, but those Germans who did feel a sense of pride focused it on the accomplishments of postwar reconstruction. During the 1950s and especially the turbulent 1960s it became fashionable for intellectuals to dismiss this West German Economic Miracle as a poor substitute for some usually undefined idealism they found lacking in the mass public. This same approach was taken by their East German counterparts such as Stefan Heym and Heiner Müller after 1989. Yet there is little doubt that economic performance, symbolized by the D-Mark, became an important vehicle for postwar identification. When asked to characterize what it meant to be German or to specify why they were proud to be German, respondents repeatedly referred to "hard work," "diligence," "industry," and the "prosperity which we have achieved."

But more significantly, surveys from the 1960s through the 1980s found an increasingly strong relationship between a West German national identity and support for democratic institutions and processes. Those citizens who expressed a sense of national pride were more likely to support the constitution, the country's laws and political institutions, the competitive party structure, and even the educational system than those Germans with little or no pride in being German. Comparative studies have also discovered that a sense of national identity and pride is an important determinant of social and political integration and stability.[60]

Comparable material on a GDR identity is not available due to the lack of survey research under communist dictatorship. The impressions of observers, policy-makers, and the fragmentary empirical data that

war period can be found in this nine volume *Jahrbuch der öffentlichen Meinung* (published between 1947 and 1992), which contains the work of the Institut für Demoskopie. The senior editor for all volumes is the Institute's founder and director, Elisabeth Noelle-Neumann.

59. *Jahrbuch der öffentlichen Meinung*, passim.

60. For German and comparative data on this point see Elisabeth Noelle-Neumann and Renate Köcher, *Die Verletzte Nation* (Stuttgart, 1987), 17-71.

were collected suggest that the regime after the Wall and especially during the early Honecker era from the early 1970s to the mid-1980s had achieved a certain collective sense of self *(Wir-Bewußtsein)* among segments of the population. But this feeling rested on a fundamental ambivalence towards the manifest successes and failures of the East German state.[61]

Honecker's "Unity of Economic and Social Policy" brought many especially young GDR families their first modern apartment with sanitary facilities that did not have to be shared. Funded by Soviet oil deliveries and helped by West German credits, the East German version of goulash communism meant improved housing and a greater supply of consumer goods in exchange for political docility. Expanded travel opportunities to other socialist countries, above all Poland, Hungary, and Czechoslovakia showed East Germans that they had the right to a certain pride in their own accomplishments *(Aufbaustolz)*. Karl-Rudolf Korte emphasizes that this feeling owed much to the satisfaction of overcoming adverse circumstances: "The majority of the East German population had to support its own identity through some kind of idea of what the GDR accomplished. It was an identity formed through the shared experience of deprivations."[62]

The GDR's leadership was never able to steer a straight or steady course on the national identity question. Throughout the 1950s and most of the 1960s it professed its commitment to unification. The 1968 constitution declared that "the GDR and its citizens ... strive for the overcoming of the division of Germany forced upon the German nation by imperialism." The GDR would pursue "the step-by-step rapprochement of both German states until their unification on the basis of democracy and socialism." Six years later (October, 1974) this passage was deleted from the constitution, which now declared that the GDR was "forever and irrevocably allied with the Union of Soviet Socialist Republics." All references to the "German nation" and to the unification of Germany were expunged. The GDR was no longer a "socialist state of the German nation," but had rather become a "socialist state of the workers and peasants."[63]

---

61. Helmut Hanke and Thomas Koch, "Zum Problem der kulturellen Identität," *Weimarer Beiträge*, 8 (1985): 1237-1264.

62. Karl-Rudolf Korte, *Die Chance Genutzt? Die Politik zur Einheit Deutschlands* (Frankfurt, 1994), 85: "Isolation from the state and withdrawal into the 'niche-society' of the GDR offered security and human warmth in a milieu remote from politics. This was a version of compensatory identification, born out of the manifold economic and democratic deficits of the GDR."

63. Timothy Garton Ash, *In Europe's Name: Germany and the Divided Continent* (New York, 1993), 189.

This constitutional change followed from a reorientation in 1971, when the SED adopted a hard-line ideology and policy of complete demarcation *(Abgrenzung)* from the Federal Republic. The goal of its ideological efforts was "to establish in theoretical terms the GDR as a nation-state in its own right." Albert Norden, the SED's chief ideologue as Central Committee Secretary for Propaganda, claimed in July, 1972 that Bonn's talk about "national unity" was a fiction because "a unified nation" did not exist any more, since the "Krupps and the Krauses no longer had anything in common." He rejected the West German claim of a "sense of community" *(Zusammengehörigkeitsgefühl),* because "the feelings of the workers in the peoples' own factories are fundamentally different from the feelings of the private-capitalistic owners of the factories, banks and ship yards of the Federal Republic."[64]

This *Abgrenzung* was complemented a few years later by an effort to coopt certain aspects of the German historical and cultural past, which it was hoped would contribute to the legitimation of the GDR regime. Under the slogan of "heritage and tradition" the statue of Frederick the Great was returned to *Unter den Linden,* a more balanced biography of Bismarck appeared, and in 1983 the 500th anniversary of Luther's death was commemorated on a grand scale. These "progressive" figures in the German historical record were seen as precursors of socialism as practiced in the GDR, but *Abgrenzung* was difficult to square with these reappropriations of a common past. By attempting to kindle some spirit of GDR nationalism, the SED was in fact encouraging East Germans to discover their buried links with the West.

Whatever *Aufbaustolz* the GDR citizenry possessed was clearly not the same as a "national consciousness." The events of 1989-1990 certainly demonstrated that when East Germans could chose, most were ready to abandon the socialist experiment. When the social contract of continuous increases in the standard of living could no longer be maintained, the weakness of loyalties to "real existing socialism" and separate statehood were exposed. The socialist facade collapsed and in its place, for at least three-fourths of the GDR population, the German nation became the basis of a common self-definition. The vacuum created by the collapse of the SED regime was filled institutionally by West Germans and psychologically by a very materialist-based national identification.

Since unification, the "identity" of East Germans has varied with their perception of how the unification process, particularly in its economic dimensions, has progressed. During 1990 and the first quarter of 1991 East Germans were caught up with unification euphoria. They

64. Ibid., 104-105.

were more likely to consider themselves German than West Germans, i.e., the proportion of East Germans who felt more "German" than "East" German was greater than the proportion of West Germans who considered themselves Germans rather than West Germans. As the prosaic consequences of unification set in, with plant closings, rising unemployment, lower wages relative to the West, and media deprecation of *Ossis*, East German identification with *Deutschland* declined. Increasingly, East Germans differentiated themselves from the West. By 1994-1995, however, the pendulum had begun to swing back towards an all-German identification.

In contrast, attempts by political leaders in West Germany to reintroduce a "normal nationalism" into the political debate were limited to occasional books and *Feuilleton* articles, which had a very limited impact. Since the Christian Democrats were winning (1949, 1953, 1957, 1961, 1965) without any national appeal, they had no intention of changing a successful formula: peace, prosperity, and no experiments!

Most mainstream Christian Democrats at this time propagated at the elite level the so-called *Staatskerntheorie:* the Federal Republic formed the nucleus for a future all-German state, with the result that the GDR was seen as situated within the territory of the FRG, the laws of which applied *de jure,* if not *de facto* to the East German territory. (Ironically, this argument was not used by German prosecutors of GDR officials, judges, generals, border guards, and secret police after 1990. This claim was found neither in the 1973 Basic Treaty nor in the 1990 Unification Treaty, which did not dispute the sovereignty of the GDR from 1949-1989). For the first two decades of its existence, this construction made the GDR a state-free territory, an occupation zone which required an official position of non-recognition toward the GDR and outright hostility to any state which did not accept Bonn's approach to the GDR (Hallstein doctrine).[65]

Such a cautious approach to the national question was unsatisfactory to some CDU intellectuals. In 1965 Eugen Gerstenmaier, then President of the Bundestag, caused a mini-flap with his book, called "New Nationalism? Concerning the Transformation of the Germans," in which he made an argument very similar to that put forth by Wolfgang Schäuble and others after 1989: "If we [Germans] want to survive as a nation, we must once again begin to know who we are and what we want." Unless a sense of national identity were to become part of consciousness, he continued,

---

65. Gebhard Schweigler, *National Consciousness in Divided Germany* (Beverly Hills, 1975).

we will, already in this century, be reduced to a perhaps quite well function-ing, but historically and nationally quite unimportant part of a European consumer society or perhaps to a provincial appendage to the American industrial society .... In such a state of consciousness a reunification of our people and thus the natural and imperative self-realization of the Germans as a nation would no longer be possible.[66]

What recovering a national identity would mean in concrete terms was never spelled out by Gerstenmaier or others during this period.

Ironically, the first explicit postwar appeal to national sentiments occurred during the 1972 campaign with the famous slogan "Germans, we can be proud of our country." Apparently written by the Social-Democratic candidate Willy Brandt himself, this phrase was quite successful, since it appealed to submerged sentiments in a moderate way. Because both Brandt and the SPD enjoyed impeccable anti-nation-alist and anti-fascist credentials, they could safely play the nation-alist card. The campaign itself was designed to focus the attention of voters on the SPD-FDP's *Ostpolitik* of reconciliation with Germany's eastern neighbors.

The SPD's success with the national theme in 1972 prompted, of course, a similar response from the Christian Democrats in 1976. Survey research commissioned by the party in 1974 and 1975 found that most voters were now comfortable with concepts like "fatherland" and "patri-otism." When asked in 1975 whether fatherland "sounds good" or "is out of place in today's world," 60 percent of West Germans responded positively to the term, but only 32 percent of voters under 30 did so.[67] From this research came the Kohl-Biedenkopf theme *Aus Liebe zu Deutschland* in the 1976 election, which was continued in various forms in the campaigns of the 1980s.

In the 1970s and 1980s the growing self-confidence of West German leaders was seen in Bonn's increased independence in foreign policy. It began with a restrained opposition to America's Vietnam policy and con-tinued with efforts to rescue detente from the "Evil Empire" rhetoric of the Reagan era. Bonn became very sensitive to any moves in Washington – even in the name of anti-Communism – which would have a negative impact on the Federal Republic's relations to the East. In spite of strong opposition from the Reagan administration, Germany in 1982 went ahead with plans to build a massive pipeline system to supply Western Europe with natural gas from Siberia. Twenty years earlier Bonn had

66. Eugen Gerstenmaier, *Neuer Nationalismus? Von der Wandlung der Deutschen* (Stuttgart, 1965), 6-10.
67. *Jahrbuch der öffentlichen Meinung*, (1976) 6: 55.

abandoned a similar project because of American opposition.[68] Following the imposition of martial law in Poland in 1981 Bonn refused to join in American-led sanctions against Poland and the Soviet Union, and instead the Schmidt government urged Germans to send food parcels. Bonn's goal, of course, was to save *Ostpolitik* even at the cost of alienating the rising Polish opposition in Solidarity. Rightly or wrongly, the Federal Republic started to assert its own interests, a behavior consistent with a growing sense of national identity.

On the eve of the collapse of the Wall the once provisional Bonn Republic had become a stable, prosperous, and self-confident democracy. As Table 1 indicates, the proportion of Germans who were proud of the postwar political system had increased substantially by 1988. In 1959 only 7 percent expressed pride in some aspect of the political system. Among Americans at that time the level of pride in political institutions was 85 percent and among British respondents 46 percent were proud of the country's political order. By 1978 the German level of pride in their political system had risen to 31 percent and in 1988 51 percent of the respondents expressed pride in the postwar constitution and political order.

Table 1   Sources of National Pride, 1959-1988 (in percent)

	1959	1978	1988
Political Institutions, Constitution	7	31	51
Economy	33	40	50
Social Welfare Programs	6	18	39
Characteristics of the People	36	25	na
Contributions to Science	12	13	37
Contributions to the Arts	11	10	22
Other, no answer	43	39	50

Source: For 1959 and 1978: David P. Conradt, "Changing German Political Culture," In Gabriel Almond and Sidney Verba, eds., *The Civic Culture Revisited* (Boston, 1980), 230; for 1988: German General Social Survey cited in Peter Mohler, "Der Deutschen Stolz: Das Grundgesetz," *Informationsdienst Soziale Indikatoren*, 2 (July, 1989): 1-4.

68. Ash, *In Europe's Name*, 248-250.

It is important to note that by 1988 the political system was the area where Germans had the most pride. On the eve of unification, the institutions of the Federal Republic had even overtaken the economy, which had been the greatest source of postwar German national pride. Support for specific national symbols had also grown since 1949. The proportion of Germans stating that they feel "joyful" or "happy" when they see their black-red-gold national flag increased from 23 percent in 1951 to 60 percent by 1989. Solid majorities of Germans now considered national feelings of patriotism and pride to be important. In January 1989, over 80 percent of West Germans felt that they could be just as proud of their country as the Americans, British, or French.[69] With unification, the final embargo on the discussion of the nation and nationalism would be lifted and a new round of discussions begun.[70]

3. The Double Burden of Memory

The unexpected return of history in 1989-90 was bound to shake the fragile foundations of the separate postwar loyalties. In 1945 Hitler's defeat seemed to have ended history, since the dissolution of the Third Reich provided a negative closure to national development. Hence the postwar period appeared to many participants as a space beyond history, a timeless moment of recovery that at best constituted a postscript to the completed master-narrative of Germany. With the fall of the Wall, history returned with a vengeance, overthrowing communism, liberating suppressed populations, and redrawing the map of Eastern Europe.[71] The democratic awakening proved not only exhilarating but also threatening, since it upset Cold War certainties and thereby reopened previously settled questions of German identity.

In spite of the resumption of the national story, unification in effect doubled the burden of the German past in the twentieth century. As if the scars of the Nazi trauma were not enough, the collapse of the GDR added another failed dictatorship, set of collaborators or victims, and demands for restitution. Just as personal memories of the Third Reich had begun to fade, fresh recollections of suffering under communist repression took their place and the whole practical set of post-1945 problems such as purging the civil service, prosecuting criminal perpe-

---

69. *Jahrbuch der öffentlichen Meinung*, (1992) 9: 394.

70. Ernst-Wolfgang Böckenförde, "Die Nation," *Frankfurter Allgemeine Zeitung*, September 30, 1995.

71. Udo Wengst, *Historiker betrachten Deutschland* (Bonn, 1992); and Jarausch, *Unverhoffte Einheit*, 278ff.

trators, and compensating their victims appeared to have returned in 1990. Some historians and publicists began to talk about a *doppelte Vergangenheitsbewältigung,* a double coming to terms with frightening pasts in which experiences in dealing with the legacy of the first profoundly affected efforts to cope with the remains of the second.[72]

The public debate during the half-decade after unity has therefore been rife with historical allusions. Overwhelmed by the unexpected rush to German unity, many Easterners tried to regain orientation by reference to a longer time-frame. Just when they most needed a stable perspective, they were forced to realize that their larger conceptions of history had also crumbled with the fall of the Wall. This loss of an accustomed past was more upsetting in the East, where the Marxist-Leninist interpretation of law-like development of a socialist nation had provided a clear direction for the future. Eventually some Western intellectuals also began to sense that the return of the national state might challenge their predictions of a post-national trajectory towards European integration as well.[73] The unification shock has therefore triggered a broad reexamination of the historical basis of German identities.

Since the shadows of the past could hardly be exorcized in general, this reconsideration surfaced in several specific debates. The ways in which painful events would be privately recalled, publicly discussed, and politically memorialized offer clues to the role of the past in shaping the identity of a united Germany. The first area of soul-searching was the commemoration of World War II which forced Germans to confront their own role in Hitler's carnage, because their neighbors insisted on celebrating their victory. In contrast to the emotional war-guilt debate about starting World War I, virtually everyone has, however, continued to accept Hitler's responsiblity for unleashing the second Armageddon. If there was a controversy, it focused on the reasons for the Russian campaign in 1941 instead. Though some rightist commentators allege that the Nazi attack only forestalled a planned Soviet invasion,[74] the public seemed unwilling to follow the tortured logic of such apologetics.

The evaluation of German resistance provoked more heated altercations. While some outside observers have remained skeptical about the

---

72. Christoph Kleßmann, "Das Problem der doppelten 'Vergangenheitsbewältigung'," *Die Neue Gesellschaft* 38 (1991): 1099-1105; Eberhard Jäckel, "Die doppelte Vergangenheit," *Der Spiegel* 52 (1991): 39ff.

73. Jürgen Kocka, *Die Vereinigungskrise. Zur Geschichte der Gegenwart* (Göttingen, 1995), 83ff, 151ff. Cf. Stefan Berger, *The Search for Normality: National Identity and Historical Consciousness in Germany Since 1800* (Providence, RI, 1997).

74. Ernst Nolte, *Der europäische Bürgerkrieg 1917-1945. Nationalsozialismus und Bolschewismus* (Frankfurt, 1987).

existence of any real opposition to the Third Reich, both German successor states had drawn their legitimacy from a specific interpretation of the *Widerstand*. Bent on proving that it was the better anti-fascist Germany, the GDR had represented itself as the fulfillment of the dreams of the Communist resistance, widespread in working-class circles. Interested in the continuity of national traditions, the FRG had instead celebrated the officers, bureaucrats, and trade-union leaders who tried to assassinate Hitler in July 1944. When the resistance memorial in West Berlin dared to dedicate a small room to Communist opponents of the NS regime, conservative circles denounced such a broadening of memory as an insult to Hitler's bourgeois opponents.[75] But after much media discussion, liberal intellectuals succeeded in upholding the more inclusive version.

The commemoration of the War's end proved equally controversial, since it posed the alternative of defeat or liberation. While most Germans were relieved to have survived the killing, many soldiers and some civilians had experienced May of 1945 as the loss of the war. In contrast to such private feelings, the official histories of both German states saw the allied victory primarily as liberation from Nazi dictatorship, disagreeing only on which savior to thank most. After unification the tenor of this debate shifted somewhat and for the first time personal memories of victimization through saturation bombing, lengthy imprisonment, or mass expulsion from the East could be talked about openly. Interestingly enough, this outpouring of recollections of German suffering did not foster revanchist sentiment, but rather reinforced President Weizsäcker's paradoxical formula of liberation through defeat.[76]

On the whole, recent remembrances of the Second World War have become more inclusive rather than more nationalist. No doubt, there were some symbolic *faux pas*, such as Chancellor Kohl's misplaced desire to participate in the Normandy observances, which François Mitterrand satisfied with a separate ceremony. But in the meantime critical intellectuals were able to attack the last taboo of the Second World War by charging that the *Wehrmacht* actively participated in the racial war of annihilation in the East. A provocative Hamburg exhibition showed countless snapshots from individual soldiers that document military participation in persecution

75. Peter Steinbach, *Widerstreit im Widerstand. Der Widerstand gegen den NS in der Erinnerung der Deutschen* (Schönigh, 1994).

76. Christoph Kleßmann, *Befreiung durch Zerstörung. Das Jahr 1945 in der deutschen Geschichte* (Hanover, 1995); Konrad H. Jarausch, "Zwischen Niederlage und Befreiung. Das Jahr 1945 und die Kontinuitäten deutscher Geschichte," *Gewerkschaftliche Monatshefte*, May 1995.

and extermination.[77] In spite of attempts to discredit communist claims so as to establish the Western version of events, the commemoration of World War II did not lead to revanchist outbursts but generally supported a reconciliation between the erstwhile belligerents.[78]

A second sensitive area of public debate, the issue of complicity in the Holocaust, continues to be more difficult to discuss. After years of NS propaganda, Germans had found the horrifying pictures, disclosed at the liberation of the camps and broadcast during the Nuremberg Trials, hard to believe. While accusations of survivors against the worst of the SS perpetrators could be dealt with through legal channels, questions about the role of the majority of the "decent" people proved disturbing, since they touched virtually everyone. In contrast to the nightmares of the victims, focused on their persecution, the recollections of most bystanders involve other kinds of suffering such as losing family members in the fighting or bombing, as well as rape, expulsion, and hunger. Supported only by a critical minority, demands for atonement were therefore seen as largely coming from the outside. (Nonetheless the public reception of the controversial Goldhagen book has been surprisingly positive.)[79]

The two successor states were therefore only partly successful in dealing with these painful questions of German guilt. In the East the SED claimed to be building a better Germany on the basis of anti-Fascist commitment that provided a clean break with the Nazi past. In spite of a rigorous personnel purge in justice and education, GDR practice did not live up to the ideal, since assigning guilt to "monopoly capitalism" absolved the majority of the people and failed to take anti-Semitism seriously.[80] In the West, the less thorough process of de-nazification allowed minor Nazis to survive and the rejection of collective guilt covered the sins of collaboration with silence. But a massive restitution program paid billions of DM to Jewish victims and eventually the critical minority succeeded in

77. "Wir hatten geglaubt, wir könnten anständig bleiben," *Die Zeit*, March 3, 1995. Cf. Jost Dülffer, *Führerglaube und Vernichtungskrieg* (Stuttgart, 1992); and Ernst Klee and Willi Dressen, eds., *'Gott mit uns'. Der deutsche Vernichtungskrieg im Osten, 1939-1945* (Frankfurt, 1989).

78. Bernd Weisbrod, "Der 8. Mai in der deutschen Erinnerung," (MS. Göttingen, 1995); Kurt Sontheimer, "Selbstverständlich war dies nicht," *Süddeutsche Zeitung*, July 21, 1995.

79. Peter Dudek, "Vergangenheitsbewältigung. Zur Problematik eines umstrittenen Begriffes," *Aus Politik und Zeitgeschichte* (1992) B 1-2: 44-53. Cf. also Richard Matthias Müller, *Normal-Null und die Zukunft der deutschen Vergangenheitsbewältigung* (Schernfeld, 1994).

80. Jürgen Danyel, "Die geteilte Vergangenheit. Gesellschaftliche Ausgangslagen und politische Dispositionen für den Umgang mit Nationalsozialismus und Widerstand in beiden deutschen Staaten nach 1949," in Jürgen Kocka, ed., *Historische DDR-Forschung* (Berlin, 1993), 129ff.

forcing a more honest confrontation with complicity in education and the media and in beating back revisionist efforts in the *Historikerstreit*.[81]

The effect of unification on this complex set of evasions and self-incriminations has been uneven. Once again the consequences have been more dramatic in the East, since the fall of the Wall exposed the "instrumentalization" of anti-Fascism by the SED. During four decades in the GDR, genuine revulsion against Hitler had turned into a justification for a one-party dictatorship that provided an unchallengeable air of superior morality.[82] Portraying the Third Reich as the product of monopoly capitalism justified the communist expropriation of Junkers and factory owners in order to destroy the social basis of Nazism. At the same time, anti-Fascism offered a brown brush for tarring the Federal Republic with accusations of neo-Nazism. Since the democratic awakening in the fall of 1989 discredited anti-Fascism as an instrument of repression, it is unclear whether it also rendered the credibility of broader critiques of the Nazi past suspect.

In the West revisionist efforts have been unable to shake the public commitment to confronting the Holocaust. Initially, Jewish fears that the crimes of the second dictatorship would overshadow the atrocities of the first seemed borne out by neo-conservative calls for an end to German self-mutilation. However, commemorations of the liberation of concentration camps such as Buchenwald have kept the issue of German guilt in the public eye. The re-dedication of the Berlin memorial *Neue Wache* from victims of Fascism to all victims of war and repression may represent some dilution of the singularity of Jewish victimhood by referring also to German suffering. But public clamor for the construction of a huge Holocaust memorial close to the Brandenburg Gate shows continued awareness of the need for a central place of symbolic memory. While this project is currently stalled by personal and artistic jealousies, its realization seems only a matter of time.[83]

The effect of the public controversies about Holocaust remembrance on popular attitudes is difficult to determine. Based on several surveys, a recent study concludes that the pessimist thesis of denial is inaccurate, since information about German responsibility for genocide is wide-

81. Charles S. Maier, *The Unmasterable Past: History, Holocaust and German National Identity* (Cambridge, 1988); and Konrad H. Jarausch, "Removing the Nazi Stain? The Quarrel of the German Historians," *German Studies Review* 11 (1988): 285ff.

82. Jürgen Danyel, "Antifaschismus und Verdrängung. Zum Umgang mit der NS-Vergangenheit in der DDR," in Jürgen Kocka and Martin Sabrow, eds., *Die DDR als Geschichte* (Berlin, 1994), 148-152; and Jarausch, "The Failure of East German Anti-Fascism," 85ff.

83. Jane Kramer, "The Politics of Memory," *The New Yorker*, August 14, 1995.

spread, and anti-Semitism is lower than in some other Western countries. As a legacy of prior indoctrination East Germans show a higher degree of anti-Fascist responses than West Germans, although even these still do comparatively well. On the Left, an unprejudiced minority of urban, younger, and educated respondents has internalized a "Holocaust-identity" that accepts the shame of its fathers. In the middle, an "ambivalent" and less clearly demarcated group knows about Nazi crimes and is not openly prejudiced, but wants "to draw a line" under the terrible past. The danger comes from the Right, where less than ten percent in the East and about double that number in the West resent the burden of guilt and show remnants of anti-Semitic biases.[84]

A third area of contention is the legacy of "real existing socialism." Coping with the debris of the GDR has proven particularly difficult, because it involves, contrary to ideological expectations, a failed dictatorship of the Left. Even if its imprisonment of much of the population seemed reprehensible, the SED-state could count on progressive sympathies, since it claimed to follow Enlightenment ideals of equality and fraternity. While dyed-in-the-wool capitalists are triumphant about the collapse of communism, leftist intellectuals are discouraged by the defeat of this imperfect version of their dreams.[85] The task is further complicated by altercations over *Ostpolitik*, with defenders claiming that the easing of human contacts undermined the East German regime and critics asserting that the de facto recognition of the SED stabilized it. Though the Left had a method to soften the border, it lacked the will to overthrow the SED, while the Right had the will but could not find a method to topple the communists.

The media have largely reduced the discussion about the GDR to the Stasi issue. Playing on victims' resentment of the secret police, sensationalist disclosures have tainted the Eastern elite with collaboration so that hardly any prominent figure has escaped unscathed. As early as 1990 GDR politicians such as CDU leader Lothar de Maizière were "outed" and subsequently such celebrities as the bobsledder Harald Czudaj or the writers Christa Wolf, Heiner Müller, and Sascha Anderson were found to have been informal informants. To establish a checking procedure the

84. Hermann Kurthen, "Antisemitism, Xenophobia and How United Germany Copes with the Past," in Hermann Kurthen, Werner Bergmann, and Rainer Erb, eds., *Antisemitism and Xenophobia in Germany after Unification* (New York, 1997). Cf. also Bernd Giesen, *Die Intellektuellen und die Nation. Eine deutsche Achsenzeit* (Frankfurt, 1993), 236-255.

85. Rainer Eckert, Ilko-Sascha Kowalczuk, and Ulrike Poppe, eds., *Wer schreibt die DDR-Geschichte?* (Berlin, 1995). Cf. Konrad H. Jarausch, "The Double Disappointment: Revolution, Unification and German Intellectuals," in Michael Geyer, ed., *The Powers of Intellectuals in Contemporary Germany* (Chicago, 1998).

unification treaty established a special "Federal Deputy for Secret Service Documents," popularly known as the Gauck-office, according to its director.[86] Bitter recriminations over the ambiguous role of Brandenburg SPD premier Manfred Stolpe or PDS leader Gregor Gysi have poisoned the climate of post-unification politics. Public furor over any Stasi connection has tended to make discussion of the actual quality of complicity difficult.

In spite of a resolve to do better the second time around, the courts have experienced great difficulties in punishing violations of human rights by officials of the communist regime. Since the mass of records left by the collapse of the GDR made it possible to document transgressions, prosecutors were able to initiate numerous cases. While the judiciary did hand down modest sentences against the soldiers who shot fleeing East Germans at the Wall, it only succeeded in condemning for minor offenses those members of the SED leadership that were not too old to stand trial. Prominent defendants like Wolfgang Vogel or Alexander Schalck-Golodkowski protracted litigation, and ultimately the Federal Supreme Court absolved most of the GDR's foreign espionage.[87] The key problem turned out to be the legal basis of the proceedings; since the Unification Treaty stipulated only that when defendants had violated East German laws, they could be held accountable, the courts proved generally helpless when contested actions were previously legal.

As a positive alternative offering information and education, the Bundestag in 1993 convened a special commission of inquiry into the GDR as political system. Led by the East German opposition pastor Rainer Eppelmann (CDU), this *Enquêtekommission*, composed of legislators and historians, held a series of hearings into the basic features of the SED-state. Prompted by numerous specialists' briefs, commission members questioned prominent figures of the prior regime such as Hans Modrow (PDS) who sought to defend their actions. Since the sessions were covered by television, these charges reached a broader audience than newspaper commentary or academic analysis. But with the approach of the 1994 election, the debates deteriorated into partisanship, with the CDU portraying communism as evil, the SPD defending its *Ostpolitik*, and the PDS claiming to be victimized.[88] Split into competing majority

86. Joachim Gauck, *Die Stasi-Akten. Das unheimliche Erbe der DDR* (Hamburg, 1991); and Albrecht Schönherr, ed., *Ein Volk am Pranger? Die Deutschen auf der Suche nach einer neuen politischen Kultur* (Berlin, 1991).

87. Dieter Schroeder, "Ein Staat – Zwei Nationen," *Süddeutsche Zeitung*, October 3, 1995.

88. Deutscher Bundestag, Referat Öffentlichkeitsarbeit, *Bericht der Enquête-Kommission "Aufarbeitung von Geschichte und Folgen der SED-Diktatur in Deutschland"* (Bonn, 1994). The dozens of Gutachten have just been published as separate volumes.

and minority reports, the verdict remained inconclusive, forcing the commission to continue its work.

Much of the public debate is dominated by an accusatory discourse which paints the GDR as a repressive regime, an *Unrechtsstaat*. This critical characterization is primarily promoted by prior opponents of the SED in the civic movement and by Western anti-communists who knew all along that it was wrong. Their language tends to be emotional, generalizing harshly about the fundamental illegitimacy of the East German regime. Its theoretical justification is a revived totalitarianism theory which, in the writings of Hannah Arendt, Carl Friedrich, or Zbigniew Brzezinski, equated Fascist with Stalinist dictatorship during the heyday of the Cold War. The political implication of such a condemnatory approach is the discrediting of everything East German and the demand for its replacement with superior Western practices. Instead of a flawed anti-Fascism, the hardliners advocate anti-totalitarianism as the political consensus of the new Germany.[89]

Against such accusations, other voices are trying to establish a counter-discourse that sees the GDR in a more positive light. For many East Germans, especially intellectuals, and some Western sympathizers, the SED-system was instead a "noble experiment" that only failed due to unfortunate circumstances and mistaken policies. The rhetoric of these GDR defenders is more subdued, citing positive counter-examples such as full employment or greater equality of incomes as the basis for a more generous judgment. The apologists reject comparisons with the Third Reich as oversimplifications and insist on the progressive aspirations of the socialist tradition while simultaneously distancing themselves from the excesses of its faulty implementation. The political purpose of this discourse is the regeneration of a post-Marxist opposition to Western colonization and the relegitimation of alternatives to capitalist exploitation.[90]

Some commentators also argue for a more differentiated view of the GDR that tries to avoid negative or positive myth-making. In the East especially reform communists and in the West primarily members of the moderate left see the East German state as a set of irresolvable contradictions between admirable and deplorable traits. Their language attempts to be more dispassionate in order to come to terms with the complexities and ambiguities of the subject. Departing from a compar-

89. Konrad H. Jarausch, "The GDR as History in United Germany: Reflections on Public Debate and Academic Controversy," forthcoming in *German Politics and Society*, summer 1997.

90. Rainer Eckert, "Strukturen, Umfeldorganisationen und Geschichtsbild der PDS," *Horch und Guck* 4 (1995): 1-15.

ative perspective of a modern dictatorship, they see one-party rule not just as repression from the top but also as cooperation and/or resistance on the bottom. In political terms, these moderates want to sort out which GDR attributes were inhumane and which others might be worth preserving for the future. Half a decade after unification, proponents of condemnation, amnesia, and critical historicization continue to struggle for public and academic ascendancy.[91]

A final battleground is the issue of re-nationalization of German identity. The unexpected restoration of the national state has posed the question of what to do with a political organization that was thought to have been left behind. The rush to German unity in 1990 not only overwhelmed the GDR theory of a separate "socialist nation" but also threw the FRG thesis of a "post-national" self-consciousness into doubt.[92] The reconceptualization of the mission of the central historical museums illustrates this dilemma. The exhibition of the East Berlin Armory, which showed the growth of socialist separatism, had to be quickly closed; but Helmut Kohl's plans for a postmodern museum of national history in West Berlin also had to be dropped so that its contents could be used to refurbish the Eastern Zeughaus as a showplace of the national past; and finally the "House of History" in Bonn, which was to celebrate a distinctive Western sense of self, had to be transformed through the addition of GDR material into a memorial to postwar partition.

Under the banner of "normalization," the Right is vigorously promoting a return to a national identity. Viewing the nation as a "natural" category, many conservatives hail unification as the end of the aberration of division and therefore call for a self-conscious resumption of a chastened version of German traditions. For instance, CDU leader Wolfgang Schäuble asserts that "the bond which holds a community together and creates identity is the nation." In foreign policy, this reorientation motivates the re-emergence of geopolitical thoughtpatterns about Germany as land of the middle and inspires calls for greater assertiveness in the name of presumed "national interests." Domestically, such an attitude supports an affirmative perspective on the German past that minimizes problematic legacies and it feeds a sense of ethnic exclusiveness towards foreigners.[93] While the rightist fringe aggressively promotes this re-

91. Jürgen Kocka, "Die Geschichte der DDR als Forschungsproblem," in *Historische DDR-Forschung*, 9-26; and "Sackgasse aus dem Sonderweg – Zum Ort der DDR in der europäischen und deutschen Geschichte," in *Die DDR als Geschichte*, 197 ff.

92. Jarausch, "Normalisierung oder Renationalisierung? Zur Umdeutung der deutschen Vergangenheit," 559-572.

93. Wolfgang Schäuble, *Und der Zukunft zugewandt* (Berlin, 1994); Heimo Schwilk and Ulrich Schacht, eds., *Die selbstbewußte Nation* (Frankfurt, 1994); and

nationalization, less extreme versions of such views are also starting to influence centrist circles to some degree.

In contrast, a defensive Left tries to cling to its rejection of nationalism. Understanding the nation as a constructed category, intellectuals blame nationalism for the disasters of German history and warn insistently against falling back into national categories. For example, Günter Grass, who once advocated the maintenance of cultural ties to the East, invokes Auschwitz as symbol of the Holocaust to oppose unification by arguing that a return to nation-state thinking would automatically lead to similar disasters. Abroad, critics oppose the use of military force on the basis of the neighbors' recollections of World War II and promote a wider European or international consciousness. At home, they advocate openness to immigration and multicultural cooperation between the various ethnic groups that make up about eight percent of all the people living in the FRG.[94] In effect, intellectuals want to retain their regional or transnational pre-unification identities.

Between these fronts, some moderates are trying to establish a democratic patriotism. Aware of the terrible excesses of nationalism in the past, they nonetheless argue for a "new foundation of the German nation" in order to stabilize the enlarged FRG. In this vein, the East Berlin SPD spokesman and theologian Richard Schröder calls for accepting his "difficult fatherland" with both its guilt and achievements. On the one hand these intermediaries find the intellectuals' "constitutional patriotism" too cold to provide a firm basis for popular loyalty to democracy, which according to Western examples also requires emotional bonding. But on the other hand, they reject the ethnic nationalism of the Right in favor of a constitutional patriotism which propagates an open conception of citizenship that accepts multicultural differences.[95] Such moderates want to prevent the return of a militant nationalism, so to speak, through an inoculation with democratic patriotism.

Five years after unification it is still unclear which of these tendencies will win out in the long run. To gain support, re-nationalization advo-

Hans-Peter Schwarz, *Die Zentralmacht Europas. Deutschlands Rückkehr auf die Weltbühne* (Berlin, 1994).

94. Günter Grass, *Ein weites Feld* (Göttingen, 1995); Peter Glotz, *Die falsche Normalisierung. Die unmerkliche Verwandlung der Deutschen* (Frankfurt, 1994); and Hans-Ulrich Wehler, "Angst vor der Macht? Die Machtlust der Neuen Rechten," Heft 8 *Gesprächskreis Geschichte* (Bonn, 1995).

95. Richard Schröder, *Deutschland, schwierig Vaterland. Für eine neue politische Kultur* (Freiburg, 1993); Christian Meier, *Die Nation, die keine sein will* (Munich, 1991); and Heinrich August Winkler, "Nationalismus, Nationalstaat und nationale Frage in Deutschland seit 1945," *Aus Politik und Zeitgeschichte* 1991, B 40, 12ff.

cates have claimed to be speaking for a more traditionalist generation of 1989, which is trying to undo the damage wrought by its rebellious predecessor, the generation of 1968. On closer inspection the fronts in this generational struggle for opinion leadership are curiously reversed. It is the aging former radicals who occupy many key positions in the media or in academe and who are now trying to defend their post-national conceptions against a neo-conservative group of younger intellectuals in their thirties and forties who use their national battle cry to advance their own careers.[96] Ironically, the really young, in their late teens and early twenties, have hardly taken sides so far, making the outcome of this conflict between the self-styled generations uncertain.

Instead of a massive shift back to the nation, there have been subtle signs of a gradual easing of the former taboo concerning national sentiments. Media anxiety about the ugly and deplorable incidents of xenophobia may be somewhat misleading, since opinion surveys show that such feelings are limited to a small minority. The electoral failure of the neo-Nazi parties and the outpouring of mass support for tolerance show that the skin-head milieu is confined to dispirited and unemployed youths, supported by some incorrigible adults.[97] Instead, what has been noticeable is greater pride and use of national symbols during international sports events such as the European soccer championships, for instance the waving of black-red-gold flags and choruses of "Deutschland, Deutschland." Also Chancellor Kohl's references to the word "fatherland" no longer seem quite as quaint as before and in a linguistic shift, the word "Germany" is making somewhat of a comeback as a self-evident category, without first having to be defined politically.

4. Living with the Ghosts

What does the burden of history suggest for the restructuring of German identities in the last decade of the twentieth century? In contrast to the legacy of other democracies, the German past is hardly a source of pride or inspiration, but rather an occasion for collective embarrassment and shame. While medieval glories seem safe enough and there is

96. Ulrich Greiner, "Die Neunundachtziger," *Die Zeit*, September 16, 1994; and Rainer Zitelmann, "Position und Begriff. Über eine neue demokratische Rechte," *Die selbstbewußte Nation*, 163ff.

97. Felix Philip Lutz, "Veranwortungsbewußtsein und Wohlstandschauvinismus. Die Bedeutung historisch-politischer Einstellungen der Deutschen nach der Einheit," in Werner Weidenfeld, ed., *Deutschland. Eine Nation – doppelte Geschichte* (Cologne, 1993), 157ff.; as well as a youth-survey in *Der Spiegel*, 38 (1994).

much early modern artistic creativity and scientific achievement to admire, more recent times are deeply problematic due to the political instability that culminated in two dictatorships. It is a continuing irritant that the bulk of the German population collaborated willingly with the Third Reich and even the SED-regime could draw some internal support from the legacy of Marx and the KPD.[98] The experience of this double repression has left more ghosts, complicating self-conceptions, than in those countries where repression was imposed largely from the outside.

From a long-term perspective, the unexpected reunification once again rearranged cultural patterns of identity. The excesses of Hitler's aggression and genocide had so discredited the Barbarossa myth as to break off the ethnic strain of nationalism after 1945. Surprisingly quickly, the very term *Reich* disappeared from political vocabulary, sounding out of place where it remained, as in the GDR railroad, the *Reichsbahn.* Instead the Germans were thrown back upon the eighteenth-century notion of the *Kulturnation,* a cultural unity sustained by intellectuals speaking a common language. Coming to terms with the terrible Nazi legacy was one of the strongest bonds, uniting East and West during division. While both postwar states claimed to carry on the Schillerian tradition, it was the Western version of capitalist democracy that eventually succeeded in realizing Tell's imperative.[99] The rejection of the imperial myth made it possible to progress from cultural community once more to political freedom combined with unity.

The historical foundation of this democratic nation-state is, however, fiercely contested. In the construction of a new master narrative, alternative memories confront one another in a battle for cultural hegemony over a united Germany. The Right generally wants to return to those national traditions that were not tarnished too badly and it promotes an assertive and ethnically exclusive stance. The slogan of normalization implies leaving behind the traumas of the past and constructing a new German identity out of the purified materials of a nation-state. In contrast the Left wishes to hold on to a postwar post-nationalism that had fled from German self-conceptions towards new American, communist, or European identities. In the critical perspectives, the terrors of history prohibit any resumption of normalcy and forever man-

---

98. Cordt Schnibben, "Das deutsche Wesen," *Der Spiegel,* 50 (1993); Irmline Veit-Brause, "Rethinking the State of the Nation: The Case of Germany," *Yearbook of European Studies* 7 (1994): 205-234.

99. Hinrich C. Seeba, "Fabelhafte Einheit: Von deutschen Mythen und nationaler Identität," in *Zwischen Traum und Trauma,* 59ff. Cf. also Otto Dann, *Nation und Nationalismus in Deutschland 1770-1990* (Munich, 1993), 297 ff.

date a German sense of guilt and contrition. In a nutshell, current struggles revolve around the issue which of these appropriations of the past will win out.[100]

Instead of subsiding, the debates about history have intensified in the wake of unification. Although remembrances of the Second World War, recollections of the Holocaust, and judgments about the GDR are separate arenas, these debates are linked by cross-cutting attitudes towards national identity. Some changes in the prior appropriations have already become noticeable. Most dramatically, the communist interpretation of history has lost credibility, personnel, and infrastructure as a result of the dissolution of the GDR Academy and the restructuring of universities. At the same time, proponents of re-nationalization, once considered a lunatic fringe, are making some inroads, and their theses, such as the critique of Westernization, are being debated more seriously. Moreover, some of the hysterical self-criticism that was fixated on German crimes alone appears to be waning and a more balanced appropriation that also allows references to German suffering seems to be emerging.[101]

Seven years after unity, only the barest outlines of a possible consensus are becoming visible. The unforeseen return of a single state is likely to re-establish the saliency of the national level of German identities that range from the regional to the European. Unlike in the nineteenth century where unity was the result of a national movement, during the second unification the common state precedes national consciousness; therefore it is the restored, if shrunken polity that is likely to spark efforts to fill it with a new shared identity. In order to justify the collection of taxes and the requirement of military service, states tend to promote the loyalty of their citizens. Though the enlarged FRG is far from unleashing nationalist propaganda, civic education is bound to propagate a sense of collective responsibility, if only to justify financial transfers to the East.[102] Does not the entire debate about the prospects of internal unity revolve around the presumption of a common destiny?

Ultimately, the current reconfiguration depends to a considerable degree upon which lessons are learned from Germany's traumatic history. So far, foreign fears of the establishment of a "Fourth Reich" have proven

100. Antonia Grunenberg, ed., *Welche Geschichte wählen wir?* (Hamburg, 1992); and Konrad H. Jarausch, "Die Postnationale Nation: Zum Identitätswandel der Deutschen 1945-1995," *Historicum* (spring 1995): 30-35.

101. Eckhart Fuchs, "'Mehr als ein Koffer bleibt:' Gedanken zu den gegenwärtigen Geschichtskulturen in Deutschland," *Z. Zeitschrift für Marxistische Erneuerung*, 5 (1994), 110-124.

102. Heinrich August Winkler, "Rebuilding a Nation: The Germans Before and After Unification," *Daedalus* 123 (Winter 1994): 107ff.

grossly exaggerated, since the neo-Nazi movement is smaller than its counterparts in Italy or France.[103] At the same time, attempts to perpetuate a post-national stance via Holocaust guilt seem to evoke fewer responses, since they imply the perpetuation of a negative German exceptionalism. The current challenge is rather to develop a chastened version of identity that accepts the entirety of the past, with all its achievements and disasters, as a mandate for a more peaceful future. In order to "pay off our debts together" the East German theologian Richard Schröder counsels: "We have to unite our histories." If they foreswear external hegemony for the sake of European cooperation and renounce internal exclusiveness in favor of multicultural openness, the new Germans at last have a chance to construct a more stable sense of their identities.[104]

103. Conor Cruise O'Brien, "Beware the Reich is Reviving," *Times*, October 31, 1989; and Helno Sana, *Das vierte Reich. Deutschlands später Sieg* (Hamburg, 1990).

104. Richard Schröder, "Gemeinsam die Hypotheken abtragen," *Die Zeit*, September 29, 1995; Jürgen Kocka, "Deutsche Entscheidungen. Rückblick und Ausblick 1995," in *Vereinigungskrise*, 170ff.

Chapter II

NATIVES, STRANGERS, AND FOREIGNERS

Constituting Germans by Constructing Others

Jeffrey Peck, Mitchell Ash, and *Christiane Lemke*

The debate in Germany about Germans and foreigners is as complicated as it is volatile. It is about peoples living inside Germany who are defined as foreign by Germans, and is therefore both about these peoples themselves and about Germans' images and treatment of them. The asymmetries involved are already embodied in the terms used to characterize each group. Germans do not describe themselves as *Eingeborene*, which translates as "natives" in English but traditionally refers to natives of third-world countries; rather, Germans use the term *Einheimische*, literally, "people who are at home here." This word is seldom if ever used to describe Turks or Jews, no matter how long such people or their forebears may have lived in Germany.

Indicative in their own ways are the generic terms used for non-Germans in Germany, *Fremde* and *Ausländer*. Both words refer to foreigners, but *Fremde*, meaning "strangers" or "people not known here" can also refer to Germans from other parts of the country, for example tourists. Most important for the following discussion, the word *Fremde* also applies to the special status of German Jews, who have been and still feel in a special sense, "strangers in their own land," as one writer put it in the 1970s. Although the majority of them are formally citizens, they are nonetheless not regarded as fully German by traditional definitions of nationhood based on culture.

The evolution of these relationships since unification makes it clear that essential notions of national identity are at stake when the status of foreigners in Germany is discussed. This is as much a struggle for discursive hegemony as for political and economic power. The debate about foreigners in Germany draws immediate attention not because of the literary production of foreign writers, but because of the apparent contradictions in official legal and political discourse. The often quoted claim that "Germany is not an immigration country" exemplifies the clash between administrative and legal "realities" and the daily lives of millions of non-Germans living and working there. Guest-workers *(Gastarbeiter)*, asylum seekers, immigrants, refugees, all conflated under the general term *Ausländer*, are different terms for a broad range of peoples who are not defined as German by the Federal Republic's Basic Law. The definition of German citizenship based on ethnic descent makes the presence in the country of large numbers of people who are not and cannot become Germans in this sense, but who nonetheless claim political, social, economic, and cultural rights, a vexing problem. Unification has raised the stakes in this debate about civic and communal identity and the principles of the legal state by adding 17 million "new" Germans to the population.

In spite of signs of growing tolerance, many Turks, Jews, and blacks still do not feel at ease due to the recent rise in xenophobia. While neither the Turks nor their current situation can be compared with the Jews or their persecution, both groups still remain "the other" among the Germans, in the case of the Turks because they are largely non-Christian, and for both groups because they are still defined as racially and culturally different. Although they are far less numerous, Afro-Germans are even more vulnerable. Normative conceptions defining "we-ness" on the basis of being "white" and Christian still appear to hold sway among many Germans. At the same time, Germans who think of themselves as liberal and progressive often confuse tolerance of different peoples with uniform acceptance. Therefore, the long-term problem of defining German citizenship and identity in a way that will give a greater measure of human dignity to the millions of foreigners and "strangers" on German soil remains unresolved.

Each of the sections of this chapter addresses this issue from a different disciplinary point of view. The historical part provides perspective by considering notions of Germanness and the non-German as well as the actual treatment of foreigners and "strangers" since 1871. It argues that otherness was constituted along nationalist-cultural, religious-ethnic, and racialist discursive axes, that Nazism simplified this complexity with murderous results, and that after the war the older, multiplex pattern was reconstituted in new ways and an East-West dimension added. The middle section focuses on how the German political system has dealt since unification with the central issues of asylum and citizenship, two of the crucial indicators for the status of foreigners. It details the differences among the various non-German groups and explores the contradiction between the lack of an immigration law and the reality of 7 million foreigners. The final part analyzes contemporary constructions of "stranger" and foreigner identities by looking at the images, myths and stereotypes created in the imagination of Germans and others. Through a close reading of *Rubensteins Versteigerung* by German Jewish author Rafael Seligmann, it shows how the protagonist's conflict and ambivalence about his dual identity become emblematic for other "strangers" and foreigners in the Federal Republic. From each perspective, resolving the tension between Germans and others remains one of the key challenges for the larger FRG.

1. Past Perspectives

Ascriptions of "otherness" or difference developed in strange ways from the first German unification in 1871 to the second in 1990. Attributions of "otherness" applied not only to "foreigners" inside and outside Germany, but also to "strangers" who were actually holding German citizenship, albeit in different ways at different times. This was most obviously the case for German Jews, but it was also true for others lacking in one or several attributes deemed to define "Germanness," such as mental or physical health, and even, in a certain limited sense, to women. Hence conceptions of alterity have remained interdependent with the multiple difficulties of defining "Germanness" in a new state with uncertain frontiers, beset by religious, regional, and class conflict.

Constructions of the "non-German" have been *multivalent*. This means, first, that multiple, at times contradictory connotations of both "Germanness" and the "non-German" could live alongside one another; it means, second, that these constructions have had multiple social and political functions and have interacted with one another in different ways. Among the axes along which alterity has been constructed are: a *national-cultural* axis, based on the widely-shared definition of Germanness as membership in a *Kulturnation* or a culturally defined *Volk*, rather than as citizenship in a state; a *religious-ethnic* axis, based on Christian belief or heritage as a defining feature of Germanness; and a *racialist* axis, based on vaguely defined "folkish" or "biological" criteria in varied combinations with one another. Each of these trajectories in turn interacted with the others, and each was structured in turn by gender and class dimensions. An adequate grasp of alterity in Germany thus requires understanding each dimension in its interrelationships with the others, as well as their transformations over time.

Otherness and the Non-German in the German Empire

According to common opinion the culture of the West has created a single continuous discourse of "otherness" incorporating so-called "primitives" or non-Western peoples as well as less privileged members of "we" groupings. But there has never been only one such text. In the discursive patterns of educated elite and middle-class Germans in the late nineteenth century, multiple "theys" were invented to help define a multivalent "we." Therefore the construction of alterity was not the result of a *Sonderweg*, but rather the German variant of a widespread pattern, the formation of bourgeois national identities. In all Western countries the dilemma was the same – how to create class identities that posited the bourgeois as the virtual representatives of humanity and also as the embodiment of what is highest and best in the nation.

In Germany, unification marked a fundamental break with earlier, more encompassing ideals of a German *Kulturnation* by creating, in Austria, a new German foreign country[1] During the Imperial era, the task thus became the recreation of Germanness. A new "we" gradually emerged through contested discourses and interests in many fields, with regional, class, gender, and status as well as national dimensions. The newness of Germany as a nation-state, the speed of that new nation's entry into the industrial world, and the conflicts between the pre-existing ideal of a *Kulturnation* and the realities of class, regional, gender, and cultural conflict in the Kaiserreich combined to intensify the ambivalences at work. A precedent for some of these tensions had been set by the ambiguous status of the predominant state in the new German Empire, Prussia, which was itself a multinational and ethnically mixed entity in which Saxon and Swabian colonists and dynastically acquired Rhinelanders lived alongside Huguenot and Bohemian immigrants and conquered Poles, Danes, and Walloons.[2] In the new Reich, Alsatians and Lotharingians involuntarily joined the other non-German residents.

1. Dieter Langewiesche, "Reich, Nation und Staat in der jüngeren deutschen Geschichte," *Historische Zeitschrift*, 254 (1992): 341-381, esp. 366ff.
2. Klaus J. Bade, *Vom Auswanderungsland zum Einwanderungsland? Deutschland 1880/1980* (Berlin, 1983); Thomas Nipperdey, *Deutsche Geschichte 1866-1918*, 2 vols. (Munich, 1990-1992); Rogers Brubaker, *Citizenship and Nationhood in France and Germany* (Cambridge, Mass., 1992).

The role of anti-Semitism in the construction of German as well as other European identities has been shown by Sander Gilman and many others.[3] Surely it is not coincidental that a German Jewish philosopher, Georg Simmel, was the first to define one of the most useful concepts for grasping its impact, the idea of "the stranger," more ambiguous and frightening than an enemy because of his/her physical presence in the same social space.[4] By law Jews in the German Empire were citizens; Jewish men voted before any women did. But equal opportunity in many elite professions remained a distant hope. Despite, or perhaps precisely because of, strenuous efforts by many of them to assimilate at least outwardly, and despite, or again perhaps precisely because of, their spectacular commercial and cultural successes, German Jews remained *in* German society but not *of* it. They were living expressions of the "failure of the German state to arrive at a satisfactory relationship between nationality and citizenship."[5] Jews frequently expressed their own awareness of this by using the terms "Germans," "Gentiles," and "Christians" interchangeably. German writers in this period managed to express the "strangeness" or "non-Germanness" of the Jews in terms of all three discursive coordinate systems just named.

In the prominent anti-Semitism of Richard Wagner, the mix of national-cultural and racialist vocabularies changed over time. Anti-Semitism and the concept of the *Kulturnation* clearly merged at first. In his "revolutionary" essays of 1848-1850, Wagner adopted and vastly expanded the Young German movement's opposition to the "Judaization," that is, the commercialization of art, when he denounced in *Artwork of the Future* the "Jewish oriental theory of Nature's subservience to human utility."[6] As German unification approached, and still more so under the Empire, Wagner altered his rhetoric only slightly by accentuating the racialist dimension, fed by his reading of Gobineau and Darwin as well as his contacts with Huston Stewart Chamberlain.[7]

A different but equally complex interweaving of discursive coordinate systems can be discerned by examining the role of gender norms and categories in anti-Semitic discourse. For example, in a speech of 1877, the founder of the "Christian social" movement and the *Innere*

3. Sander L. Gilman, *The Jew's Body* (New York, 1991); Sander L. Gilman, ed., *Anti-Semitism in Times of Crisis* (New York, 1991).

4. Georg Simmel, "Der Fremde" (1908), in *Das individuelle Gesetz: Philosophische Exkurse* (Frankfurt/M., 1987), 63-70.

5. Peter Pulzer, "Why Was There a Jewish Question in Imperial Germany?" *Leo Baeck Institute Yearbook*, 25 (1980): 138.

6. Paul Lawrence Rose, *German Question, Jewish Question: Revolutionary Anti-semitism from Kant to Wagner* (Princeton, 1990), 361.

7. Paul Lawrence Rose, *Wagner, Race and Revolution* (London, 1992).

Mission, sometime Imperial Chaplain Adolf Stoecker, repeated then-standard identifications of Judaism with capitalism, liberalism and socialism, but also noted the prominence of atheists and Jewish women in the leadership of the contemporary women's education movement. Their common bond, for him, was the suppression of "the significance of the religious (i.e., Christian) element," which he deemed central to "the true emancipation" of women.[8]

Stoecker's own movement and the other most prominent anti-Semitic political party never got more than 2.5 percent of the vote between them in Reichstag elections; but anti-Semitic discourse and the exclusion of Jews from Germanness penetrated deeply into the social life of the Wilhelmian *Bürgertum.* This was nowhere more obvious than in student life. Fraternities, many originally open to Jews, began excluding them in the 1870s, and especially when the crisis in the academic labor market of the 1880s raised fears of Jewish and foreign competition. The pattern repeated itself when women began to enter higher education in the 1890s.[9] In all cases, the cultural-national dimension predominated. In the *Antisemitenkatechismus,* a handbook widely used by anti-Semites of the period, Theodor Fritsch wrote: "It is a superficial and erroneous view to represent opposition to Jews as the expression of a stupid religion of racial hatred, when it is in truth a selfless defense based on the highest ideals against an enemy of humanity, morality, and culture."[10]

In addition to channeling fears of competition in the middle classes as well as the dissatisfaction of artisans and others in the lower middle classes, anti-Semitism in the German Empire had two closely related cultural roles. From the 1870s onward, vocal opposition by figures like Heinrich Treitschke and others to all forms of "double nationality," especially the "Jewish-cosmopolitan" variety, helped to define the unity of German self-consciousness. Later, with the open adoption of anti-Semitic positions by the Pan-German League under the leadership of Heinrich Class after 1907, anti-Semitism had become a "cultural code," a symbolic marker standing for and interchangable with all the other

8. Adolf Stoecker, "Frauenerwerb und Frauenbildung," in R. Seeberg, ed., *Reden und Aufsätze* (Berlin, 1913).

9. Norbert Kampe, "Jews and Antisemites at Universities in Imperial Germany: (I) Jewish Students: Social History and Social Conflict," *Leo Baeck Institute Yearbook,* 30 (1985): 357-394; Marion A. Kaplan, *The Making of the Jewish Middle Class: Women, Family and Identity in Imperial Germany* (Oxford, 1993), 149ff.

10. Theodor Fritsch, *Antisemiten-Katechismus* (1910), cited in Shulamit Volkov, "Das geschriebene und das gesprochene Wort: Über Kontinuität und Diskontinuität im deutschen Antisemitismus" (1985), in *Jüdisches Leben und Antisemitismus im 19. und 20. Jahrhundert* (Munich, 1990), 60.

components of anti-emancipatory and anti-modern sentiment and thus a unifying force for the political right.[11]

Another dimension of alterity involved foreigners in the proper sense of the word. In 1871, the approximately 207,000 registered non-Germans (0.5 percent of the total population, over 40 percent of them from Eastern Europe) were a tiny number compared with the four million members of national minorities with German citizenship (six percent of the total population). By 1910, however, the number of registered foreigners had risen to more than 1.25 million, over 60 percent from Eastern Europe.[12] The tensions brought about by this increase, along with the complex difficulties raised by regional ethnic disparities, were a major factor in the adoption of the German citizenship law of 1913. Precisely in order to preserve the citizenship of Germans living abroad (called *Volksdeutsche*) while excluding foreigners living in Germany, the law severed citizenship from residence and defined the citizenry as a community of culture and descent, thus applying the principle of *ius sanguinis* (literally, "law of blood"), rather than the territorial principle *(ius soli)*.[13]

Originally many of these foreigners were seasonal workers brought in from Poland by East Elbian landholders to compensate for the flight of landless German laborers to the cities or to America. These were soon joined by hundreds of thousands of Poles, Italians, and others who streamed into the booming industrial towns of the Ruhr valley. The integration patterns of the latter groups, combining tight communal and family cohesion with a relative lack of contact to the outside world other than at the workplace in the first generation, were quite similar in many respects to those of Polish and Italian immigrants in the United States.[14] As in America, the nativist reaction was not long in coming.

The imagery of these protests drew largely on the vocabulary of the *Kulturnation*, with slight admixtures of religious-ethnic and racialist elements; the "foreigner problem" was portrayed as a "Polish problem." In 1885, for example, a Leipzig editorial writer complained "that a Polonization of land areas is occuring that had already been won for German customs, culture and language."[15] In the 1890s, Max Weber reversed the

11. Volkov, "Das geschriebene und das gesprochene Wort," 62-64 and "Antisemitismus als kultureller Code" (1978), *Jüdisches Leben*, Chap. 1.

12. Statistics from Ulrich Herbert, *Geschichte der Ausländerbeschäftigung in Deutschland 1880 bis 1980* (Berlin, 1986), Table 1, 25.

13. Brubaker, *Citizenship and Nationhood*, 118.

14. Richard C. Murphy, *Gastarbeiter im Deutschen Reich* (Wuppertal, 1982); John Kulczycki, *The Foreign Worker and the German Labor Movement: Xenophobia and Solidarity in the Coal Fields of the Ruhr, 1871-1914* (Oxford, 1994); David Schoenbaum and Elizabeth Pond, *"The German Question" and Other German Questions* (London, 1996).

15. *Leipziger Tageblatt* quoted in Herbert, *Geschichte der Ausländerbeschäftigung*, 17.

actual situation when he argued that Polish workers, preferred because their lower "level of culture," low cost and undemanding behavior, were pushing out German laborers; nationalists repeated this claim again and again in the decades to follow.[16] The interaction of economic self-interest and allusions to German cultural or racial "purity" were obvious here. But anti-foreigner agitation was vigorously contested by other Germans with different economic interests. State governments responded by trying to regulate, but not by trying to stop the flow. Within the German workers' movement there was a comparable tension between international solidarity and economic self-interest. The Stuttgart congress of the Socialist International in 1907 vigorously supported the free movement of labor while opposing the importation of strikebreakers. But a minority resolution at the same congress described imported "wage reducers" as "workers from backward races (such as Chinese, Negroes etc.)," thus using language that differed little from that of their employers.[17]

Including scientistic discourse in the discussion of "otherness" and combining it with colonialism enriches the texture considerably. In spite of the assumed universalism of scientistic knowledge, nationalism, racialism, and scientism married easily in this period. The nationalist dimension consisted in competing for prestige by claiming possession of more of this universal knowledge – and hence of the power that flowed from it. Further, evolutionary biology and its claim that individual development recapitulates that of the race were extended analogically to the rise of nation-states and superior places claimed for one's own nation as a privileged exemplar on the social scale versus inferior or "primitive" groupings.[18]

Historians of racism in Germany have long emphasized the distinctive, not to say confused and confusing, mix of cultural/volkish and biologistic/pseudo-Darwinistic categories in Wilhelmine racialist discourse. By using words such as "blood" and inserting Darwinian and hereditarian language, it appeared possible, even easy, to give the long-held belief in inherent common ties of custom and culture a flavor of the unalterable. But precisely defenders of German *Kultur* often found Darwinism vulgar and "materialistic." More seriously, the primary objects of the discourse of "race hygiene" in the Kaiserreich were not foreigners, but Germans; it was the health of the German *Volkskörper* that was threatened by the "degeneration" allegedly associated with industrial civilization.[19]

16. Herbert, *Geschichte der Ausländerbeschäftigung*, 33, 66.
17. Quoted in Herbert, *Geschichte der Ausländerbeschäftigung*, 69.
18. Reinhard Fabian, *Time and the Other* (New York, 1983).
19. Paul Weindling, *Health, Race and German Politics Between National Unification and Nazism, 1870-1945* (Cambridge, 1989).

Racialist scientistic discourse was also vigourously applied to foreigners in Germany. Examples of the resulting ambivalences can be
found in the *Völkerschauen* – literally, people exhibitions – of the Kaiserreich. Most impressive of these was the German Colonial Exposition of
1896, attended by over two million visitors during its run of six and
one-half months. By far the most intriguing "exhibits" there were
Africans and Pacific Islanders in "authentic" village settings: Togo
natives cooking, forging metal, and weaving, inhabitants of Cameroon
playing drums, Hottentot huts, Massai camps, and New Guinean boats
floating on an artificial carp pond. The exhibitors clearly considered the
natives to be a slice of exotica that would appeal to a mass audience. At
the same time their commitment to scientific accuracy was part of an
effort to bring them closer to the viewing public, and thus to awaken a
sense of colonial mission by reminding German viewers of the romanticized agricultural roots of their own folk. Thus, German viewers were
encouraged to regard their colonial counterparts as idealized "primitive"
versions of their former selves, and also as commodities of the industrial
and scientific age.[20]

A gendered dimension could hardly be absent from this picture. The
exhibitors presented a New Guinean holy house, an exclusively male
domain, as analogous to German male-only clubs, and therefore as an
object of identification for German men. The characterization of
African women, on the other hand, emphasized their "abnormal" or
"degenerate" sexual organs, "mysterious" tatoos and the like, thus stressing difference rather than identification.[21] An emphasis on hypersexu-
ality in African women runs interestingly parallel to widespread images
of promiscuous Jewesses, and may thus reflect a preoccupation with
controlling German women's sexuality – part of anxiety about modernization in general.

Certain basic points stand out in the construction of alterity during
the Second Reich. First, most identifications of the "non-German" or the
"foreign" were based on simple negations of what a given speaker took
to be "German," or on projections of anxieties and uncertainties about
identity. In that sense, they said more about the speakers than about
their supposed objects. Second, the predominant vocabulary remained
that of the *Kulturnation*, sometimes though not always mixed with
religious-ethnic oppositions. Though racialist discourse came into

20. Arbeitsausschuss der Deutschen Kolonial-Ausstellung, *Deutschland und seine
Kolonien im Jahre 1896* (Berlin, 1987), 25, 356. See also Sierra Bruckner, "Colonial Exhi-
bition(ism): The Cultural Politics of German National Identity, 1890-1914" (Ph.D. diss.,
University of Iowa, forthcoming).
21. Bruckner, "Colonial Exhibition(ism)," passim.

prominence, it remained subordinate to the national-cultural and ethno-religious dimensions of alterity. The terminology of the Empire provided a fund of discursive resources from which later speakers drew in their own, changing ways.

Radicalized Racialist Alterity under Nazism

Nazi-era representations of the non-German were terrible simplifications of the multivalent identity discourses of the German Empire. In a time of economic and political crisis, Nazi-era discourse and imagery, produced by the political leadership and also by academics and intellectuals without any prodding from above, reduced that multiplicity to a primordial dualism organized around a vague and powerful notion of "race" that encompassed both cultural and biological categories. The "Germanic" "we" featured the willful supression of ethnic and class differences in favor of slogans like "one people, one state, one leader," or "You are nothing, the folk is everything." The "they" side of the equation melded racialist, ethnic, and political stereotypes by invoking a "Jewish-Bolshevik conspiracy" alongside attacks on Slavs, Sinti and Roma.[22]

In contrast to earlier racialist propaganda, Hitler and the Nazis valued the spoken over the written word, and deeds above all.[23] Hitler had already stated his aim of removing the Jewish "bacillus" from the German *Volkskörper* in *Mein Kampf.* The expulsion of Jews from the civil service and the "spontaneous" boycott of Jewish businesses in April 1933 were only preliminary steps. In 1935, the Nuremberg Laws formally denied citizenship to all Germans with at least one Jewish grandparent and forebade intermarriage or even sexual congress between Jews thus defined and other Germans. This gave the "blood" criterion already enshrined in German citizenship law an entirely new, biologistic connotation. In papers like *Der Stürmer,* what had once been decried as "gutter" anti-Semitism received mass circulation. The cynical incorporation of aspects of Wilhelmian cultural anti-Semitism, such as in the use of historian Heinrich Treitschke's famous dictum, "The Jews are our misfortune," on its front page, linked the cultural-national and racialist discursive axes. Respectable Germans may have shuddered at the Nazis' tone, but the penetration of anti-Semitic attitudes into the *Bürgertum,* along with more ordinary economic motives and a failure to grasp the

---

22. Michael Burleigh and Wolfgang Wippermann, *The Racial State: Germany 1933-1945* (Cambridge, 1991).

23. Volkov, "Das geschriebene und das gesprochene Wort," passim. Daniel J. Goldhagen, *Hitler's Willing Executioners: Ordinary Germans and the Holocaust* (New York, 1996), exaggerates the continuity of what he calls "eliminationist" anti-Semitism in Germany.

seriousness of the Nazis' intentions, shared by too many Jews, helped inhibit serious protest.[24]

In parallel to these measures, the compulsory sterilization law, also introduced in 1933, created by implication an entirely new class of "others": Germans with allegedly hereditary defects. As a result, hundreds of thousands of people, the vast majority of them women, lost their biological selfhood.[25] Shortly after the outbreak of war, the so-called "euthanasia" campaign deprived many of these people, along with tens of thousands of children, of life itself. In this act, combined with the decision to murder the Jews as well, what had once been essentially though not necessarily separate discursive coordinate systems, eugenics and anti-Semitism, merged as aspects of a single, pseudo-biologistically driven policy of "cleansing" the German *Volkskörper*. The war of annihilation waged against the Slavic peoples complemented that policy with the idea of "clearing" their territory in preparation for settlement by ethnic Germans. One fundamental distinction, however, remained: Jews, defined not only as foreigners but as outside humanity itself, were murdered or worked to death regardless of their "hereditary health."

Although in the vocabulary of "racial anthropologists" the Germans themselves had to be described as a racially mixed people, acceptance of these categorizations among ordinary people went disturbingly far. Even after the war, in their applications to permit the abortion of the fetuses resulting from rapes by Russian soldiers, German women uniformly described their attackers in racialist terms: they were never blond, but consistently "of Mongolian or Asiatic type."[26] Many parents or guardians of handicapped people selected for sterilization or "euthanasia" refused to accept state- or physician-based determinations of which German lives were "not worth living," and showed continued respect for Christian standards positing respect for life as a "German" virtue. But only a few Germans (including Oskar Schindler, for economic reasons) extended these refusals so far as to resist the deportation and murder of Jews, Sinti and Roma.

24. Otto Dov Kulka and Aron Rodrigue, "The German Population and the Jews in the Third Reich," *Yad Vashem Studies*, 16 (1984): 421-435; Michael H. Kater, "Everyday Anti-Semitism in Prewar Nazi Germany," ibid., 129-160. See also Avraham Barkai, *From Boycott to Annihilation: The Economic Struggle of German Jews, 1933-1943* (Hannover, NH, 1989).

25. Gisela Bock, *Zwangssterilisierungen im Nationalsozialismus* (Opladen, 1986).

26. Atina Grossmann, "Voices and Silences: The Rape of German Women by Occupation Soldiers," *New German Critique*, forthcoming; Atina Grossmann, *Reforming Sex: The German Movement for Birth Control and Abortion Reform 1920-1950* (New York, 1995), chap. 8.

In the realm of labor power, as elsewhere, racialist discourse and practice remained paramount. The policy decision to refrain from deliberately mobilizing German women laborers and to import foreign labor instead, discussed even before the war began, led to an unprecedented forced migration that stood in direct contradiction to Nazi population policy. By August, 1944, there were 7.6 million foreign workers in the expanded German Reich, 5.7 million civilians and 1.9 million prisoners of war; in 1943, 40 percent of the workers at Flick, IG Farben, and Krupp, and 80-90 percent of those in aircraft production, were foreign.[27] In one respect, the mass importation and murderous exploitation of foreign labor was an extension of pre-Nazi practice, since it compensated for the loss of German hands, this time not to emigration, but to the front and to occupation duty. But as statements by Nazi leaders illustrate, the hierarchy that emerged in the treatment of foreign laborers, with West Europeans highest, Poles and Russians next, and Jews lowest of all, had a certain precedent in the distinctions widely made in the Wilhelmian era between Polish and Italian laborers.[28]

Altering Alterity After 1945

Discourses of alterity in the Federal Republic during the Adenauer era marked only a partial return to the multiplicities of pre-1933 conceptions of national identity. To cite only one minor example, the word *artfremd* (meaning biologically foreign, or not "fitting") like other borrowings from Nazi vocabulary, remained, and still remains, in use. More important in official discourse, however, was the retention of a definition of German citizenship based on the fictive ideal of a unitary German culture held together by "blood." Friedrich Meinecke's classic definition of the nation resting on a "natural core based on blood relationships" had already pointed the way. "It is this factor," he argued in 1928, "that elevates a union of tribes into a nation *and makes it capable of assimilating foreign tribes and elements*."[29]

In citizenship law, such rhetoric had direct policy implications. Article 116.1 of the Federal Republic of Germany's Basic Law granted the right of repatriation not only to any German who had been eligible for or admitted to citizenship within the 1937 borders of the German Reich, but also to refugees or expellees belonging to the "German people," and to their spouses and dependents as well. Thus, West German

---

27. Herbert, *Geschichte der Ausländerbeschäftigung*, Table 12, 145; Bade, *Vom Auswanderungsland zum Einwanderungsland?*, 52ff.

28. Ibid.

29. Friedrich Meinecke, *Cosmopolitanism and the National State* (Princeton, 1970), 9.

citizenship law includes, at least potentially, persons of "German culture" and descent from all of Eastern Europe, but excludes the children of all foreigners born in Germany, even the Austrians and Swiss, who are native speakers of German.

The 1950s struggle to integrate refugees from formerly German territories in Poland, Czechoslovakia, and elsewhere made that reconstructed German identity more rigid than it might have been. Since these people were often regarded as and often felt like strangers rather than friends in Western Germany, their integration required an enormous financial and psychological effort.[30] Between 1945 and 1950, over 12 million refugees, 18 percent of the total population, crossed the borders of what still remained of Germany. Of these, 60 percent arrived in the Western zones, and 40 percent in the Soviet zone. Between 1949 and 1961, the year the Berlin wall was constructed, more than three million refugees made their way from the GDR to the FRG, raising the combined total of refugees to nearly 24 percent of its population (13.2 million in 1960).[31] The *Vertriebenen,* the refugees from the GDR, and especially the *Aussiedler* from Romania or Russia, were in effect the Federal Republic's unacknowledged foreigners. The policy that justified their influx might, with only some irony, be termed a reverse Pan-Germanism, a pulling of German peoples, or groupings so defined, inward from the East rather than expanding *Deutschum* eastward. A clear but unstated precedent for this policy, the *Eindeutschung* of "Germanized" East Europeans and children of mixed unions under Nazism, still awaits detailed historical study.

Both politics and the enormous demand for labor during the "economic miracle" underlay the extraordinary government efforts on behalf of these new citizens. The Equalization of Burdens Law of 1952, intended to ameliorate the unequal distribution of property between new immigrants and long-time residents, included measures ranging from cash payments and temporary housing to assistance in acquiring land. Comparable assistance was later extended to the 3.5 million refugees who came to the FRG from the GDR. In response to negative local reactions, based on envy of such aid, expellees organized themselves but the GDR *Übersiedler* did not. For both groups a common language and the lack of prospect for returning to their former homes eventually helped make integration work. Because the newcomers were defined as citizens, their organizations carried political weight, though they did not succeed in becoming parties in their own right.[32] Thus, an officially pro-

---

30. Albrecht Lehmann, *Im Fremden ungewollt zuhaus* (Munich, 1991).
31. Herbert, *Geschichte der Ausländerbeschäftigung*, Table 14, 181.
32. Ibid., 185.

jected, fictive identity was one of the instruments that brought about integration; it also assured the electoral support of most German refugees in the 1950s for the CDU and CSU.

Parallel to this shift was another, more awkward rearrangement in the discourse and politics of alterity – the relative privileging of Jewish victims of Nazism via restitution payments to individuals and the state of Israel, mandated in 1953 and 1954.[33] This step, hotly contested at the time, was necessary to assure the admission of the Bonn republic to the community of civilized nations. Ultimately it also allowed Germans, the majority of whom approved restitution but also ranked Jews lowest on the list of those who suffered from the Third Reich, to focus primarily on their own suffering and pay less attention to the crimes of the Nazis. Deeply ironic from the point of view of this discussion was the retention of the term "Jew" as a transnational category. This justified the award of payments from Bonn to non-German Jews, and was surely morally justified as well, but at the same time it continued and reinforced the discourse that had always classed Jews as "others." No such status rearrangement followed for Sinti and Roma, persecuted homosexuals, victims of forced sterilization, or foreigners who had been forced to work in armaments factories.

More peculiar still are the discursive transformations evident in the phenomenon widely known as *Philosemitismus,* one of the most original creations of postwar West German culture.[34] Philosemitism originally found expression in organized church groups such as the Society for Christian-Jewish Cooperation, based in part on American models such as the National Council of Christians and Jews. The phenomenon soon went far beyond this institutional framework, and now includes a wide range of seemingly pro-Jewish attitudes based on reversing the signs of old stereotypes, such as the legendary business acumen, scientific genius or cultural prominence of Jews, on fashionable folkloricisms such as klezmer music and *hora* dancing, and on romanticized victim imagery. Such manifestations may be well-meant in most cases, but they clearly continue to treat Jews, preferably safely dead and famous German Jews or comfortably foreign and exotic Eastern European Jews, as strangers and outsiders.

33. Christian Pross, *Wiedergutmachung – Der Kleinkrieg gegen die Opfer* (Frankfurt a.M., 1988); Jürgen Herbst, ed., *Wiedergutmachung in der Bundesrepublik Deutschland* (Munich, 1989); Michael Wolffsohn, *Ewige Schuld? 40 Jahre Deutsch-jüdisch-israelische Beziehungen,* 4th ed. (Munich, 1991).

34. Frank Stern, *Whitewashing the Yellow Badge: Antisemitism and Philosemitism in Postwar Germany,* tr. William Templer (Oxford and New York, 1992). See also Marion Kaplan, "Antisemitism in Postwar Germany," *New German Critique,* 58 (Winter 1993): 97-108.

Problematic in its own way was the instrumentalization of official anti-fascism in the GDR to disclaim any responsibility for or even any need to discuss anti-Semitism or the Holocaust, beyond the privileges accorded to Jews through membership in the official association for those persecuted under Nazism (VVN). That this strategy was at least indirectly a reflection of anti-Semitism in the Soviet Union is shown by the persecution of Jewish Politburo member Paul Merker in the early 1950s; the death of Stalin may have saved Merker from the show trial and execution that befell some prominent Jewish communists in Hungary and Czechoslovakia. As a result the persecution of the Jews remained a blank area in GDR historiography and political education until the 1980s, and SED functionaries of Jewish descent and their children suppressed that aspect of their identities almost completely.[35]

Yet another dimension of the postwar discourse on "otherness" revolved around the so-called "guest-workers" in West and East. Since German refugees failed to satisfy the demand for labor in the fast-growing economy of the FRG, the first agreement to import foreign laborers was concluded with Italy in 1955. Only when agreements followed with Greece and Spain in 1960, Turkey in 1961, Portugal in 1964, and Yugoslavia in 1968 did the word *Gastarbeiter* enter West German discourse. Their numbers rose from 79,600 (of 484,800 total foreigners) in 1955 to 2,070,000 (of 4,450,000 total foreigners) in 1980, declining to 1,568,000 in 1985. By 1972 Turks had become the most numerous group, though not by much (511,000 compared with 475,000 Yugoslavs and 426,000 Italians).[36] As in the past, these imported foreign workers faced a double disadvantage. In addition to being denied citizenship or voting rights, they took a disproportionate share of unskilled or lower-paying skilled jobs, thus enabling German workers to advance. In 1987, foreigners accounted for 33 percent of unskilled and semiskilled male workers in West Germany, more than ten times the share of foreign workers in the population as a whole in 1985 (2.57 percent).[37]

Especially during the early 1960s, this policy was justified as demonstrating liberality, openness, and cosmopolitanism. References to the positive impact of foreign workers on international understanding and

35. Olaf Groehler, "Der Holocaust in der Geschichtsschreibung der DDR," in Ulrich Herbert and Olaf Groehler, *Zweierlei Bewältigung. Vier Beiträge über den Umgang mit der NS-Vergangenheit in den beiden deutschen Staaten* (Berlin, 1992), 41-66; Robin Ostow, *Jüdisches Leben in der DDR* (Frankfurt a.M., 1988); Vincent von Wroblewsky, *Zwischen Thora und Trabant: Juden in der DDR* (Berlin, 1993).

36. Herbert, *Geschichte der Ausländerbeschäftigung*, Table 16, 188-189.

37. Wolfgang Zapf, "Sozialstruktur und gesellschaftlicher Wandel in der Bundesrepublik Deutschland," in Werner Weidenfeld and Hartmut Zimmermann, eds., *Deutschland-Handbuch: Eine doppelte Bilanz 1949-1989* (Bonn, 1989), Tables 1 and 2, 103, 113.

European integration were *de rigeur* in speeches of the period. For Labor Minister Blank in 1964 the presence of foreign workers in Germany aided "the blending of Europe and the friendly encounter of people of different heritages and customs."[38] Such rhetoric soon sounded increasingly hollow. After the government called a halt to the recruitment of foreign workers in 1973, it became clear that, contrary to policymakers' and popular assumptions, the vast majority of *Gastarbeiter* had no intention of returning to their homelands soon, but wished instead to bring their families to Germany. Efforts to deal with the effects bureaucratically, for example by trying to limit the number of foreigners settling in certain districts, proved easy to evade. By the early 1980s the outlines of a debate on immigration, multiculturalism, and German identity had begun to emerge.[39]

This discussion showed some peculiar discursive transformations. The term "multicultural society" itself was introduced in 1980, interestingly enough by the Catholic and Protestant churches in a statement they issued together with the Greek Orthodox church on something called the *Tag des ausländischen Mitbürgers*. In German, the word *Mitbürger*, translatable innocuously enough as "fellow citizen," means the exact opposite of what the term "fellow citizen" means in English. It applies only to members of groups that do *not* automatically qualify for *cultural* citizenship, including so-called *jüdische Mitbürger*, and thus clearly marks a boundary between them and "us" Germans. Well-meaning church officials intended to raise the level of debate beyond economic issues and persuade Germans to think of foreign "fellow citizens" as enriching, not threatening, German culture. In their very language, however, they unintentionally but inevitably continued the conflict they wanted to resolve.

On the new Right, the Heidelberg Manifesto signed by fifteen university professors in 1981 evoked a mix of biologistic and cultural nationalism with a fashionable cybernetic twist. Considering people as "living systems of a higher order with differing systemic qualities passed on genetically and by tradition" made the preservation of cultural identity seem a "natural right."[40] Far more potent, widespread, and equally resonant was the antagonism of Occident and Orient postulated by conservative politician Alfred Dregger in a 1982 Bundestag speech: "People

38. Theodor Blank, "Eine Million Gastarbeiter," *Bulletin des Presse- und Informationsamtes der Bundesregierung,* October 30, 1964.

39. Sabine Dierke, "Multikulti: The German Debate on Multiculturalism," *German Studies Review,* 17 (1994): 513-536.

40. For a citation of the Heidelberg Manifesto see Dierke, "Multikulti," 519 (author's translation).

with foreign citizenship but German culture and language" as well as foreigners from the remaining "European cultural orbit" were welcome and would "ultimately be assimilated;" Turks, Africans, and Asians were "not only unassimilable, they are also difficult even to integrate."[41] Such linguistic strategies made it possible to avoid overt racism and pay lip service to liberal notions of ethnic pluralism in order to subvert their intent by calling for territorial repatriation. On the new Left, a naive idealization of multiculturalism as a guarantor of true democracy, freedom, and world peace has only gradually given way to a more realistic recognition by Daniel Cohn-Bendit and Thomas Schmid that conflict will continue in a multicultural Germany.[42]

In the GDR, the number of imported foreign laborers remained relatively small, despite the need to mobilize replacements for workers who had fled to the West before 1961. Excluding Soviet troops, there were an estimated 170,000 foreigners in the East at the time of unification, about two-thirds of them imported workers from other socialist countries, mainly Bulgaria and Vietnam.[43] In a perhaps unconscious reversal of Nazi policy, the Socialist Unity Party chose to mobilize women and technology instead. But the strict segregation of foreign laborers in adequate but relatively poor housing suggests that the official SED view that socialist internationalism had eliminated racism was at least problematic. Similar questions could and should be raised with regard to the situation of the over 400,000 Soviet soldiers garrisoned in the GDR. However, strict non-fraternization appears to have been initiated by the Soviets themselves in order to maintain discipline.

The historical development of alterity in Germany has therefore undergone some surprising transformations. The newly founded Kaiserreich struggled to define itself positively by articulating varied notions of national identity and negatively by projecting multiple, interacting dimensions of otherness. Though the terminologies of anti-Semitism, misogyny, colonialist racism, or the language of "race hygiene" were not unique to Germany, their specific forms did yield a fund of dangerous discursive resources for the future. The Nazis simplified and radicalized this multiplex pattern by subsuming it under an all-encompassing discourse of "race," with murderous results which created its own ambivalences and contradictions. In the postwar era continuities as well as

41. Dregger speech cited in Lutz Hoffmann, *Die unvollendete Republik: Zwischen Einwanderungsland und deutschem Nationalstaat*, 2nd ed. (Cologne, 1992), 26.

42. Daniel Cohn-Bendit and Thomas Schmid, *Heimat Babylon: Das Wagnis der multikulturellen Demokratie* (Hamburg, 1992).

43. Ministry of Interior figures, January 1991, from Schoenbaum and Pond, "*The German Question.*"

transformations of older discursive elements lived alongside new versions of alterity defined by attempts to separate Germanness from Nazism and the new "enemy images" created by the Cold War.

Is alterity – the positing of "we-they" dualisms with hegemonic or at least justificatory intent – an essential feature of discourse itself, as has been contended by so many theorists? A common tendency among well-meaning liberal and some leftist West Germans has been to pretend that otherness is not only fictive but nonexistent, in Zygmut Baumann's terms to make all strangers and even some enemies into (potential) friends.[44] The dream of eliminating otherness altogether and bathing in a sea of brother- and sisterhood is a potentially dangerous fiction, since it makes enemies of those who suggest that diversity is inevitable. The naive celebration of difference is equally unhelpful, because it plays directly into the hands of the new rightists who use ethnic pluralism in order to locate the "others" somewhere else. Far more constructive seems a scenario in which multiple forms of "otherness" live alongside and also mix with one another, transcending the dualistic grids that were inherited from the past.

2. The Politics of Inclusion and Exclusion

As a result of the peculiarities of German history, two conflicting political conceptions of citizenship coexisted within the postwar consensus in the Federal Republic: the traditional ethno-cultural concept of the German nation characterized by a common history, language, culture, and descent; and a civil concept based on individual rights of citizens modeled after enlightened "Western" traditions. This dual notion, enshrined in the Basic Law, was challenged by German unification, which ended the division of the country and settled the issue of what exactly constitutes the German state by international agreement. While the incorporation of the 17 million people of the former GDR proved to be a tremendous task, millions of non-Germans entered Germany as workers, refugees, and immigrants from Eastern and Southeastern Europe. The sharp increase in violence against foreigners, along with the emotional debates about the asylum law in 1992-93, exacerbated the already complicated and volatile relationship between Germans and foreigners.

The paradoxical nature of post-unification policies in this area reflects the search for a new identity in the face of the changing order in Europe.

44. Zygmut Baumann, "Modernity and Ambivalence," *Theory, Culture and Society*, 7 (1990): 143-169.

On the one hand, the percentage of non-German residents living in the country has steadily increased in the past three decades, because Germany has received the highest number of persons seeking political asylum and has absorbed the largest group of refugees from the Yugoslav civil war in Europe.[45] Since the early 1990s, Germany has been the main destination for immigrants leaving Eastern Europe after the collapse of communism. In 1995, about 6.5 million people, or about 8.2 percent of the total population of the FRG, were residents without German citizenship. On the other hand, unlike other European countries, the U.S., and Canada, Germany has no immigration law. Although the percentage of foreign born residents has been steadily increasing since the mid-1970s, the government has repeatedly stated that Germany is "not an immigration country." The issue of the treatment of foreigners was therefore projected onto the stage of politics as an *Ausländerproblem,* or a problem with foreigners, rather than a problem of Germans and their policies towards foreigners.

A de facto Immigration Country

The relationships between German citizens and non-German residents are complex and at times confusing, since different immigrant groups are conflated into a one-dimensional perception, or singled out to serve as a (mostly negative) stereotype of a foreigner. In German politics the term *Ausländer,* or foreigner, applies to a variety of groups living in the Federal Republic. In a strictly legal sense, a foreigner is a non-German resident. In political discourse, the meaning of *Ausländer* has changed over time, including different peoples migrating to Germany voluntarily for work or family reasons, or involuntarily to seek refuge from war or persecution on political, religious, or ethnic grounds. The term *Ausländerpolitik,* or policies concerning non-German residents, was introduced in the mid-1970s, whereas the notion of *Asylpolitik,* policies involving political asylum, first became a contentious issue in the mid-1980s.

Three major groups of immigrants can be distinguished. The first, guest-workers *(Gastarbeiter),* who came to the FRG to work but stayed to live with their families and dependents, are the largest group of resident foreigners today. The major unanticipated effect of this worker recruitment has been the emergence of a multi-ethnic society in Germany, since temporary guest-workers became permanent resident *Ausländer* during the 1980s. About two-thirds of all foreigners living in

---

45. For an explanation of the terms, see *Bericht zur Integrations-und Ausländerpolitik,* Senate of Berlin, ed., (1995).

Germany today came from those countries in which the federal government actively recruited labor. The largest non-German ethnic group is the Turkish minority, with 1.7 million people. Some 60 percent of the foreigners have resided in Germany for ten or more years, almost half are women, and more than two-thirds of the children called *Ausländerkinder* were born in Germany. Repeated attempts by the CDU/CSU-FDP government to encourage the return of immigrant laborers to their countries of origin have had only marginal success. Foreign labor accounts for roughly eight percent of the total work force, a crucial support of the economy. Despite high unemployment and recession, the number of foreign workers working and contributing to the social security system in 1993 was 2.23 million, a record high since 1972-73.[46] Different forms of contract labor, mainly from neighboring Poland, are widely used to support Germany's industrial and construction businesses.

In the former GDR, contract labor recruitment was also practiced, but on a much smaller scale and under different political circumstances. In 1989, about 200,000 foreigners living in the GDR made up 1.2 percent of the population. About half of them were contract workers, mostly living in socially isolated compounds and housing units separated from the rest of the population. The largest group came from Vietnam (60,000); others were from Mozambique, Poland, Hungary, and the former USSR. After unification, the German government pursued a rigorous policy of return, reaching agreements with the countries of origin wherever possible. Yet, many of the former contract workers have stayed in the country.

In West Germany *Ausländerpolitik* has been a partisan issue since the mid-1970s. Problems of integration of the mostly working-class immigrant workers were first addressed by the Social Democratic government as early as 1978, resulting in the creation of a federal office for policies concerning foreigners. Since 1982 the governing CDU has framed the issue as an *Ausländerproblem*, stressing the country's limited capacity to absorb newcomers and integrate minorities into society. Despite the long residency of immigrant laborers and their dependents, they do not enjoy the rights of political citizenship, such as the right to vote or stand in local and national elections. Following regulations established by the 1992 Treaty on European Union (Maastricht Treaty), only EU nationals enjoy greater political rights such as voting in the country of residency. Thus, representation of minorities in German politics is weak. Social

46. Karl-Heinz Meier-Braun, "40 Jahre 'Gastarbeiter' und Ausländerpolitik in Deutschland," in *Politik und Zeitgeschichte*, B 35, (1995): 21. Also see Klaus Bade, ed., *Deutsche im Ausland – Fremde in Deutschland. Migration in Geschichte und Gegenwart* (Munich, 1992).

rights, such as health care, education, and pensions are more easily granted to foreigners than political rights.

The second major group of foreigners in Germany are refugees and persons seeking political asylum. This group has been at the center of the extensive debate about immigration that followed unification. In Europe, the FRG was unique, because it granted individual claims to asylum for all those who were politically persecuted. The asylum regulation embodied in the Basic Law of 1948-49 most clearly embodies the liberal, civil rights approach to conceptualizing citizenship rights in West Germany.

The rising number of refugees seeking political asylum has, however, been a source of concern for the German government for some years. Since the early 1980s the number of asylum seekers has increased from about 108,000 in 1980 to 193,063 in 1990. In 1992, it peaked with an astounding 438,000 persons applying for political asylum. All attempts to tighten admission procedures were overwhelmed by the increase of global problems, human rights abuses in many European, Asian, and African countries, and the sweeping changes in Eastern Europe. In 1993 it took a change in the constitution to severely restrict the right to political asylum, and since then the number of asylum seekers has been declining: 127,000 in 1994, and 128,000 in 1995.[47] However, with half of all refugees within Western Europe entering the Federal Republic, Germany remains the major receiving country for asylum seekers.

Among the refugees coming to Germany recently in large numbers were Bosnians and other groups fleeing the civil war in the former Yugoslavia. Of the 800,000 refugees leaving the war-torn regions after 1992, about 400,000 came to the Federal Republic. Half of them were women. In contrast to the skeptical reception given to individual asylum seekers, these refugees were widely accepted by the German public despite their large numbers. They were granted temporary residency on humanitarian grounds without an application for political asylum.[48]

A third group of immigrants in Germany are ethnic Germans from Eastern Europe. According to the ethno-culturalist notion of citizenship in the Basic Law (Article 116) and special provisions established in

47. The largest group of applicants in the first half of 1996 came from Turkey (11,714), many of whom belonged to the Kurdish minority. The second largest group came from Serbia and Montenegro (Yugoslavia), followed by Iraq, Afghanistan, Sri Lanka, Iran, Armenia, Zaire, India, and Pakistan. Two-thirds of the applications were rejected and in only 7.5 percent of all cases was asylum granted. *(Pressemitteilung des Bundesministeriums des Inneren,* July 4, 1996.)

48. Following the Dayton peace accord on Bosnia-Herzegovina, the Federal Government in 1996 negotiated for return agreements and extended residency until they would be concluded.

the 1950s, these immigrants are not considered foreigners, but rather Germans, due to a common heritage. Basing citizenship on descent led to a remarkable openness to ethnic German immigrants from Eastern Europe and the Soviet Union, but also fostered a negative attitude to non-German immigrants. In the immediate postwar years, a liberal view of German identity allowed for the integration of millions of German refugees *(Flüchtlinge)* and expellees *(Vertriebene)* from Eastern Europe to the FRG. During the "economic miracle," these refugees were quickly integrated into society with the help of the Equalization of Burdens Law of 1952, which tried to equalize the war-time burdens between new migrants and earlier residents.[49] In addition to the ethnic migrants from Eastern Europe, about 3.5 million refugees *(Übersiedler)* came across the inner-German frontier from the GDR. The integration of these refugees and migrants is one of the great success stories of post-war political development.

One of the unintended consequences of these earlier regulations was a sharp increase in the immigration of Eastern Europeans to the Federal Republic in the late 1980s and early 1990s: about two million relocated to Germany after the collapse of communism. In 1990, a total of 397,075 people claiming to be Germans came to the FRG, and in the years 1991, 1992, and 1993 a quarter of a million ethnic migrants, *Spätaussiedler,* who invoked German ancestry, arrived each year. Due to stricter regulations, the number of ethnic German immigrants has declined in recent years to about 180,000 in 1995, and the downward trend is continuing in 1996. Policies towards German minorities in post-communist Europe have shifted; the FRG government is now encouraging these groups to stay in their home countries and advocating attentive monitoring of minority rights, such as learning the German language.

In contrast to the partisanship surrounding the inclusion of migrant workers and their descendants, political incorporation of ethnic Germans has remained almost undisputed. This pattern exposes most clearly the predominance of the ethno-cultural conception of citizenship and "Germanness," extending more solidarity to newcomers who can claim German ancestry than to those non-ethnic German residents living in the Federal Republic. One of the effects of this attitude has been that the government has repeatedly rejected designing a coherent immigration law, or *Zuwanderungsgesetz.*

In spite of indications of growing acceptance of minority groups, a series of unexpected attacks on foreigners in the early 1990s suddenly

---

49. Douglas B. Klusmeyer, "Aliens, Immigrants, and Citizens: The Politics of Inclusion in the Federal Republic of Germany," *Daedalus* (Summer 1993): 86.

challenged the civic integrity of German society. Immediately after unification, an outburst of xenophobic and racist violence sent shock waves
through the country, exposing a hostility unprecedented in postwar Germany. One of the most violent outbreaks occurred in the fall of 1991 in
Hoyerswerda in East Germany, where neo-Nazis and skinheads attacked
a housing unit for foreign workers from Vietnam and Mozambique, as
well as homes for asylum seekers with firebombs, rocks, and bottles.
Another ugly incident that drew attention abroad occurred in the summer of 1992 in Rostock, where neo-Nazis attacked a home for asylum
seekers and burned down a housing unit for Vietnamese guest-workers
while hundreds of onlookers stood by and cheered. In November 1992,
five Turkish women and children were killed and several people were
wounded in a firebombing by neo-Nazis in Mölln. According to official
sources, a total of 656 fire attacks involving right-wing extremists were
recorded in 1992, and 284 in 1993.[50] Violent attacks by neo-Nazis and
skinheads caused the deaths of six people in 1992, and 20 people in
1993. Even though the level of violence has decreased overall since then,
attacks on foreigners have continued in both West and East Germany,
including a number of anti-Semitic acts.

The wave of right-wing actions set in motion a broad countermobi-
lization against the rise of xenophobia *(Ausländerfeindlichkeit)*. Church
groups and human rights organizations, neighborhood groups, unions,
and political parties joined to organize several large-scale public actions.
A demonstration against the rise of xenophobia and in favor of the liberal asylum law and the integration of minorities in society in December
1992 in Berlin drew half a million people to the streets. This was the
largest demonstration in Germany since the peace movement mobilized
the same numbers in 1981, protesting in Bonn against the deployment
of nuclear missiles.

The sharp increase in racially motivated attacks on foreigners in the
FRG after German unification has been a cause for great concern about
civil rights. Once again the treatment of minorities and attitudes towards
them have served as a litmus test for the strength of civil liberties in
united Germany. The concept of a multicultural society, introduced in
political debates in the mid-1980s, is one framework for assessing the
demographic changes of German society. Multiculturalism acknowledges the fact that society has changed, and proponents of this concept
stress that minorities should receive full social and political rights, even
if this necessitates a more complicated structure of conflict resolution
and problem solving in politics.

50. Bundesministerium des Inneren, ed., *Verfassungsschutzbericht 1993* (Bonn, 1994).

Revising the Asylum Law

The asylum law debate in 1992-93 revealed the continuing strength of traditional conceptions of nationhood and citizenship and the notion of ethno-cultural solidarities. But it also reflected the ongoing efforts to redefine German identity in the context of a more culturally diverse society. On which grounds should the FRG admit the entry of migrants and asylum seekers? Does Germany have a special responsibility among the European states to pursue a liberal path, given its political history? Or should the country close the gates to avoid a potential destabilization after the opening of Europe? Proponents of restrictive regulations stress the limits of social solidarity for fear of overloading the welfare state, while supporters of openness emphasize the fundamental constitutional commitment to human rights. Since the right-wing Republicans reject "foreigners" altogether whereas some members of the Left call for an unrestricted right to entry, the asylum debate mirrors the clash between different attitudes that have characterized the postwar consensus in German politics.

Until 1993, asylum applicants came to Germany by asking for political asylum under Article 16 of the Basic Law ("Every politically persecuted individual has a right to asylum"). This constitutionally granted *individual* right, drafted with fresh memories of persecution in Nazi Germany, was unique in Europe and embodied a liberal conception of citizenship. It remained uncontested until the early 1980s, when the numbers of refugees significantly increased and the new CDU/CSU and FDP coalition government began to stress national interests in its policy towards foreigners. Since applications for constitutional rights require careful consideration of each case, the legal system soon was overburdened, and dissatisfaction with some immigrants' practices, such as illegally remaining in the country despite refusal of asylum, resulted in an erosion of political support for liberal practice.

Partisan rhetoric soon focused on the problem that persons not actually threatened by persecution were increasingly seeking asylum as a means of getting into Germany. Because of the absence of other immigration provisions, increased demand for asylum created concern about the potential exploitation of a liberal policy by those seeking economic gain. The center right parties rejected the right to asylum altogether, and part of the media stigmatized the asylum regulations as subject to misuse *(Asylmißbrauch)*. The term *Asylant* for those seeking asylum, charged with negative connotation, replaced the more sympathetic concept of *Flüchtling* or refugee. Fueling welfare chauvinism, critics argued that asylum seekers were only hoping for economic advantage as *Wirtschaftsflüchtlinge*, and that the country could not become a haven for poverty migrants from around the world. Since persons seeking political asylum do not receive work permits, their dependency on state social support created a negative image of welfare dependence. Especially after the opening of Europe in 1989, popular perceptions shifted to questioning the asylum law.

Proponents of a curb on political asylum argued that the postwar provisions were not designed for the large influx of refugees that Germany witnessed after the opening of Eastern Europe. Stressing the limits of the state's capacity to absorb the increasing numbers of non-German nationals coming to the Federal Republic, they argued that only a stricter asylum law could save the country from internal turmoil and destabilization. Faced with both the sharp increase of immigration on one hand, and rising hostility or outright violence against foreign nationals living in Germany on the other, the German government called for quick measures to resolve the issue. In the fall of 1992 Chancellor Kohl used the term *Staatsnotstand* (state of emergency) and proposed a much stricter policy in which the constitution would be amended to abandon the liberal asylum law.[51] In this context, the problem of increasing migration to Germany after the opening of Eastern Europe was framed as an issue of asylum rights rather than immigration law.

Opposition to the new law on political asylum came from a variety of political groups, including the Social Democrats, the Greens, and the post-communist Party of Democratic Socialism (PDS), as well as from left-liberal intellectuals, journalists, and other representatives of public life. But due to pressure from working-class members, the major opposition party in the Federal parliament, the SPD, eventually abandoned its opposition to an amendment and finally allowed the passage of the constitutional changes. Social Democrats had sought to resolve the issue by changing and streamlining the procedure through which asylum was granted, and by passing an immigration law *(Zuwanderungsgesetz)* with quotas for different groups. After long and heated debates, an "asylum compromise "was finally reached between the governing parties and the opposition to secure the two-thirds majority in the Bundestag necessary to amend the Basic Law. Vocal public opposition to the proposed changes continued to express itself in mass demonstrations, public statements, and in parts of the media. On July 1, 1993, the reform of the asylum law nonetheless went into effect.

The compromise keeps the liberal provision of Article 16 in place, but restricts the individual right to seek asylum in a revised Article

---

51. It is interesting to note that popular support for the liberal asylum law increased after the violent attacks on foreigners in 1991-92.

16 a.[52] Major changes include the provision that a person coming to Germany via a "safe" third country such as Denmark, France, or Poland will be returned to this country without consideration of his or her case. This so-called *Drittstaaten-Regelung de facto* abolishes the formerly constituionally guaranteed right of each individual to apply for political asylum. Since all countries bordering the Federal Republic are considered to be safe from persecution, it is now impossible to enter Germany as political refugee by land. Furthermore, the federal government has established a list of countries in which, according to the German government, no persecution exists *(sicheres Herkunftsland),* allowing nationals from these country to be turned away immediately. Among the countries conidered free from persecution are, for example, Gambia, Ghana, Hungary, Romania, Senegal, and Slovakia. To speed up the decision process, refugees have to stay in the airport, where their case has to be decided within two weeks *(Flughafenregelung).*

In May of 1996, the Federal Constitutional Court had to decide whether these new regulations were in accord with the German Basic Law, since in several cases complaints challenged the new law on humanitarian grounds. Critics of the regulations included the Protestant Church, which considers the right to asylum one of the oldest human rights, several civil rights organizations, such as "Pro Asyl," as well as the UN-High Commissioner for Refugees, UNHCR. The authority attributed to the Court in German politics and by the public made this a crucial decision, since opposition to the revised asylum law was widespread. The Court ruled that the tightening of the asylum process was constitutional, but it demanded better protection of human rights for those applying for asylum at the port of entry. The Court also requested that the government monitor human and minority rights developments in the bordering "safe" countries, and allow for exceptions to the strict rules for returning asylum seekers.

The asylum conflict can also be read as a struggle between two different conceptions of immigration policy.[53] One concept holds a mono-cultural, ascriptive view, rooted in a "culture of ethnicity." Traditionally in

52. "(1) Those who are politically persecuted enjoy the right of asylum. (2) Whoever enters from a member state of the European Union or from another state that guarantees the application of the agreement on the legal position of refugees and of the convention of human rights and basic freedoms cannot invoke paragraph one. Those states outside of the European Union to which the prerequisites of the first sentence apply are determined through a law which needs to be approved by the Bundesrat ...." Article 16 a, *Basic Law of the Federal Republic of Germany.*

53. Daniel Kanstrom, "Wer sind wir wieder? Laws of Asylum, Immigration, and Citizenship in the Strugggle for the Soul of the New Germany," *The Yale Journal of International Law,* 16 (1993): 201-243.

postwar West Germany, the proponents of this conception have argued for an inclusive policy towards ethnic Germans in Eastern Europe, and an exclusive policy towards non-German and non-EC nationals concerning immigration and naturalization practices. In the debate on asylum, this view was expressed in the claim that Germany is not a country of immigration and should not extend solidarity towards foreigners. Granting political asylum in the new Europe was viewed as a threat to the order of the national state. From the perspective of supporters of an ethnocultural view on immigration, the FRG does not have a special moral responsibility to maintain a generous policy of entry to everyone since – as was argued in the case of the asylum law – the national order itself is presumably threatened by the influx of foreigners.[54]

The second conception is rooted in the postwar West German vision of a liberal, open society strongly committed to a constitution protecting human rights and the rule of law. Since in the "post-national era" identity grows not out of an ethnically based nation but from commitment to democracy and civil rights, Germany should be inclusive of others, such as migrant workers settling in the country. Political philosopher Jürgen Habermas, for example, rejected the policy of *Abschottung,* the closing of gates, on potential immigrants.[55] He argued that the more prosperous nations of Europe have a responsibility to allow entry by adopting generous policies. Since the world is becoming one society, global responsibilities demand liberal asylum policies on the part of wealthier nations. Because of the increasing imbalance between wealthy and poor nations, the amendments to Article 16 of the Basic Law are not only politically flawed, but morally wrong. Though it has reduced the number of asylum seekers, the tightening of legal provisions has neither ended the controversy nor solved the broader issue of immigration policies.

Revising the Citizenship Law

Because substantial groups of minorities have come to stay in the Federal Republic, recent debates have focused on revising the law on citizenship to grant immigrant laborers and other foreigners equal political rights. This discussion involves a redefinition of German identity in the absence of a legal concept of citizenship that goes beyond the 1913 law,

54. In the parliamentary debate in May 1993, the Minister of Interior, Wolfgang Schäuble, referred to the asylum law as a measure to save the country from internal turmoil. "Zur Änderung des Asylrechts – Debattenbeiträge und Hintergründe," *Der Tagesspiegel,* May 27, 1993.

55. Jürgen Habermas, "Die Festung Europa und das neue Deutschland," *Die Zeit,* May 28, 1993.

which still defines who is to be "German." Citizenship has become an increasingly salient political, social and cultural issue in European countries, and as such an instrument to include or exclude individuals in a society. The perception and definition of who is a "foreigner" and the framing of the issue of citizenship are very much shaped by Germany's troubled past.

German notions of nationhood and citizenship emerged historically before the founding of the modern German state, and they were tied to the idea of a "cultural nation" or *Kulturnation*. Originally, nation and state were distinct, posing more of a problem for creating a concept of citizenship than in France, where the nation developed out of a single state.[56] Due to its longstanding political fragmentation, Germany was able to formulate and implement a national citizenship law only on the eve of World War I. In the context of rapid industrialization after the first unification of 1871 and the rise of imperialism, Wilhelmine Germany codified national citizenship in the *Reichs- und Staatsangehörigkeitsgesetz* of 1913.[57] In order to facilitate the preservation of citizenship by Germans living abroad, the 1913 law severed citizenship from residence and defined citizenry clearly as a community of descent or *ius sanguinis*.[58] This ethnic rather than territorial conception became the defining basis for the modern understanding of citizenship, a principle that has endured political ruptures in Germany until the present time.

The constitution of the Federal Republic of 1949 was drafted to reflect the postwar realities of the new international order.[59] The dismemberment of the *Reich* after the defeat of Nazi Germany, the mass flight of refugees and expellees to the West, and the division of the country resulting from the Cold War once again put the "German question" of state and nationhood on the agenda. The framers of the Basic Law envisioned the FRG as only a "provisional state" until the "entire German people" could "achieve in free self-determination the unity and freedom of Germany" as the preamble states. Since many prior citizens were not included in the small territory of West Germany, the framers recognized a certain class of rights inherent to the quality of being Ger-

56. Rolf Grawert, *Staat und Staatsangehörigkeit. Verfassungsgeschichtliche Untersuchung zur Entstehung der Staatsangehörigkeit* (Berlin, 1973), 216

57. Brubaker, *Citizenship and Nationhood*, 118

58. Gerard-Rene de Groot, *Staatsangehörigkeitsrecht im Wandel* (Cologne, 1989), 54-75. Citizenship is passed by descent, originally from father to child; in 1974 mothers received equal status in passing on citizenship and their individual rights as citizens were instated.

59. The 1913 citizenship law was reintroduced in the FRG as well as in the GDR after the defeat of Nazism. The GDR in 1967 revised the law, restricting the term citizen to GDR residents in order to legitimize the forced adoption of children of refugees and the loss of citizenship of dissidents through expatriation.

man, irrespective of formal state affiliation. Article 116.1 of the Basic Law therefore grants the right of repatriation to any person who had been admitted "to the territory of the German Reich within the frontiers of December 31, 1937, as refugee or expellee of German stock *(Volkszugehörigkeit)* or as the spouse or descendent of such person." In the aftermath of World War II this stipulation allowed Germans expelled from the Soviet Union and Eastern Europe to settle in the FRG.

As a result of this ethnic understanding of citizenship, the FRG has one of the lowest naturalization rates in Europe. Whereas assimilation and naturalization is expected, for example, in France, the federal government has viewed naturalization of foreigners not of German descent as the exception. Naturalization rates are four to five times higher in France than in Germany for migrant workers and their dependents. The gap is even greater for second- and third-generation immigrants.[60] Because of the dilemma Germany was facing in respect to integrating migrant workers and their families, some procedural changes were eventually introduced.[61] In 1990, a revised Aliens Law *(Ausländergesetz)* provided for easier naturalization of second- and third-generation foreigners and dual citizenship is now more often granted by the administration. Naturalization rates have increased, especially in cities with larger ethnic minorities such as Berlin and Frankfurt, but assimilation still faces high cultural, social, and economic hurdles. The Aliens Law was widely criticized by reformers as insufficient to assure the integration of foreigners, keeping the reform of citizenship on the agenda.

During German unification, regulations concerning citizenship rights were shaped again by the ethno-cultural tradition.[62] Despite the fact that the territory of the German state was now clearly defined by international law in the so-called "2 plus 4" settlement, neither the citizenship law of 1913, nor the Basic Law provision for ethnic Germans (Article 116) was revised.[63] The reason was two-fold: First, the openness towards ethnic Germans in Eastern Europe has become a feature of partisan politics in the FRG, since the governing CDU/CSU has long enjoyed the electoral support of former expellees. Bonds with ethnic

60. Brubaker, *Citizenship and Nationhood*, 79-80.

61. Werner Weidenfeld and Olaf Hillenbrand, "Wie kann Europa die Immigration bewältigen? Möglichkeiten und Grenzen, eines Einwanderungskonzeptes," *Europa-Archiv*, 1 (1994): 1-10.

62. Christiane Lemke, "Crossing Borders and Building Barriers: Migration, Citizenship and State Building in Germany," in Louise A. Tilly and Jytte Klausen, eds., *Paths to European Integration: Migration, State, and Citizenship in the Nineteenth and Twentieth Centuries* (forthcoming, 1998).

63. See Article 1 (1) of the "Treaty on the Final Settlement with Respect to Germany" (New York, 1990).

German communities and enclaves in Eastern Europe are still strong and pressure to maintain an inclusive policy is continuing.

Second, the encompassing notion of Germanness laid down in the Basic Law provided for easy integration of East Germans from the GDR. West German center-right and conservative political parties who had kept "the German question" open during the Cold War and insisted on the notion of one *Volk* saw their position reaffirmed, whereas those who had wanted to recognize a separate GDR citizenship in the 1980s according to a territorial definition were put on the defensive. Moreover, legal unification arrangements were easier because the GDR had never been a "foreign" country by international and German law. The legal integration of the 17 million East Germans into the Federal Republic was thus facilitated, even though East Germans often see themselves as "second class citizens." The ethnically based ascriptive notion promoted by the CDU and CSU has been less contested by popular opinion since unification, whereas the "post-national" approach to political inclusion of all minorities has become increasingly difficult to sustain.

In legal terms, the key question for the future is whether the FRG will revise its traditional practice of granting citizenship on the basis of descent. Incremental changes proposed by the SPD, FDP, and a minority within the CDU would include granting dual citizenship more easily, and making naturalization easier, especially for second and third generation foreigners. The most far-reaching proposals include the introduction of the *ius soli* principle in German citizenship law alongside the traditional *ius sanguinis,* an approach that is most sharply rejected by the Bavarian CSU and the governing CDU. Since migration into the wealthy FRG is bound to continue, the issue of immigration and the integration of newcomers to society will be on the agenda for years to come.

3. German Jews as Foreigners or Strangers

Scholars trained in literary criticism have tended to examine the representations of foreigners' lives and milieus in texts by foreign writers in Germany or by Germans in a field called *Ausländerliteratur.* However, recently the interdisciplinary impulse of cultural studies has redirected critics dealing with the so-called "foreigner literature" to question such limiting categories and nomenclature.[64] More than just a semantic shift,

64. In an article in *Die Zeit* entitled "In mir zwei Welten," (June 24, 1994) the respected critic Fritz J. Raddatz presented writers such as José F. A. Oliver, Gino Chiellino, Zehra Çirak, Sinasi Dikmen, and Zafer Senocak, indicating their respectability. But these artists were frustrated by being recognized only as "foreign writers," wanting their work

the study of minority discourses, as a broader and more theoretical category, views representations of the foreigner as caught up in complex political, economic, and cultural relations that play themselves out in the ways that their experiences are represented, and then in the production and reception of such texts.

German cultural studies has gone beyond traditional notions of culture as a mere background, a stage of customs and behaviors upon which the literary text played itself out. Abandoning the old *Landeskunde*, anthropology, interpretive ethnography, and postcolonialist studies have rethought the study of culture as an organized system of signs, symbols, and representations and offerred methodological and theoretical tools for analysis drawn from social scientific as well as the humanistic disciplines. Cultural critics ask how the experience of the foreign is rendered into a "textual" form (fictional literature, personal narrative, ethnography, film, theater, and so on) that makes sense for those who have not themselves experienced a foreign culture. As a result of this border crossing, the complex relationship between natives, foreigners, and strangers can now be understood as a rich discursive field called culture, in which relations and meanings between these groups are constantly shifting, being redefined, and renegotiated.

The tensions between a supposed homogeneous people and the many ethnic, religious, and racial groups who are asserting their own identities make Germany a particularly interesting terrain to explore the ambiguities of multiple identities. In Central Europe such hyphenated self-definitions are obvious, although inadequately acknowledged. One obvious example are German Jews. Their position is complicated by the creation of new identities that are ethnically different due to the changing character and composition of the Jewish community. The heavy immigration of Jews from the former Soviet Union creates additional burdens and tensions both within and outside the community. While Jews may well be German citizens and even (although today it is less likely) of German heritage, their status, while secured politically and legally, remains uncertain, and they often still feel like strangers in their own country. The Afro-German is an equally hybrid category that confounds bifurcation that would make it impossible to conceptualize a "black" German. While citizens, fluent speakers of the language, and residents for their entire life, black Germans are difficult to fit into traditional stereotypes, yet they evoke xenophobic attacks.

---

read as literature as such. Cf. also the criticism of Ülker Gökberk, a Turkish Germanist trained and teaching in America, republished in a special volume of Zafer Senocak's journal *Sirene. Zeitschrift für Literatur* (Berlin).

The Turks in Germany are the most numerous "foreigners." Though the notion of a Turkish-German is becoming more prevalent as second- and third-generation Turks become German citizens, the Turk is still seen as the generic foreigner. Violent attacks or prejudice against foreigners do not take into consideration citizenship rights. In short, anyone who looks different from stereotypical norms identified with "the German" is suspect. Thus physical characteristics such as color play an important role beyond the purely racial or ethnic criteria. Since color, dress, or habitus mark the foreigners as other, their representation in cultural products such as literature, film, and the media, as well as in the public sphere are highly significant.[65] Novels such as Aysel Özakin's *Die Leidenschaft der Anderen* or Emine Sevgi Özdamar's *Mutterzunge* express the schizophrenic position of the Turk living in Germany.[66] The Turkish-German Zafer Senocak's collections of essays and poetry, and the essays by other non-German writers such as the Italian Franco Biondi, form a canon that is becoming increasingly well-known.[67]

While judicial, legal, and administrative systems determine the status of foreigners and natives, cultural discourses play a much greater role than is generally admitted. Many of the attitudes behind economic or political conflicts are based on cultural conceptions which create the familiar tensions and hostilities. Literary and cultural analyses of the symbols, myths, and images [*Bilder*] that represent the foreigner to the world, as well as the relationship of these cultural signs to political discourses, may sharpen consciousness of the origins and effects of such perceptions of natives and foreigners. Often the images and words used to speak, write, and imagine Germans, Jews, or Turks influence their behavior towards each other. Though it did not coincide with reality, Nazi propaganda depicting Jews with dark hair, big noses, and humped backs had terrible physical consequences. By creating characters, events, and situations that are not necessarily "real" but rather extreme, an author can show alternative ways of seeing everyday experiences with Jews and Germans that may challenge well-worn assumptions. For instance, for the Jews living in Germany today, as well as those outside, such insights mediate the subjective experience of those inside to those

65. See also Jeffrey M. Peck, "Rac(e)ing the Nation: Is There a German Home?" *New Formations*, 17 (1992): 75-84.
66. It must be mentioned here that in 1991 Özdamar won the prestigious Ingeborg Bachmann prize for literature written in German, which aroused some controversy.
67. See Senocak's works such as *Ritual der Jugend* (Gedichte, 1987); *Das senkrechte Meer* (Gedichte, 1991); *Atlas des tropischen Deutschlands* (Essays, 1993) among other works. Biondi has written poetry, a novel, and essays, such as "nicht nur gastarbeiterdeutsch," (Gedichte, 1979); and "Die Unversöhnlichen –Im Labyrinth der Herkunft," (1991).

outside, those who cannot know themselves what it feels like to live as a Jew in Germany.

An exemplary text by a German Jewish writer may help explain the complexities of trying to define who is German and who is foreign, and what the experience of non-Germans living in Germany might be like. Positing the German Jew or the Jew in Germany as "foreign" is already problematic and the term "stranger" fits more precisely their status, at least from their own perspective. [68] No other writer communicates the ambivalence of this situation as well as Rafael Seligmann in his ironic novel *Rubensteins Versteigerung* (1989).[69] The identity crisis he presents is compounded by the fact that the Jew living in Germany, unlike the Turk, is indistinguishable from the population since s/he is more likely to speak the same language, is less visibly "foreign," and often of a different social status.[70] While Turks living in Germany bear the brunt of prejudice, it is precisely the fact that German Jews appear to be able to occupy both subject positions simultaneously – be both German and Jewish – yet still confront anti-Semitism and suffer from insecurity, that confounds the question of identity.[71]

Like Seligmann himself, Jonathan Rubenstein, the anti-hero of the novel, returns to Germany from Israel as a child. As a young man he reproaches his parents for having brought him back to what he calls "Naziland." Feeling displaced, Jonathan vents his frustration by his hostility, especially towards his mother, to whom he refers crassly as "jackass." Unhappy with his relationships with women, especially Jewish women and even his teacher,[72] he falls in love with a gentile German.

68. The distinction between these two phrases is significant, since the former term was used to describe the Jewish population before the War, and the latter indicates the heterogeneous mixture of today's Jews in the country. The discussion today in Germany is precisely about the creation of a new German Jewish identity composed of a variety of Jewish peoples.

69. For a similar analysis see Sander Gilman's *Jews in Today's German Culture* (Bloomington, 1995).

70. While this has been the case historically in Germany, the establishment of a Turkish middle and professional class and the influx of Soviet Jews who cannot practice their professions and are required to work below their status influences potential changes in the place of Turks and Jews respectively.

71. Jeffrey M. Peck, "The 'Ins' and 'Outs' of the New Germany: Jews, Foreigners, Asylum Seekers," in Sander L. Gilman and Karen Remmler, eds., *Reemerging Jewish Culture in Germany: Life and Literature since 1989* (New York, 1994) and the paper on "Comparing Turks and Jews: The Question of Tolerance," presented at a conference at the German Historical Institute, Washington, D.C.

72. Jonathan and his teacher are attracted to each other but he auctions his sperm in order to appear more powerful to his classmates (thus the title *Versteigerung*). She abandons her idea to meet him privately since it will compromise her ability to grade his papers.

His desire for many amorous liaisons, coupled with his brazen sexuality is finally tempered by his deep affection for Susanne, a non-Jew who also feels strongly for Jonathan. But the relationship is not meant to be. When Jonathan takes his girlfriend to visit his mother, she brusquely insults both her son and his girlfriend immediately upon their arrival. Is this a Jewish mother's jealousy of a woman who might steal her son, especially a German *Schickse* (non-Jewish woman), whom she calls a "Nazi daughter?" Or is she just angry that her son and his girlfriend are late because they have been having sex? The mother insults Jonathan and Suse, Jonathan insults his mother, and Suse is left crying. Jonathan's reaction is telling:

> My euphoric mood of this afternoon is gone. Screwing hasn't changed a thing. And I had hope that it would solve all of my problems. Only new complications. *Esel* won't be happy until she destroys my relationship with Susi. Also nothing has changed regarding my situation as a Jew in Germany. Everyone here can be a murderer, even the doctor. The same guy who cures me has perhaps killed *Esel's* brother and sisters through injection. And I fall in love possibly with his daughter and produce children with her here. German children? Jewish children …? My hate is absurd …. How can I continue to hate – I am in love with a German woman! But for sure there was somebody from her family who was present, if not the SS then in the SA or the Party or in some other shit. Is there no way out? Is one condemned as a Jew in Germany to insanity?[73]

A disturbed relationship to his parents; sexual fixation on performance, especially with a German girl; failure in school. For Seligmann Jonathan's problems – the academic, the familial, the sexual, the interpersonal – are all linked to his being a Jew in Germany after the Holocaust.

Throughout the novel there are many such examples, repeated discussions about his circumcised penis, his unsuccessful sexual exploits, his misunderstandings with Jewish friends about life in Germany versus life in Israel. No doubt Seligmann wants us to see how divided Jonathan Rubenstein is. Like Portnoy in Philip Roth's American best seller, *Portnoy's Complaint*, Jonathan is caught between childhood and manhood and between being Jewish and living in a Gentile world. Yet Jonathan has an additional weight to bear: being Jewish in Germany. The exaggeration of sexual exploits, the tone of his hostility towards his parents expressed in language no child, much less the traditional obedient Jewish child would use, is purposeful. Seligmann, like many who would try to represent the situation of Jews in Germany, is caught in a bind. How can a German Jewish writer today address the problem of intense dis-

73. Rafael Seligmann, *Rubensteins Versteigerung* (Munich: DTV, 1991), 177. All further references to this text are by page number.

orientation in a conventional tone? The hyperbole is an ironic attempt to redress the imbalance that exists for Jews. How could one write about this topic without such shrillness if one wanted the audience to seriously think about what it means to live this double life?

Straightforward accounts fall too easily into maudlin or pathos-ridden chronicles of suffering and trauma. The latter are certainly there with Seligmann's Jonathan, but the reader is forced to step back, to reflect on Jonathan's turmoil while simultaneously laughing at his exploits. The humor is black; the smiles are tinged with the tragic-comedy of his dilemma. The response is filtered, mediated through the lens of the author's own ambivalence. Seligmann is coming to terms with the past, performing a Jewish version of dealing with the burden of memory. Thus come the accusations of fellow Jews in Germany toward Seligmann that he was "dirtying the nest" that is, betraying his own people by portraying Jews in such crass terms and revealing the contradictions to non-Jews of Jewish life in Germany. But Seligmann also does not let his fellow Jews get away without criticism. He fumes about the unnecessary reticence of Jewish authors in Germany: "Not a single Jewish writer in the Federal Republic dared to express rage or hate in public."[74]

One passage is central for understanding this unique situation of Jews in Germany today:

> This complete abstinence from hate unmasks both Germans and Jews. Could the German critics really accept the idea that "their" Jews were better than those beyond their borders? That the German master race had come to be replaced by a Jewish master race that was morally pure, forgiving of everyone, loving everyone – even the murderers of their own families? Nobody, not even a German intellectual could be so immeasurably naive.

And it is the following where Seligmann treads on sensitive but very important ground:

> Many so-called friends of the Jews are voyeurs of the Holocaust and the life of its survivors. They remind one of butterfly collectors: they know a lot about the object of their love – age, history, behavior, structure – but they are most comfortable when the specimens are dead. There are countless experts on German Jewish literature in Germany .... All of them should have noticed that Jewish writers in Germany were afraid to write about their feelings toward Germans, to the extent, of course that they were interested in living Jews at all. It is remarkable that this body of experts [German critics, some Jewish], along with legions of ordinary readers, overlooked the fact that no Jewish writer in Germany could muster the courage to say what he or she

---

74. Seligmann, "What Keeps the Jews in Germany Quiet?" in Gilman and Remmler, *Reemerging Jewish Culture*, 177.

thought and felt about the mass murderers and their children. *That there was not a single line of German Jewish literature about the feelings of Jews in contemporary Germany.* (emphasis in original)[75]

Can anyone but a Jew in Germany be critical of their acquiescence to being used by politicians and church leaders, as what the sociologist Y. Michal Bodemann calls "ideological capital?" Can anyone but Seligmann at the same time criticize German "philosemitism" expressed in the preponderance of Christian-Jewish dialogues (with very few Jews) and the almost prurient interest in the Holocaust at the expense of understanding the Jews living in Germany today? Can anyone but a Jewish academic in America be critical both of the supercilious position of German conservatives that the Jews are indeed "Germans" different from other "foreigners" and of the single-minded rejection by American Jews of the idea that Jews can live in Germany today or that there is no difference between guilt and responsibility when considering "the Germans?" Here is an important parallel between the author and the critic.

Seligmann aims precisely at the intersection and ambivalence of two positions – German and Jew – a distinction and opposition that is still maintained from pre-Nazi times and ironically has more legitimacy today, when a small percentage of Jews in Germany are German Jews. Being a German Jew or a Jew in Germany may well be different, according to Seligmann, for him and other Jewish writers such as Maxim Biller and Irene Dische, who also immigrated to Germany, the former from Israel and the latter from the U.S. Having not grown up with anti-Semitism may well be why he "writes directly against the avowed enemies of the Jews, and why [he] has the fewest qualms about describing Jewish fears and phobias."(180) Nevertheless, the position of all Jews living in Germany today, whether German or other, represents the dilemma of ambivalence for the Jew and the German because they are living, present, and part of everyday life, even only as 50,000 out of a population of approximately 82 million.

For his negative portrayal of Jonathan Rubinstein, Seligmann was himself accused of anti-Semitism. One letter asked pointedly: "What are you doing with us Mr. Seligmann? Finally, we have created a positive image of the Jew and now you come along and ruin the pretty picture!" And yet, as if to emphasize Seligmann's controversial position in between, another Jewish reader, this time an Israeli, said: "How can you live with your own consience and live in this country?" Seligmann takes

75. Seligmann further deals with these topics in "Die Juden leben," *Der Spiegel* 47 (September 1992): 75-76, "Wie in der 'Judenschul'," *Der Spiegel* 10 (March 1995): 62, 66, "Neue Heimat Deutschland," *Der Spiegel* 15 (April 1997): 57-60.

the heat on both counts: he lacks solidarity with his fellow Jews by presenting a German Jewish family fraught with parent-child hostilities and with a son whose sexual appetite is out of control, and on the other hand is berated for living in Germany at all. Isn't Seligmann's position, caught in between, the situation of all Jews living in Germany? Isn't the dilemma for Jews in Germany not just anti-Semitism, but the inability to have an honest and open dialogue with Jews as well as Germans about their mutual schizophrenia? Jonathan discusses this with his friend Motl, who complains about life in Israel and prefers to live in Germany – which he admits is not his country and his people – as the eternal Jew, the world citizen, the diasporic Jew. Jonathan can only continue to question: "Can't one live anywhere as a Jew, as one likes – without having to be crazy or normal to a fault?"(88)

Like Jonathan, Seligmann recognizes the ambivalences and contradictions of living as a Jew in Germany today. Unlike Jonathan who feels trapped in a country that he does not belong to, Seligmann, as the author of a fictional character, provides German and Jewish readers with a critical point of view towards themselves and each other. Seligmann is in Germany as a committed voice of opposition. While in principle Jonathan can always leave, it no longer seems an alternative. Ultimately Jonathan is even forced to break up with Suse who teaches him that the force of history and their individual identities 45 years after the end of the war cannot be disengaged from their parents' experiences; her father was indeed, as it turned out, in the *Waffen SS*. Suse convinces him that "the past is also still very alive in you."(185) The relationship ends. Jonathan realizes that he has been robbed of the two things that kept him going: his hate of Germany and his sexual desire. What is left? In the last line of the novel he declares emphatically, "*I am a German Jew!*" (189) Is this merely resignation? The acceptance of a situation that he cannot escape? Naming himself a German Jew after the dramatic experiences leaves him with an identity that remains an anomaly. The alternatives are neither being only German or only Jewish. He is a third identity composed of both simultaneously.[76] His declaration at the end of the novel seems to stop him.

At this point Seligmann and his anti-hero Jonathan differ, and author of the novel cannot be identified with a literary character, no matter how autobiographical the novel may seem to be. Seligmann wants more, or perhaps he uses Jonathan as the vehicle to a more critical consciousness. Jonathan's self-awareness, which concludes the novel, is the beginning of self-definition, one however that for Seligmann is not defined by the

---

76. John Borneman and Jeffrey M. Peck, *Sojourners: The Return of German Jews and the Question of Identity*, (Lincoln, Nebraska, 1996).

Germans negatively, but one that can be defined positively by the Jews, ambivalent as it may be. Seligmann defines himself by making a conscious decision to be a German Jew, live in Germany, and confront the daily personal insecurities around belonging, difference, and home. Therefore Seligmann's novel is a literary venue for change, a cultural program for what living in Germany can be for a Jew.

Admittedly, Seligmann is only one man. All Jews living in Germany are not as aggressively outspoken or willing to bear the brunt of criticism from both sides as he. He calls upon Jews in Germany to become more critical, more openly provocative, and to engage in serious dialogue with each other and with Germans. To do this, however, one has to give up notions of harmony, of fears of anti-Semitic reprisals, and to allow oneself as a Jew to be seen as a human being, with good and bad qualities. Philosemitism that lionizes all Jews leaves no room for dissension and dispute: where is self-reflection and change without questioning stereotypes and norms, whether all positive or negative? Liberal and left-leaning Germans are as guilty of such positive stereotyping as conservatives, only the former love all Jews (and foreigners) and deny their own Germanness, thus identifying exclusively with the "other," while the latter love the German Jews because they are supposedly German and can legitimize conservative policies to a broader Jewish constituency in countries like the United States.

While the concerns of the literary critic may deal with the place of such literature in the canon of German classics, cultural critics are more concerned with the real lives of foreigners making a life in Germany and the anomalies and contradictions between what is stated and what is lived. In particular, American Germanists are occupied with these works because they want their American students who are learning about Germany to know that German society is not one-dimensional ethnically, religiously, or racially. Against assumptions of ethno-racial Germanness explicitly and implicitly represented by government policies, on the one hand, and traditional German teaching materials such as textbooks, on the other hand, American German teachers feel a responsibility to address cultural diversity. Their urge to do this is influenced by American assumptions about multiculturalism and cultural pluralism, which one should not forget are increasingly being questioned in American society today. In fact, the legitimacy of comparing attitudes, values, and policies in the two systems is itself a contentious issue.[77]

77. A conference on "Multiculturalism in Transit" at the Center for German and European Studies of Georgetown University brought together American German Studies scholars and German American Studies scholars from different disciplines with common interests in studying culture and minorities.

Most literary and cultural critics are convinced of one central point, namely that the question is not a foreigner problem but rather a German problem of identity. In fact, more progressive observers in Germany as well as in America are no longer using the term *Ausländer*, but rather "non-German," since debate is really about assimilation or integration of those who are strange rather than those who are foreign. Since many of these foreign peoples have by now become *Inländer*, the former designation does not adequately represent their experience residing in Germany. Isn't an ethnic German from Russia or Romania who has never lived in Germany and does not speak German more of a foreigner than a third generation Turk born and raised in Germany? Should privileges of citizenship, voting rights, and social welfare be based on ethno-racial notions considered questionable in a modern civic society?

Such controversies prove the centrality of cultural questions for a topic that is largely dominated by administrative, judicial, and legal discourses. German identity, or defining German identity, has to be understood historically as a concept that has evolved and is still in the process of evolution. Cultural approaches grounded in interpretive ethnography emphasize that any claim to totality misrepresents the ways cultures are constructed and that notions of universal or unified German identity are misleading. It is often forgotten that Germany has a long history of receiving various ethnic and religious groups – Jews and Huguenots into Prussia in the eighteenth century, Poles in the next century, and Russians in the Weimar period – because most of these immigrants became "Germanized." Since the negation of the so-called German-Jewish symbiosis by the Holocaust shows the possibility of undoing assimilation, it must be possible for ethnic groups to retain their "native" identities while integrating themselves into the dominant German culture. As long as German identity can only be gained through birth rather than from place of birth or residence, German culture will remain trapped in the myth of homogeneity.

Today color and other visual characteristics combine with the older distinctions of race and religion to undermine the imagined uniformity of the white, blond-haired, and blue-eyed German Christian that became the Nazi icon. While Jews, even German-Jews, are white, the urge to talk about Jewish visual characteristics moves them from a religion to ethnicity and finally to race. Hitler had to make the Jews wear the yellow star to distinguish them from the rest of the German population. They then could be marginalized like the Turk who is "white" i.e., racially Caucasian, but whose skin color, dress, and other markings set him apart ethnically and racially. By virtue of being a Moslem, the Turk, unlike the other guest-workers from Yugoslavia, Italy, and Portugal, has had a more difficult time being accepted. The sheer numbers of Turks also emphasize the impact of Turkish Moslem culture on the Christian Germans. The Turks have become the generic dark foreign other and the media has played on the fear of large numbers of foreigners invading Germany by emphasizing mass movements of foreigners overrunning the borders of Germany from the East and the South.

The above reflections indicate that the native/foreigner debate is replete with myths, symbols, and images that incite the imagination of a German people that is insecure with its own identity. The shadow of the Holocaust complicates any attempt to conjure up a more positive German sense of self. Reactions tend to be absolutized, politically dichotomized on the left and the right, in favor of foreigners and necessarily against being German, or on the right the reverse. If the debate about natives and foreigners teaches anything, it shows us that gradations between such poles have to be accepted. Shades of light and dark quite literally require more careful and differentiated responses.

The German discussion also symbolizes the ability of democratic citizens and institutions to recognize that their treatment of people who are different reveals their understanding and respect of themselves. Tolerance does not necessarily mean acceptance without rules or standards or unconditional love of one's neighbors, but rather accepting differences even when they diverge from our long-held norms. Literary texts like the example analyzed above show that it requires more patience, self-reflection, and tempered thought. Behaviors, practices, and attitudes can be explained best, by understanding how their meanings are constituted by culture and shaped by history. The multiple collisions of signs, symbols, and discourses require serious attention as to how they are made and understood. If relations between natives and foreigners are to be more peaceful in Germany in the future, some cultural decoding and translation are necessary between the various groups.

4. Discourses and Discrimination

Though different in their disciplinary orientation, the three sections of this essay show remarkable similarities in their analysis. There is no question, for example, that the political and social reality of Germany is – to use an overworn phrase – multicultural. With approximately 7 million "foreigners," the German population, especially in urban areas like Berlin, Frankfurt, and Cologne, no longer constitutes a homogeneous ethnic, racial, or religious country. Interior Minister Manfred Kanther's statement that a multicultural society creates "terrible stress and often

much more suffering and quarrels among different ethnic groups" illustrates an unwillingness on the part of many Germans to acknowledge
the realities of everyday life. The insistence that Germany cannot be "an
immigration country" because it officially has no "immigrants," immigration policy, or immigration laws, but only foreigners, asylum seekers,
refugees, former *Gastarbeiter*, and Jews of various sorts, leads to contradictions that confound all reasonable discussion.

There is equal agreement among critical observers that the discussion
of foreigners and strangers essentially revolves around questions of German identity. Posing the question in that way is not to be taken for
granted. The American focus on "identity politics," played out in feminism, and ethnic and postcolonialist studies, has raised important questions of agency, power, contingency, and representation that can be
helpful in analyzing German developments. Even beyond the obvious
comparisons between America's multicultural heritage and Germany's
newly developing identity, American theoretical perspectives emphasize
a cross-cultural aspect that can broaden the ground of debate. Although
this brand of theorizing is not always welcomed in Germany, it has
encouraged a wide range of scholars at American universities to address
the issue of multiculturalism. Some German academics are venturing in
a similar direction, but public discourse about foreigners is still dominated by journalists and politicians, many of whom see things in more
traditional terms.

It is therefore not surprising that attention to discourse is central to
any analysis of this question. Though elites and institutions as well as
laws and policies are undoubtedly important, the issue of foreignness is
played out not only in the effects of politics on particular individuals or
communities, but also in the language used to represent Turks, Jews,
Poles, or Afro-Germans. The notion of discourse, whether political or
cultural, needs to be recognized in any serious discussion, since a term
like *Ausländer* insufficiently describes the wide range and variety of
groups who are composed of non-Germans. Such an overdetermined
category already establishes specific relations of power that are conditioned by particular social interactions and practices, as well as public
representations, that are still largely dominated by the governing elites.
In short, the power of the word is not equally dispersed.

In shifting the focus to the German quest for identity, it would be
unfair to present "the Germans" as a monolithic group, unsympathetic
to the interests or rights of "foreigners." Distinctions need to be made
among various political parties in their attitudes towards, for example,
citizenship and asylum, and the vocal and public opposition by German
citizenry to attacks on foreigners in recent years. Similarly, it must be

pointed out that among the distinct groups of non-Germans, whether categorized ethnically, religiously, or racially, significant differences exist, namely whether one is a Turk or a Jew, black or white, Christian or Moslem, eligible for political asylum or not. Each category presumes a unique relationship to that group's history in Germany, the conditions that brought them there, and their present political, economic, and cultural status. This essay therefore pleads for the need for further differentiation of the simple binary opposition between natives and foreigners, Germans and all others.

A closer analysis of "foreigners" and "strangers" reveals many different ways of belonging and not belonging. Comparing Turks and Jews in Germany raises thorny questions about the historical specificity of two groups who define themselves very differently and are viewed by the dominant society in distinctive ways. Turks were brought to Germany as guest-workers in the 1960s and 1970s, do not as a group hold citizenship, and are largely Muslim. While Jews are citizens by virtue of being German or, as in the case of immigrants from the Soviet Union, receive refugee status, they are in an anomalous position because of memories of the Holocaust, which make them strangers in their country. Though granting them legal rights, German citizenship does not guarantee their belonging to the native community. Poles, ethnic Germans, and East Germans, who are physically indistinguishable from West Germans, also feel strange in their adopted country. Due to differences in habitus, even the conception of filiation through descent can be undermined by time, space, and political ideology. Belonging must not only be understood in terms of objective criteria such as laws, statutes, and policy, but also in terms of subjective experiences of marginalization and discrimination, even if many Germans would wish it otherwise.

Eventually changes in the law might narrow the gap between discourse and reality. In the summer of 1996 politicians from a wide spectrum of parties, including young members of the CDU, were encouraging revision in the citizenship law and acceptance of the complicated question of dual citizenship. The CSU, however, balks at these encouraging moves from its partner party. Whatever the outcome of these deliberations, Germany will have to confront the demographic changes within its borders and its status under laws established by the European Community. This broader perspective, whether it be inter-European or trans-Atlantic, is necessary to detach the issue from its focus on German identity. Perhaps interdisciplinary and international analyses such as the above can contribute to overcoming the stalemate of the current debate.

Chapter III

EAST AND WEST GERMAN IDENTITIES
United and Divided?

Helga A. Welsh, Andreas Pickel, and Dorothy Rosenberg

Most liberal democracies are able to define key characteristics of national identity along territorial and/or political system dimensions, but this has long been troublesome in the German case. Whether one attributes this to specific German character traits or to repeated border and regime changes over the past 150 years, the fact remains that in the past, for both German states, references to nation, patriotism, and nationalism have been problematic. Likewise any reference to German identity was certain to evoke anxieties. These are closely related to the perennial inquiry about the exceptionalism of German political development; those who question German identity seem equally concerned about its ramifications when it is identified and when it escapes clear conceptualization. This ambiguity reveals the uneasiness both inside and outside of Germany, which often equates clearly-defined (national) goals with lust for power and the lack of them with a dangerous unpredictability that requires vigilance.

As a result, uncertainties about the character of national identity loom large in historical and political writings about Germany, more so and over a longer period of time than in any other Western democracy. As is true for most aspects of political debate about Germany, looking into its future remains closely tied to remembering its past.

The division of Germany after World War II and the unanticipated unification in 1990 added new complexity to the century-old puzzle. In this chapter we are particularly concerned with the impact unification has had on the understanding of German identity. Are there substantial differences in "identity" when comparing East and West? What developments account for the similarities and which ones are responsible for the differences? Which trends can be discerned in the relationship between East and West since unification has taken place? What effects have political, economic, and cultural differences had on expressions of identity? Last but not least, does an answer to these questions matter, and if so, in what ways?

The following sections approach the question of identities in the eastern and western parts of Germany from political, economic, and cultural perspectives. The authors agreed that understanding established and emerging identities in the previously divided parts of Germany is important for comprehending the process of unification and of Germany's current and future political direction. We concurred that any analysis of multiple identities remains incomplete if it is looked at solely from a political, social, or cultural perspective, but, as expected, our methods, research questions, and findings overlapped only partly. Should identity be interpreted mainly as the product of conscious construction and reconstruction by elites or, rather, as the outcome of influences from the political, social, economic and cultural environment?

The authors continued to debate the selection and interpretation of political, economic and cultural trends as well as the choice of symbols and their intended, subliminal, and unintentional "messages." For example, economists and other social scientists who analyze the economic results of unification do not differ as radically in their evaluation of the situation as do cultural theorists, who examine questions of identity formation and change. This is perhaps not surprising since it is much easier to agree on measurable attributes than on their social and political consequences and their cultural significance. In the course of discussion it became clear that the lines of contention were both related to specific scholarly disciplines and to political differences in interpreting the development of German identities. Because of a multiplicity of methodologies and viewpoints, this chapter conveys a mixture of optimism on some and pessimism on other indicators concerning the future trajectory of the differences between East and West.

1. Political Perspectives

Most social scientists are quick to assert that national identity should not be equated with national character but that it refers to common political, social, and cultural characteristics that are observable over time and space and which differ from those of other political entities. When analyzing East and West German identities it is important to recognize that the territorial integrity of the nation-state is not in question: there are no signs that a return to the East-West division is on the agenda of any political group or of large segments of the population.[1] Ethnicity, language, a partially shared history, and culture provide common ground.[2] More to the point is the question whether the German nation-state is also characterized by shared political values that cross the East-West divide. Thus, the question remains whether divergences in East and West German identities undermine a sense of community and common national goals – in short, whether the differences are serious enough to affect the political stability of the Federal Republic or whether ethnic and civic identity coincide. Framed in such a way, political culture studies[3] can provide a useful approach since they focus on the analysis of attitudes towards the political system with the intent of explaining political behavior and identifying political interests within nation-states.

That political culture captures only part of the German reality (and thus identity) is clear to all those who observe the birth pangs that are associated with community-building in the two parts of Germany. Since unification it has become commonplace to argue that many obstacles to the integration of the two Germanys are to be found in the different conceptions of German identities – and, by implication, different interests – in German politics. The question remains to what extent East and West identities differ and converge and to what extent the "new" Germany is able to define legitimate national interests. Thus, the study of East-West identity is supposed to track progress or the lack thereof in the political integration of the two German societies. Finally, it relates to similarities and differences in the support of democracy between eastern and western Germans.

1. In 1995 only 15 percent of eastern Germans regretted that unification had taken place. See *Der Spiegel*, 27 (1995): 42.

2. Marc Howard provides a provocative view (as he himself admits) of the East-West German division. However, his application of ethnicity to the German political landscape is fraught with problems. While he is careful in setting out his definition of ethnicity, he fails to give adequate attention to the fact that the principle of ethnicity served as the rationale for unification. In addition, his definition sets aside commonly acknowledged elements of ethnicity such as culture, religion, language, and common ancestry. Finally, his interpretation highlights differences only. But East-West German relations are characterized by a complex set of differences and similarities. See his "An East German Ethnicity? Understanding the New Division of Unified Germany," *German Politics and Society*, 13 (Winter 1995): 49-70.

3. The concept of political culture is explained, among others, by Gabriel A. Almond, *A Discipline Divided: Schools and Sects in Political Science* (Newbury Park, 1990), 138-156.

Contemporary political concerns aside, German unification can also be regarded as an important laboratory in which to test theories of political socialization and political culture. Clearly forty-five years of political socialization under a communist regime and international isolation must have left enduring influences. But what are these influences? How important was counter-cultural socialization – in opposition to the officially prescribed political culture – and in what ways has it manifested itself in post-communist eastern Germany? Did media exposure to and communication with the West (pre-)socialize eastern Germans into a democratic political culture? Are conceptions of democracy primarily derived from expectations and perceptions associated with socialist democracy, a concept which was fostered by the now-defunct communist regime but never realized, or by western conceptions of democracy?[4] Finally, what are the effects of exceptional developments such as the eastern German "revolution" in 1989 and the process of unification on political attitudes?[5]

Although there is relatively broad agreement on the relevant research questions, responses to them have been much more varied. Any assessment of the extent of political differences between eastern and western Germans was and continues to be hampered by several interrelated factors: a) the uncertainties of identities in both Germanys prior to unification; b) insufficient reliable longitudinal data regarding political attitudes in the eastern part of Germany; c) the expectation of relatively high volatility regarding political attitudes due to extreme political, economic, and social uncertainty and stress for most eastern Germans; d) the coincidence of unification and economic recession.

Uncertainties About Past Definitions

Up until 1990 it was characteristic of both Germanys that uncertainties about the true extent of identity formation and expression prevailed. Neither state completely succeeded in imposing the officially-desired version of identification on its people. Thus, a major reason for the difficulties isolating elements of German identity in the new, unified Germany is lack of clarity about its past definitions. To the East, identity formation was closely linked to a moralistic approach about Germany's past and to

---

4. See in particular Bettina Westle, "Demokratie und Sozialismus. Politische Ordnungsvorstellungen im vereinten Deutschland zwischen Ideologie, Protest und Nostalgie," *Kölner Zeitschrift für Soziologie und Sozialpsychologie* 46 (1994): 571-96.

5. Possible explanations for democratic attitudes in the East are summarized by Russell J. Dalton, "Communists and Democrats: Democratic Attitudes in the Two Germanies," *British Journal of Political Science* 24 (1994): 480-81.

a narrow version of anti-fascism. Efforts to widen the identity spectrum to include contemporary manifestations of GDR-socialism proved difficult. Therefore the recognition of nationhood (as opposed to statehood) for the GDR remained contested among its own citizens.

In the West, an initial identification with economic success was gradually superseded by an increasing commitment to democratic procedures, institutions, and attempts to introduce elements of a European identity. The phrase "constitutional patriotism" that was initially coined by Dolf Sternberger and later adopted by Jürgen Habermas and others emphasizes the decline in national attachment among West Germans. This assessment was supported by consistently low levels of national pride and by the experience of unification. The lack of enthusiasm aroused by unification and the matter-of-fact assumption by practically all West Germans that the united Germany would be modeled closely after the old Federal Republic revealed a substantial degree of identity with and legitimacy of the postwar West German state and its constitution and not a historically-derived notion of nation. Before 1989, the likelihood of unification seemed remote and the desire to build a unified nation was not responsible for the collapse of the GDR nor was it inspired by Western demands. Taken together, these trends have inhibited the resurgence of nationalism in all but a youthful fringe.

The Experience of Unification

Unification has contributed to a heightened awareness of both similarities and differences in political identities in the two Germanys. Not surprisingly, some legacies of a 45-year long relationship, which was artificially constrained and shaped largely by external factors, have been enduring.[6] But the unification process has added new dimensions to an already strained relationship, since it was characterized by perceived as well as real time pressures, marred by Western elite dominance, the unconditional transfer of the western German political, economic, and social model to the East, and created a great degree of uncertainty regarding most aspects of daily lives for Easterners. The latter has brought severe interruptions into practically every aspect of eastern German lives whereas disruptions for most western Germans were limited to financial sacrifices. As a result, the current eastern German identity is only partially identical with that of the former GDR. Five years of experience with a unified state have amended as well as altered the former identity.

6. See Helga A. Welsh, "The Divided Past and The Difficulties of German Unification," *German Politics and Society* 30 (Fall 1993): 75-86.

For some, the experience of rapid political and economic transformation and the devaluation of life under communism have intensified rather than lessened feelings of an identity that is separate from that shared by Westerners, but not necessarily one of GDR nostalgia. Many eastern Germans continue to feel inferior to western Germans. This strengthens separate identity patterns and reinforces the estrangement between eastern and western Germans. The difficulties of adjustment have fostered a sense of community among citizens of the former GDR. For others, an already weak identification with the former communist state has diminished even more. Most western Germans have seen little reason to adjust their identity but, likewise, the experience of unification has heightened the recognition of differences between eastern and western Germans.[7] To this date, however, the exact processes and their outcomes are little understood.

The Identification of Similarities and Differences

On the institutional level, matters of political and economic integration can be addressed by laws, administrative decrees, and executive decisions, but the societal acceptance of these measures often lags behind the institutionalization of the new political order. Indeed, integration theorists presume that community-building precedes and inspires attempts towards formal political integration. In the German case, however, major steps towards community-building can only follow legal integration. Thus it should hardly come as a surprise that the process of integration emphasizes dissimilarities at least as much as similarities between the two German populations.

It can be argued that the greatest barriers against community-building do not reside in political or social differences, but in the cognitive distance between East and West Germany, the *Mauer im Kopf* (wall in the mind).[8] Since the contrasts have become more apparent with the removal of the wall, recent research emphasizes the significance of distinct behavioral patterns, cognitive differences, and the feeling of estrangement *(Fremdheit)* between the Germans in East and West.[9] However, it is important to

7. The difficulties are illustrated in a quote from former dissident Jens Reich and the response by the West German reporter: "Mit dem Zusammenbruch der DDR werde er innerlich DDR-Bürger, werde es bleiben, 'bis ans Ende meiner Erdentage.' ... Ja, gewiß. Das gilt in gewissem Sinne aber auch für unsereins, der das fröhlicher sagen kann, für die Bundesrepublikaner ...." *Die Zeit,* September 7, 1990.

8. See Hans-Dieter Klingemann and Richard I. Hofferbert, "Germany: A New 'Wall in the Mind'?" *Journal of Democracy* 5 (January 1994): 30-44 and Michael Minkenberg, "The Wall after the Wall: On the Continuing Division of Germany and the Remaking of Political Culture," *Comparative Politics* 26 (October 1993): 53-68.

9. See Lothar Fritze, "Irritationen im deutsch-deutschen Vereinigungsprozeß," *Aus Politik und Zeitgeschichte* B 27/95 (June 30, 1995): 3-9; and Rosmarie Beier, "Bericht zur

remember that psychological distance is not identical to political distance, although it may reinforce the latter.

So far, the clearest indicator of East-West political differences is the electoral success of the Party of Democratic Socialism (PDS). During 1994, in eastern Germany, the PDS garnered 19.8 percent of the vote in the federal elections and between 16.5 (Saxony) and 22.7 percent (Mecklenburg-West Pomerania) in the elections at the *Land* level. The PDS is a significant political actor at the state and communal level in the former GDR. However, with one percent of the vote, the party continues to be relegated to political obscurity in western Germany. As is true for other formerly communist Central and Eastern European polities, the reasons for the comeback of post-communist forces are manifold: they relate to opportunities provided by the structure of party and electoral systems, to the advantages associated with financial and membership strengths carried over from the communist period, and, last but not least, to the chances to occupy political spaces being neglected by other parties. In eastern Germany, extensive grassroots activities and the political portrayal of itself as the representative of regional interests and of a particular milieu being generally ignored and misunderstood by the other, Western-based and Western-oriented parties have contributed significantly to the electoral success of the PDS.[10]

At the end of 1994, the PDS remains the largest party in the East, with slightly more than 121,000 members. But it is smaller than most post-communist parties elsewhere, has been as affected by membership attrition like the other parties, and its membership base in the West is limited to approximately 2,000 members. The inability to attract new party members in eastern Germany is characteristic of both the former bloc parties and the newly-established parties SPD and Alliance 90/The Greens. It also extends to institutions of civil society, including trade unions and other interest groups.

Political participation remains below levels customary for the West. The fact, however, that these processes are not limited to the former GDR but are characteristic of practically all post-communist societies emphasizes political volatility in times of transitions. A "mishandling" of political integration on part of western German politicians may have contributed to the problems but may not have been its primary cause. Lower levels of political activism are related to political alienation but

---

(mentalen) Lage der Nation. Was die Besucher einer Berliner Ausstellung über die deutsch-deutsche Vergangenheit, Gegenwart und Zukunft denken," ibid., 10-18.

10. Hans-Georg Betz and Helga A. Welsh, "The PDS in the New German Party System," *German Politics* 4 (December 1995): 92-111.

have sources in many other factors as well: lack of clear party identification, freedom not to get involved politically and, not least, the preoccupation with issues of economic and social adjustment.

Despite similarities in electoral outcomes between eastern and western Germany which favor the two dominant parties CDU and SPD, the differences go beyond eastern Germans casting votes for the PDS. Because of diffuse party identification, the success of Manfred Stolpe and Kurt Biedenkopf suggests that the personality factor in voting is more striking in the East than in the West. Some voting patterns that have been established in the West were not confirmed in the East. For example, working-class votes in the East are cast more often for the CDU than for the SPD. Religious affiliation has little significance in the eastern part of Germany but continues to be an important predictor of voting preferences in the West. At least in 1994, the FDP seemed to have lost its power base in the East – which, in 1990, it had largely borrowed from previous bloc parties and which had been amplified by the "Genscher" factor, the popularity of the East German born foreign minister of the FRG. Other electoral outcomes have reinforced the slow but consistent erosion of some voting patterns that also have been visible in the West. For example, the decline of partisan and class affiliations, which is characteristic of recent Western developments, has been reinforced by the addition of the former East Germany.

Although many seem to be surprised at the articulation of differences between East and West, one might be at least as astonished at the relative ease with which – seven years after formal unification – the new Germany has found some common political ground.[11] Basic features of the German party system are accepted – and the center holds. Fears of unabated nationalism have proven exaggerated. Despite differences in political behavior, political culture studies undertaken in the two parts of Germany often reveal remarkable similarities in attitudes toward the political system and lately a growing trend toward greater assimilation. This is not to deny differences, and, depending on the questions asked, they can be substantial. Contrasts remain, for example, as to the evaluation of socialism, satisfaction with democracy, and trust in political institutions. But the extent of these differences does not signify serious legitimacy deficits in the political system. In addition, as Tables 1 and 2 indicate, in many areas the differences are narrowing rather than widening.

11. This point is emphasized by Hans-Joachim Veen and Carsten Zelle, "National Identity and Political Priority in Eastern and Western Germany," *German Politics* 4 (April 1995): 1-26.

Table 1: Trust in Public Institutions* (Mean Score)

| | 1991 | | | 1995 | | |
Public Institutions	West	East	Diff.	West	East	Diff.
Federal Constitutional Court	2.5	1.1	1.4	2.1	1.1	1.0
Land Government	1.4	0.7	0.7	1.1	0.9	0.2
Federal Council	1.7	1.1	0.6	1.2	0.9	0.3
Police	2.0	-0.2	2.2	1.9	0.8	1.1
Courts	2.2	0.1	2.1	1.7	0.6	1.1
Federal Army	1.3	0.9	0.4	1.0	0.6	0.4
Trade Unions	0.8	0.8	0	0.6	0.5	0.1
Federal Government	1.1	0.4	0.7	0.8	0	0.8
Federal Diet	1.6	0.5	1.1	1.1	-0.1	1.2
Television	0.7	1.1	-0.4	0.4	-0.2	0.6
Political Parties	--	--	--	0.1	-0.6	0.7
Print Media	0.5	0.5	0	0.2	-0.6	0.8
Churches	0.7	0.6	0.1	0.6	-0.7	1.3

*Based on a scale extending from -5 (absolutely no trust) to +5 (complete trust).

Source: IPOS, *Einstellungen zu aktuellen Fragen der Innenpolitik 1995 in Deutschland. Ergebnisse einer repräsentativen Bevölkerungsumfrage in den alten und neuen Bundesländern* (Mannheim, 1995), 42-43.

Table 2: Satisfaction with Democracy and Selected Societal Conditions* (in percentage)

| | 1991 | | | 1995 | | |
	West	East	Diff.	West	East	Diff.
Democracy	78	52	26	68	53	15
Educational Opportunities	84	69	15	84	57	27
Equality of Rights	71	79	8	73	44	29
Economic Situation	87	14	73	51	29	22
Crime Protection	63	58	5	43	14	29

*Responses: Very satisfied and satisfied only

Source: Ibid., 16, 30.

Indeed, on many policy issues – ranging from European integration to state financed children's allowances – East-West contrasts are no more striking than the breakdowns according to party affiliation suggest for Germany as a whole. In addition, main characteristics of the political self such as levels of pride in nationality and of identification with national and European identities show remarkable similarities (see Table 3). The financing of the East through tax increases and "solidarity" contributions has been less controversial than one might have expected. Most importantly, East and West Germans share a basic understanding that policy-making should be rooted in cooperation and consensus; they also have in common a preoccupation with security and stability, although these very same principles may mean different things to different people. Indeed, what caused many of the problems in the last several years has been the violation of these principles in the eyes of many eastern Germans: unification was master-minded by the West and based on the premise of expedience and efficiency. In the East, the principles of cooperation and consensus were shaped by the successful roundtable experiences which were crucial in the peaceful transfer of power in 1989 and 1990. But in the unified Germany they soon took on different forms as well: bargaining became more competitive and reminiscent of patterns established in the West. Much of this competitive edge in politics has been attributed to the elite dominance and elite transfer from the West to the East.

Table 3: Pride in Nationality and Level of Identification with National and European Identity

	West Germans	East Germans
Very proud to be German	13	9
Fairly proud to be German	32	39
Not very proud to be German	21	24
Not at all proud to be German	14	12
Nationality only	28	34
(Nationality) and European	43	44
European and (Nationality)	15	12
European only	9	5

Source: European Commission, *Eurobarometer. Public Opinion in the European Union: The First Year of the New European Union. Report on Standard Eurobarometer 42* (Fieldwork: December 1994; Release: Spring 1995): B.50 and B.51.

Finally, on some issues currents have emerged that create potential unifying identities among groups in the East and West in spite of other differences. For example, those in the West who favor a liberalization of the abortion law have been strengthened by political support from the East. Xenophobic attitudes have been fueled by developments in both parts of Germany. Cooperation and discord among the federal states have begun to defy East-West divides, as seen in the Saxon-Bavarian alliance that emerged in the 1995 media debate.

One of the most interesting of those alliances deals with the issue of *Vergangenheitsaufarbeitung* in the old GDR. Almost ironically, those dissidents who most despised the former communist regime have perpetuated a picture of repression that plays into the hands of those in the West who use the totalitarian framework to de-legitimize experiences in the former GDR in its entirety. In turn, this has strengthened anti-communism in the West and alienation from the West in the East. Thus, in reference to eastern German identity it might be useful to distinguish elements of identity *in opposition to or in defense of* the old system. The former favors a German identity based on the old Federal Republic, the latter emphasizes the differences between East and West. Those cleavages can also be discerned in the treatment of *Stasi* agents and in the handling of politically motivated purges more generally.

The Search for Explanations

The postwar creation of two Germanys coupled with the leveling effects of industrialization has reduced the importance of traditional differences based on history, religion, class, and culture in German politics. This has encouraged the emergence of identities that are no longer seen as exclusive but as complementary and/or in competition with each other. The (re)emergence of regional ties at the *Land* level, attachments to some aspects of the old GDR *and* to the Federal Republic, as well as to Europe, more often than not complement rather than contradict each other. In other words, East and West German identities are only one of several competing identities.

At the same time some particular social milieu patterns of the former GDR persist. For example, in comparison to the western part of Germany, the old German Democratic Republic is still characterized by a relatively large traditional working class, a small middle class and an inflated, hierarchically-based class of elites (in particular the former *nomenklatura* and intelligentsia). The social and political milieus associated with these strata strengthen East-West differences.[12] Taken together, these uncertainties have heightened our awareness that processes of identity-formulation take place at different levels, according to spatial as well as societal dimensions.

12. See Michael Vester et al., eds., *Soziale Milieus in Ostdeutschland. Gesellschaftliche Strukturen zwischen Zerfall und Neubildung* (Cologne, 1995), ch. 1.

The analysis of identities in the two parts of Germany also suffers from a confusion that tends to equate political estrangement with political differences. It has to be kept in mind that the expression of regional interests has not undermined the political stability of the Federal Republic, nor have East-West political differences been a serious impediment to the articulation of national interests. Differences between East and West German identities remain indicative of the process of community building, and thus of unification, but are only partially reflective of problems associated with national interests.

Last but not least, knowing about the origins of the differences between eastern and western Germans may provide important clues as to their longevity. In other words, is it just a question of time until eastern Germans are assimilated to Western patterns, once they have caught up with "modernization"? Along this line, it has been argued that "East Germans appear to be the West Germans of yesterday."[13] This reference not only alludes to lifestyle issues but even more to political attitudes, which are compared to those of West Germans until the early 1960s. Such comparisons are based on the premise that the experience of the democratic process is important for political socialization and that eastern Germans, just as western Germans in the fifties, show a particularly strong correlation between economic performance and democratic attitudes. But such comparisons tend to oversimplify the complex circumstances of regime transitions after World War II and after 1989. For example, conditions of regime collapse and transition to democracy and market economy differ significantly.[14] Nevertheless, there is practically unequivocal consensus that the economic dimension is crucial to identity building, particularly in Germany where economic performance has always been a major source of regime identification. In addition, economic hopes by far outweighed any nationalist motives in the pursuit of unification in 1989 and 1990. Thus, it is important to ask to what extent recent economic changes since unification may have influenced identity formation.

2. Economic Perspectives

One source of stability and change in identities is economic, though such objective economic realities are always mediated politically and

13. Anne-Marie Le Gloannec, "On German Identity," *Daedalus* 123 (Winter 1994): 139.
14. See Bettina Westle, "Changing Aspects of National Identity in Germany," in Dirk Berg-Schlosser and Ralf Rytlewski, eds., *Political Culture in Germany* (New York, 1993): 291-94.

symbolically, and often with quite unexpected results. Thus one some-what puzzling phenomenon has been the recent coincidence of eastern Germans' subjectively felt and objectively measurable improvement in the standard of living, on the one hand, and their growing reassertion of an East German identity, on the other. It may nevertheless be useful to ask what systematic economic differences between the two parts of Germany are likely to persist, not in order to draw any firm conclusions about what this will entail for the reconfiguration of German identities, but rather in order to focus attention on structural disparities and lines of division that can be expected to have some bearing on Germany's East-West integration.

Clearly, the new East German economic reality is so complex that many interpretations are plausible. Consumption is up, so is the standard of living and travel, and levels of personal satisfaction are relatively high. Thus, one can argue with some justification that unification has on balance been a success. At the same time, employment is down, personal security is lower, solidarity and social cohesion have declined. This is why others can arrive at a much more negative conclusion about the outcome of unification. Moreover, "the (West German) other" continues to be experienced by many East Germans in a very real and immediate fashion as the boss at work, the superior in the office, the landlord at home, political leaders in Bonn and the new Länder capitals, and public opinion dominated by the West. From a Western point of view, "the (Eastern) other" is primarily experienced as the drain on "Western" revenues and income.

Unemployment

The radical strategy of marketization followed by the Kohl government, in particular the overnight revaluation of the East German currency and the economy's full exposure to Western competition, meant that by 1992 East German employment levels had fallen drastically. In just two years, 3.6 million jobs were lost, the number of employed declined from 9.75 million to just over 6 million, and of these almost one million were underemployed (on work creation projects [ABM], or involuntary short-time work).[15] Another 260,000 were added to the unemployment rolls in 1993.[16] In December 1994, the number of unemployed, short-time workers, as well as individuals involved in ABM, retraining and further

15. Jörg Roesler, "Privatization in Eastern Germany – Experience with the Treuhand," *Europe-Asia Studies*, 46 (1994): 505-17.

16. Dagmar Sakowsky, "Arbeitslosigkeit im vereinten Deutschland," *Deutschland Archiv* 27 (February 1994): 122.

training in the new Länder was 2.5 million. According to a study by the Economic Research Institute in Halle (Saxony-Anhalt) in 1994, this added up to an unemployment/underemployment rate of 30 percent of the work-force in the East, compared to 9.3 percent in the West.[17]

Job losses in industry and agriculture were particularly great. Due to previously hidden unemployment, the number of employed in the agricultural sector decreased from approximately 985,000 (1989) to 218,000 (1994), affecting the rural economic regions in general and women, who represented a high percentage of the agricultural workforce, in particular. Employments trends in eastern Germany are shown in Table 4.

Table 4: Employment in Eastern Germany by Sector (in thousands)

SECTOR	1989 1ST HALF	1991 1ST HALF	1992 1ST HALF	1993 1ST HALF	1994 1ST HALF
Agriculture & Forestry	985	469	300	245	218
Energy & Mining	306	204	181	145	124
Industry	3,265	2,170	1,357	1,138	1,063
Construction	846	701	797	887	998
Trade & Transport	1,652	1,252	1,160	1,129	1,115
Services	962	920	1,014	1,091	1,179
Public (State)	1,750	1,514	1,442	1,358	1,320
Total	9,766	7,230	6,251	5,933	6,017

Source: Karl Eckart, "Der wirtschaftliche Umbau in den neuen Bundesländern," *Deutschland Archiv* 28 (June 1995): 585.

While in the East 82 percent of working-age women want to work, in the West only 60 percent wish to be part of the labor force. This disparity has led some to conclude that part of the unemployment problem is simply due to the "unnaturally" high workforce participation rate of eastern German women. After having been pushed out of many positions by men in eastern Germany's post-unification scramble for jobs, at the end of 1994 women accounted for two-thirds of the unemployed and three-quarters of those out of work for more than a year.[18] In the GDR more than 90 percent of women were employed, rarely in top positions, but frequently in middle management and often highly qualified. Their qual-

17. Gisela Helwig, "Sozialstaat auf dem Prüfstand," *Deutschland Archiv* 28 (January 1995): 1.

18. Ibid., 1.

ifications, however, have been devalued; university or professional degrees are sometimes only partly or not at all recognized; and retraining often means downgrading, such as engineers or artisans being retrained as secretaries or florists. The result has been a considerable deskilling of the workforce[19] and the demoralization of many individuals.

Income and Assets

The unemployment picture in the East would suggest a high level of dissatisfaction among eastern Germans with their personal economic situation. Surprisingly, most surveys do not bear out such a conclusion. One clue that may help resolve this apparent paradox of personal satisfaction under conditions of economic depression is that since the currency union of July 1990 household income in eastern Germany has more than doubled while the cost of living has increased only by about 35 percent, leaving a still considerable increase in real income.[20] At the same time, average household income in the East is still only between 60-70 percent of western German levels.

A less frequently noted disparity that is certain to continue for generations to come is related to one of the central provisions of the unification treaty. First, the principle of restitution of private property over compensation has meant that buildings and land that for many years were used and maintained by East Germans were now returned to their West German owners. The resulting new injustices, insecurities, and legal battles have reinforced a sense of victimization on the part of many eastern Germans. Second, the Treuhand, the agency in charge of privatizing GDR state enterprises, at the end of 1994 had managed by and large to complete its task. In addition to speed, the Treuhand was interested in negotiating some job guarantees and investment commitments from the new owners. But no attempt was made to ensure that former GDR citizens would have opportunities to acquire ownership in or of these state enterprises. The result has been what some have called a "second expropriation" of East Germans.[21] More than 80 percent of privatized enterprises were purchased by non-eastern Germans. Management buy-outs by eastern Germans, a privatization method adopted by the Treuhand only after a drying up of western German investment interest, accounted for 2,360 firms, almost all of them of medium or small size

19. Sakowsky, "Arbeitslosigkeit," 122-23.

20. Klaus Asche, "Zur wirtschaftlichen und sozialen Lage in den östlichen Bundesländern," *Deutschland Archiv,* 27 (March 1994): 232-37.

21. Rüdiger Liedtke, ed., *Die Treuhand und die zweite Enteignung der Ostdeutschen* (Munich, 1993).

with 50 or fewer employees, and many of them continuing to operate on the verge of bankruptcy.[22]

In this context, it is revealing to contrast the wealth gap between East and West. According to one source, western German households own 93 percent of Germany's DM 8.9 trillion in privately held assets. While eastern Germans represent 19 percent of the population, they own barely 7 percent of assets. Specifically, an average western German household has financial assets worth DM 64,000 and real estate worth DM 215,000. The corresponding figures for eastern German households are only DM 23,000 and DM 59,000, respectively.[23] While income for those employed may approximate western German levels over the next few years, it is likely to require several more decades for the wealth gap between East and West to be reduced significantly. It is true, of course, that significant regional disparities in income and wealth also exist in the West, since per capita income in Hamburg, for example, is almost twice as high as in the regions of Weser-Ems or Oberpfalz.[24] But the crucial difference is that economically underdeveloped regions in the West are small, isolated pockets, without anything even approaching a potential common identity.

Transfer payments

In return for giving virtually unconditional control over the reorganization of property rights to the Federal Government, the last GDR government received for its citizens the full and equal inclusion into the West German welfare state and federal system of equalization payments. This bargain, in addition to offering a veritable smorgasbord of subsidies to investors, has required the German government to transfer to the East in one form or another over US$ 100 billion annually, adding up to approximately US$ 600 billion by the end of 1995 (see Table 5).[25] As a consequence, the federal budget deficit has grown continuously and tax increases became unavoidable.

Not surprisingly, this one-sided flow of resources, with no end in sight, continues to reinforce the impression of a zero-sum game between West and East and, from the viewpoint of the West, is probably the single most important factor that structures political conflicts along East-West lines. The relative intensity of this identity-reinforcing clash will

---

22. Roesler, "Privatization," 511.

23. *Neues Deutschland*, February 15, 1995.

24. Asche, "Lage," 237.

25. The annual East-West flow excludes taxes remitted from East Germany. The transfer payments include funds from the federal government, Länder and local governments, the Federal Labor Office, the Pension Fund, and the European Union.

Table 5: Transfer Payments to Eastern Germany (in billion DM)

YEAR	PAYMENTS
1990	48.0
1991	144.5
1992	187.8
1993	199.9
1994	200.6
1995*	210.0

*estimate

Source: Westdeutsche Landesbank. Cited in *Süddeutsche Zeitung,* June 30, 1995, 15.

depend, from an economic point of view, on two basic questions: How well will the (West) German economy perform in the future? And when, or to what extent, can the eastern German Länder become economically self-sustaining? During the last several years, East Germans have grown decidedly more pessimistic regarding a short-term assimilation of living standards between East and West whereas West Germans continue to exhibit greater optimism. (see Table 6).

Table 6: Expectations Regarding Assimilation of Living Standards between East and West Germans (in percentages)

	1991		1995	
	West	East	West	East
Up to 5 years	30	39	38	15
5 to 10 years	50	49	41	48
More than 10 years	18	10	17	37

Source: IPOS, *Einstellungen zu aktuellen Fragen der Innenpolitik 1995 in Deutschland. Ergebnisse jeweils einer repräsentativen Bevölkerungsumfrage in den alten und neuen Bundesländern* (Mannheim, 1995), 92-93.

Economic structure

The eastern German economy is dominated by highly efficient and technologically advanced western German branch plants. Sometimes described as "cathedrals in the desert," these enterprises are however directly linked to the western German economy and barely integrated into their regional economic structure, thus having only a limited development effect for the eastern German regions.[26] Under the slogan "preservation of industrial cores," in 1993 the federal government began intervening directly to save industrial dinosaurs in some particularly hard-hit regions from privatization and liquidation. This policy has produced a number of Land-administered quasi-state enterprises, such as Jenoptik in Thuringia or the former Trabant car plant in Saxony.[27] Since the end of the Treuhand, eastern Land governments are rediscovering the virtues of industrial policy and state capitalism. In an ironic replay of the SED's policy of preserving ideologically questionable, semi-private enterprises until the early 1970s, eastern Länder are propping up weak enterprises by buying up shares through their own industrial holding companies.[28] Harsh economic realities – an industrial base that has already slipped to contributing less than 30 percent of eastern Germany's GNP – and a self-sustained recovery still out of sight make such unorthodox initiatives politically palatable, at least to eastern Länder governments.

The new middle class *(Mittelstand),* or an eastern German capitalist class, has not yet emerged in strong enough force to take advantage of the return to the market. By mid-1993 about 490,000 new businesses existed,[29] a figure that would need to be broken down in order to give any indication of the size and kind of ventures included here, the large majority of which at any rate are small firms in the local service sector. It is interesting to note the fact that approximately 100,000 of these private businesses already existed under the old regime.[30] The eastern German *Mittelstand,* which includes the almost 2,400 management buy-outs mentioned earlier, is growing slowly, in most cases dependent either on the fortunes of large firms or on the health of still fragile regional economies.

On the one hand eastern Germans are subject to high levels of unemployment and underemployment and have suffered substantial deskilling. This is particularly the case for women. Income, on the other hand, has on average increased considerably since 1990. While still lower

26. Gernot Grabher, *The Elegance of Incoherence – Institutional Legacies, Privatization and Regional Development in East Germany and Hungary,* Wissenschaftszentrum Berlin, FS I 94-103 (1994).

27. Roesler, "Privatization," 513.

28. *WirtschaftsWoche,* 4 (1995): 23-6; and Andreas Pickel, *Radical Transitions: The Survival and Revival of Entrepeneurship in the GDR* (Boulder, CO, 1992).

29. Asche, "Wirtschaftliche und soziale Lage," 232.

30. Thomas Koch and Michael Thomas, "Transformationspassagen. Vom sozialistischen Ingenieur und Manager zum kapitalistischen Unternehmer," *Deutschland Archiv* 27 (February 1994): 154; and Pickel, *Radical Transitions,* passim.

than in the West, it can be expected to converge in the not too distant future. Strong differences between East and West, however, are likely to remain due to the availability and type of jobs and their corresponding salary level. The wealth gap between East and West will be further solidified by the stark differences in assets held by private households. One manifestation of this is the fact that most productive assets in eastern Germany are owned by western German corporations and individuals. The restitution of property, which has been mentioned above, is a well known and particularly acrimonious instance of this. Transfer payments to the eastern Länder have been enormous and have led to tax increases, affecting particularly those living in the West. Deindustrialization and what appears to be an emerging pattern of regional underdevelopment will make any significant reductions in the extent of these disparities unlikely in the near future.

The Interplay of Politics and Economics

Regardless of exactly how unique the eastern German mentality and exactly how strong eastern Germans' collective consciousness may be at this time, systematic economic disparities of this magnitude will offer great opportunities for identity building and reinforcement. But this perhaps conveys too simplistic a picture. For it assumes that an eastern German identity thrives primarily on such objective economic disparities, and that it is itself an expression of victimization and defeat. Clearly, these mechanisms play a role, and the well-documented resentment directed against western German managers and civil servants working in the East, especially by the "losers" of unification, provides support for such a view.[31] Other evidence, however, suggests that there is no direct relationship between personal economic situation and eastern German identity.[32] The comparative case of Quebec indicates forcefully and in more general terms that economic development and equalization may well strengthen rather than weaken collective identity.

As the post-unification transfer of East German assets to western German ownership proceeded virtually without public comment (at least in the West), the media overflowed with discussions of German national identity. From a cultural studies perspective, a "reading" of the symbols selected by post-unification political elites and the process of their presentation to German citizens as icons of "historical memory"

31. Siegfried Grundmann, "Zur Akzeptanz und Integration von Beamten aus den alten in den neuen Bundesländern," *Deutschland Archiv* 28 (January 1994): 36-38.

32. Laurence McFalls, *Communism's Collapse, Democracy's Demise? The Cultural Context and Consequences of the East German Revolution* (New York, 1994).

can offer insight into the particular difficulties of reconstructing an official version of German national self-understanding.

3. Cultural Perspectives

Although it seems merely to involve intangibles, the cultural bridging of differences between East and West may ultimately take longer than political or even economic integration. Many observers claim that during the first half-decade after unification the mental gap between both Germanys appears to have grown rather than diminished. Perhaps this finding should be less surprising, if one remembered that deeply held outlooks, values, and ideologies cannot change overnight. Beliefs of a lifetime that are rooted in a wealth of experiences are not likely to be jettisoned quickly, since they also involve strong feelings that resist rational appeals at reorientation. The public disparagement of the neck-twisting bird *Wendehals* is one indication of a deep-seated suspicion against too quick a change.

Preoccupied with the differences between *Ossis* and *Wessis*, the media have reveled in discussing the problems of reconstructing a joint German national identity. A favorite topic has been the collaboration of prominent literary figures such as Christa Wolf, Sascha Anderson, or Heiner Müller with the Stasi in order to diminish their moral authority. Though the question of a separate eastern German identity is debated at length, the normative nature of a western German identity, based on commitment to the democratic system, has often been taken for granted, since it seemed to be the necessary goal of assimilation by the Easterners. Due to a lack of reliable data on the East and the failure of most Western survey instruments to adjust for the avoidance responses of the postwar generations to explicit (as opposed to indirect) nationality-based self-identifications, the discussion was characterized primarily by assertion, speculation, and polemic.

Perhaps a symbolic approach to cultural debates could help make some sense of these discordant voices. According to Bourdieu,

> the aim of political activity is to create and implement representations (mental, verbal, pictorial, dramatic) of the social world by which the thinking of the actors in society, and thereby the social world itself, can be influenced; or more precisely, to create and remove social groups – and with them the social actions by which these groups could change the social world in accordance with their interests – by producing, maintaining, or destroying the representations which enable these groups to see themselves or to be seen by others.[33]

33. Pierre Bourdieu, *Was heißt sprechen? Die Ökonomie des sprachlichen Tausches* (Vienna, 1990).

The public display of symbols, slogans, or physical objects makes broad communication possible, while the careful creation, selection (or omission) of symbolic objects or phrases can convey multiple, ambiguous, contradictory, and even taboo meanings. The avoidance of explicit articulation allows symbolic communication to produce emotional responses or associations without activating the demands of rational logic or violating the conventions of acceptable public discourse. Therefore a careful "reading" of the symbols selected by post-unification elites as icons of "historical memory" can offer insights into the current effort to reconstruct an official German national self-understanding.

Clashing Traditions

As Hobsbawm has noted, during periods of revolutionary change, new traditions are invented through "a process of formalization and ritualization, characterized by reference to the past."[34] All complex societies carry through time a variety of interpretations of who or what they are, put forward by different groups and political actors contesting for dominance or legitimacy, and all periodically rewrite their dominant national mythology to reflect shifts of power, political expediency, and taste.[35] Since the past is a central battleground for the contestation of cultural identities, it might be helpful to take a closer look at the different ways in which East and West Germany dealt with their common antecedents as well as their diverging developments.

From the early postwar period, historians, politicians, and other public figures in the two Germanys were actively engaged in the struggle to shape a historically-derived sense of national identity into a serviceable vehicle for political identification with their respective states. These efforts produced two highly selective oppositional valorizations of German social, political, and cultural history to which the East and West Germans who confronted one another in 1989 had been acculturated. It needs therefore to be recognized more clearly that the forty years of division created two virtual mirror self-images, locked in mutual antagonism. Many of the current debates about the past can therefore be understood as efforts to negotiate a reconciliation of these long-held, contradictory norms of German identity.

This process is complicated by both the exclusivity of the two prior co-dominant versions and by the taboo nature of their common prede-

---

34. Eric Hobsbawm, "Introduction: Inventing Traditions," in Eric Hobsbawm and Terence Ranger, eds., *The Invention of Tradition* (Cambridge, 1984), 4.

35. Mitchell Ash, "Becoming Normal, Modern and German (Again?)," Paper presented at Johns Hopkins University, September 1992, forthcoming in Michael Geyer, ed., *The Power of Intellectuals in Germany* (Chicago, 1998).

cessors, the undigested National Socialist vision of the German *Volk*. It is further made difficult by the circumstance that in each case, a new orthodoxy was imposed by external rather than internal forces (political or economic defeat). In the old Federal Republic, an *ex post facto* internal debate beginning in the late 1960s resulted in a degree of consensus. A similar process may well develop in the current case. Thus far German unification has, however, not led to a reevaluation of the distortions and elisions of the postwar political polarization, but to an attempt to simply replace the Eastern version with its Western mirror image.

One telling indicator of the difference in Eastern and Western self-conception was the way in which each successor state dealt with the crimes of the Third Reich. Explicit nationalism remained taboo in both systems, which shared different but equally complex systems of repression and denial. Thus, the vast majority of the population in both German states escaped any explicit confrontation with its toleration of – or participation in – the crimes of National Socialism.[36] Despite both shared experience and shared repression, postwar conditions dictated that the political activity of the dominant elites of the two German states represent pre-1945 history in radically different ways.

The German Democratic Republic, founded in 1949, based its claim to legitimacy primarily on its resistance to fascism. Its post-Soviet occupation government was composed of communists, socialists, social democrats, and labor organizers who had fled to the Soviet Union in 1933 and returned in the wake of the Red Army. They were joined by a smaller number of exiles returning from Western countries and political prisoners who had survived the Nazi period in prisons and concentration camps as well as representatives of bourgeois democratic parties (CDU, LDP, and later NDPD). The new state justified its separate existence with the goal of building socialism on the ashes of the Third Reich and grounded its founding mythology in an "unbroken" historical tradition of the German labor, socialist, and communist movements.

In contrast, the Federal Republic that combined the British, French, and American sectors considered itself the legitimate legal successor to the Weimar Republic. The West embraced its Cold War role as the bulwark of anti-communism and elaborated a history which placed it in a tradition of social reform, economic liberalism, parliamentarianism, and democracy. While not central to this founding mythology, the bour-

36. Holger Schick, "Zum Umgang der Deutschen mit ihrer NS-Vergangenheit (1945-1949)," in Ulrike C. Wasmuth, ed., *Konfliktverwaltung ein Zerrbild unserer Demokratie?* (Berlin, 1992), 227-239; and Elizabeth Domanski, "'Kristallnacht,' the Holocaust and German Unity: The Meaning of November 9 as an Anniversary in Germany," *History and Memory*, 4 (1992): 60-94.

geois-conservative resistance provided a thread of continuity through the period from 1933-1945 and served as a proxy for the nation. The resistance to fascism was portrayed as heroic, but doomed, a fig-leaf rather than a foundation.[37]

Just as the East failed to honor bourgeois-conservative resisters, so the West refused to acknowledge the existence of any opposition beyond its own narrow selection. The *Kreisauer Kreis* and the Officers of July 20 became the iconic figures of resistance in the West, while the Red Orchestra and the Herbert Baum group were so stylized in the East. The White Rose was apparently regarded as politically neutral and was commemorated by both sides. Resisters who fell into neither political category, such as the several thousand German women who successfully demonstrated in front of the Rosenstrasse prison in Berlin-Mitte in 1943 to win the release of their Jewish husbands, were ignored until discovered by the daily life history movement in the late 1970s and 1980s.[38]

Both postwar states quickly positioned themselves as allies (rather than as vassals) of their occupiers. Given popular anti-communism and anti-Slavic racism, poorer economic conditions, and political upheavals in the East bloc, this was a difficult task demanding intense propaganda and police efforts in the East. One psychologically effective method was the condemnation of fascism and iconization of the resistance, offering compromised citizens a (false) identification with heroic German antifascists. Aided by the Cold War, West German elites found common ground with their occupiers/allies in the conflation of fascism with Stalinism under the heading of "totalitarianism." The creation of a common racialized and political enemy facilitated the psychological shift of the Western population via (false) identification, especially with the economically powerful United States, to the winning side in a continuing war against communism.[39] Despite steps taken toward partial normalization of relations between the two German states beginning after both

37. Ulrich Doelfs, "Die 'Wende' oder die nationale Aneignung von Geschichte?" in Wasmuth, *Konfliktverwaltung*, 240-255.

38. The funeral of Marlene Dietrich, a German cultural icon, was denied official recognition. Press coverage of the event reflected a widespread attitude that Dietrich, far from being celebrated as a resister, was regarded as a traitor for having made anti-fascist broadcasts from exile and entertaining Allied troops.

39. Konrad Adenauer saw Korea as "just one more place along the same front" that began in East Germany; Moscow was not part of Europe but rooted in the "culture of the most backward part of Asia;" the Soviet Union represented the "monstrous power of Asia" and "Asia stands on the Elbe." Only an "economically and spiritually healthy western Europe ... that includes as a vital part that portion of Germany not occupied by the Russians can stop the further forward pressure of Asia ...." Comments made in 1950, 1946 and 1948, all cited from Robert G. Moeller, *Protecting Motherhood. Women and the Family in the Politics of Postwar West Germany* (Berkeley, 1993), 102-103.

were accepted into the United Nations in the early 1970s, the relationship remained one of mutual antagonism.

Attempts beginning in the 1980s to reposition West Germany internationally as a "normal" nation have tended to meet with more success in German eyes than in those of its neighbors.[40] The efforts of various conservative politicians and historians to rehabilitate nationalism by relativizing parts of this taboo Nazi past have regularly produced detonations in what can best be described as a political minefield. One telling example is the speech made by President of the Federal Parliament Philipp Jenninger on the fiftieth anniversary of the *Kristallnacht* pogrom which sought to provide a relatively straightforward and accurate description of the anti-Semitic violence. But when he tried to evoke the attitude of the average German toward the Jews without appropriate quotation marks, he was profoundly misunderstood:

> And as far as Jews were concerned: After all, hadn't they in the past presumed to a role – that's what it was called then – which they did not merit? Shouldn't they finally have to accept some limits, for once? Didn't they even perhaps deserve being shown their place? And above all: aside from wild exaggerations which were not to be taken seriously, didn't the propaganda in the main agree with one's own suspicions and convictions?[41]

Forced to resign by a firestorm of domestic and international criticism, Jenninger mused: "One has to learn from this example. Not everything can be called by its name – in Germany."[42] As one foreign commentator wrote: "Germans today would much prefer *not* to be completely clear in their understanding of their history."[43]

Since West Germans perceived the division as a result more of the Cold War rather than of the Second World War, its end could be interpreted as the return of the country to "normalcy." The pervasive conflation of Stalinism and fascism allowed unification to be presented as the symbolic closure of both the Third Reich and the East-West conflict. At a special party caucus of the CDU in October 1993 Kohl said: "I believe that the postwar era has come to an end. Germany had a distastrous special role forced upon it after 1945. As far as I am concerned that time is past."[44] When Steffen Heitmann, a conservative Eastern candidate for

---

40. See Ash, "Becoming Normal'; and Domanski, "'Kristallnacht'," 60ff.

41. Philipp Jenninger, Speech to the German Bundestag, November 10, 1988.

42. Philipp Jenninger, *Der Spiegel*, November 14, 1988, 23.

43. Conor Cruise O'Brien, "Denounced – for the Truth," *The Times*, November 16, 1988, 12.

44. Quentin Peel "German Postwar Era 'At An End'," *Financial Times*, October 21, 1993, 16. See also Stephen Kinzer, "Kohl Turns Right to Face Elections," *New York Times*, September 15, 1993, A6.

President of the united Germany, too boldly enunciated this logic in public, a domestic outrage, aggravated by his sexist and racist comments, forced him to resign.[45] Well aware of the taboo nature of explicit speech on these matters, Chancellor Kohl has instead preferred to operate at the level of symbolic representation, which while not foolproof (e.g., Bitburg), offers a number of advantages.

Removing the Perpetrators: The Example Neue Wache

Though the debate among the intelligentsia over German identity has had little if any direct relevance to the majority of the people who live in the East, the political project of replacing the East German founding mythology with the West German variant did evoke a wider response. As noted above, the crimes of fascism and the resistance to it constituted the bedrock upon which the legitimacy of the GDR leadership was founded and formed part of the "historical memory" accepted by the population. In the wake of unification, this foundation has been physically as well as ideologically obliterated.

The recent renovation of the Neue Wache war memorial on Unter den Linden, the processional avenue of East Berlin, provides an example of complex symbolic communication. Until 1990, the former war memorial consisted of a bare room containing an eternal flame and the dedication "To the Victims of War and Fascism" above a crypt holding the remains of an unknown German soldier and an unknown concentration camp victim. The post-unification renovation, following a design personally chosen by Chancellor Kohl, replaced the specific terms "War" and "Fascism" with the generic "Terror" and "Tyranny" and the confessionally neutral flame with an oversized version of a Käte Kollwitz' sculpture "Mother with Dead Son," or "*Pieta*."[46]

45. Shortly after he was announced by Kohl as the CDU candidate, Heitmann was cited as saying that Germany can accept "only a limited amount of penetration by foreigners," and that Germans have a "right to protect their identity." Rounding things off in another statement, Mr. Heitmann asserted: "For women, caring for children and self-realization are not compatible. One can only be done at the expense of the other." Kinzer, ibid., A10.

46. Arne A. Kollwitz, "Symbole, die unvereinbar sind," *Frankfurter Allgemeine Zeitung*, March 28, 1995, 43. In response to the Berlin Senate's plan to return statues of the Generals Scharnhorst and Bülow that had flanked the building prior to 1945, the Kollwitz' heirs made public their agreement with Chancellor Kohl and the Berlin Senate which gave permission to enlarge the piece in return for a guarantee that the Neue Wache would not emphasize militarism. The heirs have threatened to remove and destroy the sculpture if the statues of the generals are returned. See also: "Berlin Debates the Message of the Neue Wache ...." *This Week in Germany*, May 5, 1995, 6; and Jane Kramer, "The Politics of Memory," *The New Yorker*, August 14, 1995, 48-65.

After Ignatz Bubis, the leader of the Central Council of Jews in Germany and Jerzy Kanal, leader of the Berlin Jewish Community, refused invitations to participate in the re-dedication ceremony and protests were received from other Jewish organizations, a plaque enumerating those being memorialized within was affixed to the facade of the building.[47] By expanding the list to include civilians, soldiers, gypsies, homosexuals, sectarians, resisters and anti-communists, this effort at concreteness so diluted the prior reference to the Jews as principal victims of German fascism that it symbolically displaced them from any central role in a memorial dominated now by an over-dimensional Christian symbol.

At issue is a curious competition for victimhood. In spite of official philo-Semitism, most Germans have shown relatively little interest in the principal targets of fascist persecution. As Schick has noted, "the discussion almost always centered on what suffering the German people had experienced through the Nazi criminals."[48] Openly reclaiming the role of victims-of-fascism both connects the German population with their own experience or family history of bombing raids, occupation, and forced relocation, and places the Germans together with other Europeans as having suffered under the Nazis. Rather than simply repressing the complex dissonance of complicity or toleration, it obliterates them, for if the Germans are officially victims, the perpetrators are obviously others.

The post-unification Neue Wache has been reconfigured as a memorial to the German Christian victims of unspecified (but implicitly unmistakable) violent and tyrannical forces. Chancellor Kohl called his creation a monument to "reconciliation" and in fact, the new Neue

---

47. The full text of the plaque reads: *"Die Neue Wache ist der Ort der Erinnerung und des Gedenkens an die Opfer von Krieg und Gewaltherrschaft.*

Wir gedenken der Völker, die durch Krieg gelitten haben. Wir gedenken ihrer Bürger, die verfolgt wurden und ihr Leben verloren. Wir gedenken der Gefallenen der Weltkriege. Wir gedenken der Unschuldigen, die durch Krieg und Folgen des Krieges in der Heimat, die in Gefangenschaft und bei der Vertreibung ums Leben gekommen sind.

Wir gedenken der Millionen ermordeter Juden. Wir gedenken der ermordeten Sinti und Roma. Wir gedenken aller, die umgebracht wurden wegen ihrer Abstammung, ihrer Homosexualität oder wegen Krankheit und Schwäche. Wir gedenken aller Ermordeten, deren Recht auf Leben geleugnet wurde.

Wir gedenken der Menschen, die sterben mußten, um ihrer religiösen oder politischen Überzeugung willen. Wir gedenken aller, die Opfer der Gewaltherrschaft wurden und unschuldig den Tod fanden. Wir gedenken der Frauen und Männer, die im Widerstand gegen die Gewaltherrschaft ihr Leben opferten, wir ehren alle, die eher den Tod hinnahmen als ihr Gewissen zu leugnen.

Wir gedenken der Frauen und Männer, die verfolgt und ermordet wurden, weil sie sich totalitärer Diktatur nach 1945 widersetzt haben."

In the event, Bubis did attend, while Kanal remained absent in protest.
48. Schick, "Umgang," 234. See also Domanski, "'Kristallnacht,'" 60ff., and Kramer, "The Politics of Memory," 48-65.

Wache is the successful realization of the gesture that went awry at Bitburg. The appearance of wreaths and flowers dedicated to the memory of fallen officers[49] is an appropriate response to the official iconization of German victimhood. It is neither unique nor an isolated incident, but the most visible physical representation of the current revision of German historical memory. At other sites in Brandenburg and Saxony-Anhalt there have been similar conflicts over the dismantling of monuments to the victims of fascism and memorials to anti-fascist resisters from public squares and street signs, parks and graveyards. However, the bulk of the protest against the revision of the Neue Wache, located in the official ceremonial public sphere, came from foreign observers and German Jewish groups.

Rewriting the Resistance: Street Names

A parallel example of post-unification reconstruction of memory is the renaming of the streets in the center of Berlin, examined from an urban anthropological perspective in a case study by De Soto.[50] Here, the intrusion of the new dominant culture into the lives of East Berliners has provoked more significant local resistance, because in this case, official "historical memory" is embedded in individually lived experience and personal space. De Soto interprets the "unequal dispute between political elites and urban residents"[51] as a classic case of the power of symbolic politics.

In July 1990, that is, three months prior to unification, the (West) Berlin Council of Mayors initiated an action to rename the streets of East Berlin. This first plan, based on the idea that residents of these districts would suggest acceptable new names, failed due to lack of cooperation. A second plan, that new names were to be suggested by elected district representatives, also failed when these insisted that suggestions be developed in consultation with their constituents and voted on in district meetings. The city Senate, with the support of the Chancellor's office in Bonn, responded by appointing its own "Independent Commission" and directed it to select exemplary "democratic" names. Despite protests against this procedure, the commission produced a list

49. Kramer, "Politics of Memory," passim.
50. Hermine G. de Soto, "Symbolic Productions in the New East Side of Berlin, 1990-1994," Grazyna Ewa Karpinska, ed., *The City: Today, Yesterday and the Day Before* (Lodz, 1995), 162-178. I would like to thank Dr. Hermine de Soto, Women's Studies Research Center, University of Wisconsin-Madison, for generously sharing with me a pre-publication manuscript reporting on her research in Berlin-Mitte on the street name controversy.
51. De Soto, "Symbolic Productions," 164.

of monuments to be removed and of correct new names for now unacceptable streets. This led to further objections, letter writing campaigns, several postponements of actions, and numerous changes of street signs without notice.[52]

The West German version of history now being dictated to the East tars the GDR with the brush of "totalitarian dictatorship," at times implicitly equating it to the National Socialist regime. Despite disagreement among representatives of the different political parties on the Commission over the pedagogical and historical symbolic value of individual replacement names, none seem to have questioned the appropriateness of the procedure or the conviction that "communists" were taboo. Such reverse polarization still produces black and white images. Hence passages in the Independent Commission's Report read like self-parodies, such as the explanation of why some leaders of the labor movement, a cornerstone in the development of German democracy, were nonetheless found to be "undemocratic," or the rationalization of why members of the aristocracy provided better "democratic" models.[53]

In fact, many names were changed quickly and without protest. Otto Grotewohl, Otto Nuschke, Klement Gottwald, Karl Maron, Heinrich Rau, and Hans Marchlewski (among many others), disappeared with no sign of widespread public regret, all of them party officials either little known or little-loved by the general population.[54]

Those streets which became objects of serious contention were named after historical figures of considerable significance – Karl Liebknecht, Rosa Luxemburg, Clara Zetkin, Karl Marx, Friedrich Engels, and V.I. Lenin. Many public spaces in the GDR were named in honor of members of the German and international labor movements, those who fought in the

52. The seven-member commission included one East Berlin member and used the following guidelines to evaluate present street names: 1) persons who actively helped to destroy the Weimar Republic should not be honored; 2) persons who fought after 1933 against the National Socialists in order to construct a communist dictatorship should not be honored; 3) only those persons should be honored who fought for human as well as citizen's rights and for the rule of law and democracy; 4) new names for streets would be suggested from those persons who fought for a state of law, who defended the Weimar Republic and who fought against the dictatorships of the National Socialists and the German Democratic Republic. *Abschlußbericht, 17. März 1994. Berliner Senat Abteilung für Verkehr und Betriebe,* (Berlin, 1994), 5 (cited and summarized from de Soto, "Symbolic Productions," 167-169).

53. Ibid., 7.

54. A report listing by district the final results of the Commission dated June 1, 1995 (*Senatsverwaltung für Verkehr und Betriebe III A 33, Stand 1,* June 1995, with handwritten corrections, November 12, 1995) shows the following totals: Mitte: 17; Friedrichshain: 6; Hohenschönhausen: 4; Treptow: 4; Lichtenberg: 14; Köpenick: 1; Marzahn: 10; Prenzlauer Berg: 7; Hellersdorf: 14; Pankow: 4; Weissensee: 1.

Spanish Civil War or the anti-fascist resistance, or others who were forced to emigrate, persecuted, or murdered by the Nazi Regime. While these names were intended to legitimize the postwar East German state, they were also based upon a socialist tradition with which the population had come to identify. Through education, habituation, or active identification, these figures had been accepted as legitimate representatives of the German tradition in a way that the postwar party functionaries had not. Therefore, the signs recalling these names had become part of the normal physical landscape and geographical orientation of the local population.

One of the first physical actions was the removal of a large red granite statue of Lenin, located on Leninplatz (renamed United Nations Square, in an awkward display of substitute internationalism), off Leninallee (renamed Landsberger Allee) in Friedrichshain. Petitions, letters of protest, and demonstrations by the residents of the surrounding apartment houses (prized by the *nomenklatura* for their solid construction and spacious rooms) failed to prevent the removal and destruction of the memorial. Local comment at the time expressed resentment at the intrusive aspects of the procedure as well as the ironic expression of regret that they hadn't taken Ernst Thälmann instead, who was only a few blocks away in Prenzlauer Berg, much larger, far uglier, and not exactly a great political thinker.

Eventually the controversy moved from coverage only in the local East Berlin media to the West Berlin press and thus to the level of "real" politics. Mrs. Laurien, the conservative President of the Berlin House of Representatives, expressed outrage at the prospect of mail being addressed to Representatives at a street bearing the name of Käthe Niederkirchner. As a child, Niederkirchner had fled to exile in Moscow with her parents, members of the German Communist Party. In 1943 she had parachuted as a partisan into occupied Poland behind German lines, was captured, tortured, and executed at Ravensbrück in 1944. Since these resistance credentials were impeccable, a compromise was reached by using a side street as a new mailing address.

For De Soto, street names are on the one hand "symbols of memory [which] have become ideological instruments" for political elites. On the other hand she sees them as a part of the "everyday culture" of ordinary East Berliners, "their lived history or … experiences."[55] The struggle over the representation of German history in the names of central Berlin threatens to silence this "lived history," provoking a personal resistance which becomes politicized in the process. For De Soto this is a case in which the dominant culture is still non-hegemonic:

55. De Soto, "Symbolic Productions," 175.

the new dominant culture is perceived by the natives as ideology rather than [hegemonic] culture because the dominant culture has not yet connected with the experience and understanding of those people who do not produce it, who lack access or have sharply diminished access, to wealth and power.[56]

The street names controversy offers to the local population a highly problematic demonstration of the West German practice of parliamentary democracy. The intervention of the Berlin Senate violated the principle of subsidiarity (by suspending the well-established right of Berlin boroughs to assign street names within their boundaries) and effectively excluded residents from voting on, or even influencing the choice of the names of the streets on which they lived.[57] The East has received democratic forms, but the unequal distribution of power makes the resulting decisions appear less than democratic in practice. Moreover, the Senate intervened only in the East. While the Marx-Engels Platz elevated train station in Mitte has long since become Hackescher Markt and both Marx-Engels Platz and Karl-Marx Allee are on the list for removal, the Karl-Marx-Straße subway station and Karl-Marx-Straße in the West Berlin district of Neukölln remain serenely unremarked upon.

In the renaming of streets and the planned reconstruction of the central downtown, even the formalities of public participation in city planning and development decisions have been set aside. This perception is shared by other observers. Janice Bockmeyer wrote in response to a recent *New York Times Magazine* article on the redevelopment of Potsdamer Platz:

> When I lived in Berlin from 1989 to 1992, I attended a community meeting in which stunned former "East Berliners" were told of planned changes and demolition in their neighborhood. Without input into these decisions, the residents soon saw the parallel with earlier centralized-planning experiences. "Is this democracy?" someone whispered.[58]

The two examples of symbolic communication discussed above are both located in the center of Berlin, previously the center of East Berlin. As the capital of the former East German state and the future capital of the united Germany, this physical territory is a uniquely contested space which must be cleared of the symbolic residue of the prior occupants

56. Ibid., 165.

57. See *Ausführungsvorschriften zu PP5 des Berliner Strassengesetzes – Benennung* 6 (December 1985), AB1, 2466/DB1 VI, 156, changed by *Verwaltungsvorschriften* 16 (August 1991), AB1, 1966/DB1 I, 309.

58. Janice Bockmeyer, "Reimagining Berlin," *New York Times Magazine*, February 26, 1995, 10.

and prepared for the new tenants. It is vital to the normalization and legitimation of the unified German state that the post-unification elaboration of (West) German founding mythology be projected in the center of its ceremonial capital.

Ideology, however, has often proved to be a blunt weapon. The process of obliterating the icons of the GDR state in the popular self-identification or geographical orientation of eastern Germans threatens to eliminate the communist tradition and much of the resistance to fascism from "historical memory." Equally disturbing is the fact that the residents of Berlin Mitte and many other districts in the five new states are receiving lessons in the mechanics of a "democratic" process which stand in crass contradiction to the democratic model of an informed and active citizenry. The lack of credibility of the justification of the "Independent Commission" for finding Dorothea, a Dutch princess and second wife of a Prussian grand duke, a more appropriate democratic role model than Clara Zetkin,[59] is outweighed by the counterproductiveness of the procedure. New citizens are unlikely to gain respect for or identify with the "pluralistic values and ... West German rules of law and democracy" (the commission's declared goal) by having their right to vote on neighborhood issues disregarded.

As the Federal Republic continues to rewrite its own history, many East Germans feel that they are being offered assimilation into a Western-defined "German identity" rather than allowed an active role in creating a common founding mythology for the unified state. At the same time, social, political, and especially economic conditions continue to reinforce clear distinctions of opportunity and status between East and West. Identity, however, cannot simply be dictated by a new elite. It must in some way connect with, confirm or be confirmed by the experience of the population.

The reconfigured Neue Wache appears to connect with the genuine experience of many people in both parts of the united country of having suffered in the Second World War and with a shared inclination to take refuge in vagueness as to cause and effect. In contrast, the renaming of Berlin streets and removal of other resistance memorials actively intervenes and visibly clashes with both lived experience and its own ostensible ideological message. Such interventions, which claim to promote the

---

59. Clara Zetkin was a leader of the movement for female equality and women's suffrage in Germany. She was a member of the Reichstag from 1920 until 1933; in 1933 she was forced into exile. Autorenkollektiv, *Geschichte der Sozialistischen Frauenbewegung* (Berlin, 1982). While her contributions to the feminist movement were acknowledged, members of the Independent Commission highlighted her role in the Communist Party and the Comintern which helped destabilize the Weimar Republic.

integration of the eastern German population, are more likely to provoke the opposite: cynicism, resentment, or a sense of powerlessness. Lack of identification can lead either to a withdrawal from the political process or to resistance, hastening the consolidation of alternative or oppositional group identities which contest the control of the dominant elites. This result may not please those who seek to impose an unchanged version of the dominant culture, but may ironically better integrate the citizens of the former GDR via the mechanisms of civil society.

4. Future Prospects

In 1990, Chancellor Helmut Kohl invited eastern Germans to become western Germans, and a large majority responded favorably, unaware as yet of the fundamental differences that had developed between East Germans and West Germans during forty years of political division. Not surprisingly, this transformation of identities proved too radical for most East Germans to complete overnight. In fact, seven years after the two German states unified, it is evident that the prior identities have considerable staying power – in both East and West. An identity, however, can be maintained only as long it can be convincingly separated from "the other." Reality has to continue to correspond to this conceptual and emotional separation to some degree.

There are many signs that the crisis of unification has given way to a more gradual approach toward the integration of the two German societies. Social and economic trends that emerged in the last few years suggest that the assimilation of social and economic circumstances in the two parts of Germany are well underway, although it will take at least until the end of the decade until pre-unification levels are reached in areas such as marriage and birth rates and economic output. Social and economic developments, however, are also indicative of political trends. But it is important to remember that the methods by which German unification was achieved and implemented and the continued dominance of western Germans in every aspect of life, including their demographic dominance, will perpetuate political interests that are predominantly determined in and by the West. Thus, it is likely that political differences between East and West will not widen. However, neither will they disappear, but should acquire a greater degree of certainty and therefore predictability.

Depending on one's political position, the manifestation of an eastern German identity is considered a "bad" thing or a "good" thing, but in either case proof that unification is "not working." In the former case, it is the weak, insufficiently adaptable, and unwilling citizen of the former

GDR trying to hide behind eastern German identity, a best-forgotten remnant from a poor and repressive past. In the latter case, the ill-treated and downtrodden, the colonized and exploited, rise up against the new oppressors under the banner of a new eastern German identity. These stylizations may be politically more or less useful tools, though even in that capacity their attraction seems to be limited to the simple-minded and the angry. A clever variant of the first position is to accept eastern German claims to cultural difference and to draw the conclusion that the economic cost of such cultural distinctiveness should not be borne by the West. In other words, if you don't want to be like us, don't expect us to keep sending money.[60]

A stronger eastern German identity is in fact not a somehow passive and negative reaction to a unification process gone sour. This would simply be inconsistent with what a majority of eastern Germans say. Rather, a growing collective consciousness is better understood as an adaptation strategy to the problems and conflicts that have been created by unification. Eastern German identity is not necessarily embraced as a way of opting out of the new Germany, of celebrating cultural distinctiveness, or of waxing nostalgic about a paradise lost. From a functional point of view it may instead be a constructive response: an Eastern German self-consciousness does not question the rules of the game in any fundamental sense but rather facilitates integration by empowering individuals and collective actors in the ongoing conflicts of interest, many of them along East-West lines.

The reawakening of eastern German consciousness has grown out of a recognition that the two societies are distinct, that the West cannot or at any rate should not simply be copied, and that in addition to undeniable successes, the attempt to do so has created a wealth of serious and long-term problems. Growing support for an eastern German identity can be understood as a demand for recognition of these basic facts. Whether the East-West division will continue and for how long, will depend on many factors, including the answers to the following questions: Will traditional social milieus erode as part of the ongoing assimilation process, and if so, how much time will it take? Can potentially unifying, cross-cutting alliances between East and West be strengthened? Can the process of integration be changed from perceptions that are primarily based on past stereotypes to a feeling that allows openness and exhibits a degree of confidence and understanding?

60. This is an interpretation forcefully suggested, for example, by Meinhard Miegel at the Fourth Transformation Conference of the Berliner Institut für Sozialwissenschaftliche Forschung. See his article, "Wie realistisch und wünschenswert ist die Angleichung der Lebensverhältnisse in West und Ost?" *BISS public* 14 (1994): 5-9.

Economic, social, and political conditions continue to reinforce clear distinctions of opportunity and status between East and West. The media discussions and surveys indicate that identity cannot simply be dictated by a new dominant group. Dominant cultures and societies never find it easy to understand, let alone recognize, the distinctiveness of subordinate cultures and societies. This myopia is unfortunate, since successful examples like the Ruhr Poles in the German past indicate that it is the recognition of such distinctiveness that greatly facilitates the process of integration in the long run.

Chapter IV

WOMEN, MEN, AND UNIFICATION

Gender Politics and the Abortion Struggle Since 1989

Joyce Mushaben, Geoffrey Giles, and *Sara Lennox*

I have always thought that abortion acquires political volatility in periods when the social position of women generally is under siege. This is because the abortion decision epitomizes the capacity of individual women and women collectively to control fertility and to control the consequences of heterosexual sex ....

Rosalind Pollack Petchesky

The over-determined, contradictory elements of German identity, refracted along gender lines, have been nowhere more apparent than in the struggle over the legality of abortion in united Germany. What was at stake in this controversy, which has been called the "most emotional issue of unification?"[1] In a recent book examining the contours of German reproductive rights campaigns between 1920 and 1950, Atina Grossmann stresses that Weimar debate derived from a process in which high unemployment and a rise in the number of illegal abortions were articulated as the "twin emblems of Germany's crisis of social policy and political legitimacy."[2] Grossmann reads the intensity of birth control debates during the 1920s as an expression of a problematic transition in which "the new woman" – outfitted with voting rights

1. Konrad H. Jarausch, *The Rush to Germany Unity* (New York, 1994), 172.
2. Atina Grossman, *Reforming Sex: The German Movement for Birth Control and Abortion Reform 1920-1950* (New York, 1995), 79.

under the Weimar Constitution – became the focal image of a general "crisis of modernity."

This essay rests upon the analogous assumption that the FRG abortion controversy since 1990 has served as a focal point for multiple conflicts over the character of this "new" Germany, particularly as they pertain to gender identity. While the abortion debate per se seems to concentrate on contending notions of appropriate female behavior in the unified nation, the struggle over women's rights to bodily self-determination simultaneously invokes a conflict over the future course of the Body Politic, over the lessons to be derived from two German histories, over economic restructuring, and over the meaning of German "citizenship" in a united Europe. On a more practical plane, it is also important to remember that this ideological confrontation has profound implications for the career chances and quality of life of women in East and West Germany.

To provide a tighter focus for this interdisciplinary investigation of the reconstruction of gender identities after unification, this essay concentrates primarily on a single text, namely, the Bundestag's plenary debate over the Law on Assistance for Pregnant Women and Families on June 25, 1992.[3] This was the first full scale debate of the emotional issue by the parliament of the united Germany that offered eastern and western deputies an opportunity to reflect on their differing experiences. A close reading of the verbatim protocol of this pivotal legislative discussion makes it easier to overcome the differences in respective methodological approaches, since the common theme helped reconcile the divergent historical, literary, and political science perspectives.

The joint analysis of the abortion struggle after unification involves three distinct dimensions. The first part of the essay explores the development of the issue by searching for clues to the present in the past. Already the debates of the Weimar era reveal an unbroken continuity of gender images which portrayed women as morally weak, "naturally" subordinate to men, and in need of male guidance and control. In the center of this chapter stands a close textual analysis of the Bundestag discussion of 1992, focusing on multiple blind spots inherent in the ostensibly "coherent" maternalist discourse which came to dominate the debate.[4] This reading reveals the extent of the contradictions of this framing of the discussion: on the one hand, women are destined *by nature*

---

3. Deutscher Bundestag, *Plenarprotokoll/Stenographischer Bericht*, 99th Session, Bonn, June 25, 1992, 8233-8384.

4. Sara Lennox wishes to acknowledge that her part of the essay could not have been written without the generous help of Marlene Fried, Atina Grossmann, Lester Mazor, Meredith Michaels, and Linda Morgan.

to be mothers and thus deemed ethical, life-preserving beings; yet women abort and hence prove their incapacity for ethical judgment, on the other. The concluding section traces the ways in which the abortion debate remains tied to many political-institutional, constitutional-legal, and market-economic conflicts inherent in unification. That examination of its links to the larger systemic context suggests not only that women have been the most dramatically affected by the immediate process of *de jure* unification, but also that gender will continue to serve as a battleground for re-contesting East-West identity questions for several years to come.

1. The Abortion Issue in Historical Context

The abortion debate after unification was structured in implicit and explicit ways by its own complicated history. The earlier discussions of the Second Empire, the Weimar Republic, and the Third Reich left a confusing legacy of claims and counter-claims that continued to reverberate through later discussions. Framed mostly by male speakers, the arsenal of arguments from the past contained such different dimensions as a medical rhetoric, dealing with the health of the potential mother and child; a demographic rhetoric, concerned with population growth and quality; a moral rhetoric, preoccupied with the transgressions and vices of individual women; a religious rhetoric, focused on personal sin and redemption; and a legal rhetoric, privileging the protection of life and the upholding of community standards over the rights of the individual woman. At what times did these different claims originate, what motivated opponents and supporters of abortion, and what were the political consequences of their arguments?

In modern Germany, male sentiment against abortion coalesced as part of the general reaction to the upheaval of the French Revolution and the Napoleonic wars. Conservative thinkers traced this whole cataclysm back to the dissemination of liberal ideas in the Enlightenment, and since that upheaval had also seen women leaping aggressively onto the political stage, the question of women's rights was conveniently bundled by its opponents into the same package as the condemned revolution. The encyclopedia, *Meyers Konversations-Lexikon*, a useful bellwether of middle-class opinion, since it was regarded as a benchmark in tens of thousands of homes by both men and women, clearly locates in its 1894 edition the start of the women's movement in the French Revolution. For all his general sympathy, the author of the article on the "women's question" intoned with an almost perceptible shudder: "It wanted nothing less than the wholesale implementation of a complete equality of both sexes in public and private life." A revolution indeed! The article went on to link the resurgence of women's issues to the July Revolution in 1830 in France, and generally to French socialism.

Introduced first in 1851, legal prohibition of abortion was therefore part of the response to the "springtime of the peoples," 1848, when women quickly began demanding rights. When the Frankfurt Parliament fizzled out in 1849, and the Prussian government settled down to a period of conservative restoration, one of its early legislative acts was directed against the right of women to have an abortion. Such a personal decision must have seemed in the government's eyes to be one of the worst examples of unbridled individualism *à la Olympe de Gouges.* Allow women to act against the public good in that way, and more socialist and revolutionary ideas and action would follow. It comes as no surprise to learn that the lawmakers of the new German Empire twenty years later took over the Prussian ban on abortion (along with most sections of the Prussian criminal code), adopting it in the Imperial code as "Paragraph 218" (the term that has become a rallying cry to opponents ever since).

Even at the end of the century, most men viewed it as anathema that women should be accepted as full equals in the political realm. Indeed women's participation in various "good works" in Germany's moral purity movement in the 1880s had been encouraged as a means of diverting their mainstream political aspirations. It seemed quite sufficient to many men to move toward equality in civil law, regarding property matters etc., and to open up more employment opportunities in such areas as the postal and telegraph services – and with that women should be content! "The desire for political equality derives less from a practical need than from a theoretical perspective of dubious worth," noted *Meyers'* essayist. The very nature of women was different and left them "little suited for an active participation in public life." Men were really doing them a favor in protecting their maternal role. All this was summed up in the slogan: "To the man the state, to the woman the family!"[5]

In the second half of the nineteenth century, the denial of the right to choose an abortion was closely woven with a more general opposition, not just to women's rights, but to liberal, individualistic ideas as such. Abortion itself was not such a central question as it became after the First World War, nor had the debate over whether this was a public

5. Entry on "Frauenfrage" in *Meyers Konversations-Lexikon: Ein Nachschlagewerk des allgemeinen Wissens,* 5th ed., vol. 6 (Leipzig/Vienna, 1894), 818-823.

or private issue come to the foreground, but the strategies that continued to be employed under the Weimar Republic, stressing "family values," were grounded in these earlier arguments. If a mother was tied down to the home, raising children, she would not have time to meddle in politics. Therefore any action such as abortion which freed her from these domestic duties worked against the maintenance of the male monopoly on politics.

Another important dimension in attitudes toward abortion was the propaganda of the eugenics movement. Though in retrospect associated with the biopolitics of the Third Reich, this concern with declining population growth and increasing hereditary disease at the end of the demographic transition was shared also by progressive thinkers in all European countries and the United States. Under the influence of Malthus, Spencer, and Darwin, commentators became increasingly anxious about their own national population as it compared with that of others in terms of both numbers and quality. While the growing importance of eugenic thinking suggested the need for some quality control over reproduction, political concern over the falling birth-rate inspired a strong concern for keeping up raw numbers of the population above else. Such fears increased during the imperialist competition of the *fin-de-siecle* and predominated after the distastrous loss of life in both world wars. While eugenic arguments supported terminating what was considered to be diseased offspring, more generally they opposed abortion as such on seemingly medical grounds of the maintenance of a healthy polity.

In the wake of the societal upheavals following the First World War, which increased male insecurities, abortion became a burning national issue for the first time. Cornelie Usborne has identified around twenty motions and bills concerning abortion in the Reichstag between 1919 and 1932, though most of them were either rejected or not even debated in the first place.[6] It was almost entirely the Social Democrats and the Communists who can be thanked for bringing to the fore these issues, whose rejection by the other parties became more or less automatic as part of the whole slate of left-wing demands. Despite this, a compromise revision of German abortion law did occur in 1926, which succeeded in reducing the punishment for female offenders from penal servitude to straightforward imprisonment. While this extremely hard-won concession may seem a small gain, it in fact made Paragraph 218 the most lenient abortion law in Western Europe at the time, since all political parties except the communists accepted that abortion was in fact a

6. Cornelie Usborne, *The Politics of the Body in Weimar Germany: Women's Reproductive Rights and Duties* (Basingstoke, 1992), 217-219.

crime. Throughout the period, it must be remembered, the discussion of sexual matters remained embarrassing and distasteful in the extreme to many middle-class parliamentarians.

Weimar's new openness about sexuality was welcomed especially by working-class women, whose sex education from their mothers had been more confusing than helpful. The first step toward correcting the pain of ignorance was taken by Dr. Magnus Hirschfeld, who set up his Institute for Sexual Science in Berlin and held monthly meetings offering public answers and explanations in response to anonymous questions dropped in the institute's mailbox.[7] Much greater accessibility was offered by the Marriage and Sexual Advice Centers set up in cities all over Germany in the Weimar years. Associates of Hirschfeld, usually committed socialists like Dr. Max Hodann, were instrumental in supporting the foundation of the more liberal and open of these, while a more conservative school around Alfred Grotjahn and Max Hirsch sought to restrict advice on sexual matters to married couples.[8]

A born populist as a writer, Hodann published a number of innovative books on sex education, including a frank, sensible and unsensational one for young children, called *Is It Really the Stork who Brings Us?*, which was promptly banned.[9] In his books for young adults, he often framed his message as a homely chat between doctor and patient or advice-seeker. One such chapter dealt with the abortion question in this manner. After the doctor explained to a young man the difficult fight in the Reichstag for the abolition of Paragraph 218, the latter responded:

> Well, what you're telling me is really the sort of material with which you could not fail to win over for the Left the female section of the electorate, because after all it's their weal and woe that you're dealing with here.

To this argument the fictional doctor replied:

> Sure, but unfortunately the women are for the most part, a great deal more than men, under the thumb of superstition, be it of Protestant or Catholic complexion – and you know that the Lord God has always stood with the battalions of the ruling classes; in Germany he's either solidly German National or Catholic.

7. See for example the announcement with dates of meetings for 1928 inside the back cover of Magnus Hirschfeld and Richard Linsert, *Empfängnisverhütung. Mittel und Methoden* (Berlin, 1928).
8. Kristine von Soden, *Die Sexualberatungsstellen der Weimarer Republik 1919-1933* (Berlin, 1988), 58 and passim.
9. Max Hodann, *Bringt uns wirklich der Klapperstorch? Ein Lehrbuch für Kinder lesbar* (Rudolstadt, 1928).

Hodann was always transparently partisan, while at the same time dispensing easy-to-understand and invaluable advice on practical matters of sexuality, making him a hero especially in working-class circles.[10]

Perhaps surprisingly for such a radical, Hodann was nevertheless not prepared to ignore the law and perform "therapeutic" abortions on demand. And here he was at one with the majority of the German medical profession, as even women physicians who were fighting Paragraph 218 generally rejected abortion as an easy method of birth control. Hodann's strategy was to win supporters for the political fight to amend the law. In one "political morality tale", as Atina Grossmann aptly describes it, the young woman, to whom the doctor has just refused an abortion as medically unnecessary, goes away and commits suicide.[11] Naturally Hodann's books went straight onto the bonfire in 1933, their frankness and political lobbying epitomizing for the Nazis all that was wrong with Weimar. Yet his stories were not pure fiction: there were countless actual cases of women dying at the hands of quack abortionists after bona fide physicians had refused to carry out the operation.

Nonetheless, anti-abortion views persisted as well during the Weimar Republic. In 1926 another popular encyclopedia, *Brockhaus,* showed continued hostility to the political aims of the women's movement such as pacifism, and patriarchical conceptions of female work: "The highest goal of woman has been seen at all times to be in her vocation as mother."[12] The reaffirmation of Catholic religious opposition to the termination of pregnancies in response to the rising abortion numbers during the Great Depression served a similar purpose. The New Year's Eve encyclical of Pope Pius XII in 1930, *Casti Conubii,* condemned outright not only abortion, but also contraception and female emancipation, insisting on women's rightful, subordinate position within the family as their sacred duty.[13] This authoritative restatement of church doctrine reinforced the resistance of the large Catholic population of southern Germany to further reform and made it receptive to racist arguments, advanced by the NSDAP.

Yet the Papal prohibition had a galvanizing effect on the supporters of abortion, and the practice became more frequent than in previous years.

10. Max Hodann, *Geschlecht und Liebe in biologischer und gesellschaftlicher Beziehung* (Rudolstadt, 1927), 127-8.

11. Berlin women doctors seem to have been an exception in their call for abortion on social and eugenic, as well as medical grounds. Grossmann, *Reforming Sex,* 89-91, 96-7.

12. Entry on "Frauenfrage" in *Brockhaus Handbuch des Wissens,* 6th ed., vol. 2 (Leipzig, 1926), 109-113.

13. Atina Grossmann, "Abortion and Economic Crisis: The 1931 Campaign against Paragraph 218," in Renate Bridenthal, Atina Grossmann and Marion Kaplan, eds., *When Biology Became Destiny: Women in Weimar and Nazi Germany* (New York, 1984), 71.

In response 356 Berlin physicians called for the addition of a "social hardship" indicator to dispensations granted to save the life of the mother and to end pregnancies involving rape, incest, or fetal deformity. Two doctors, Else Kienle and Friedrich Wolf, were arrested for practicing "commercial abortion" in Stuttgart in February 1931, right after the appearance of the encyclical, and were convicted and imprisoned. Women were outraged, and the *Berliner Volkszeitung* received 45,000 letters condemning the law, and only 150 in support of it.[14] As the worldwide depression hit Germany, the demand for abortions surged parallel to the increase in severe economic distress. Although the latter was not viewed as a valid reason by opponents of abortion, over one million such operations were now being performed illegally every year.

After coming to power in 1933, Hitler had an opportunity to implement his anti-abortion policies, which were based on a curious mixture of eugenic and misogynous ideas. Nazi ideology was intensely concerned with the declining size and mixed racial composition of the German population; at the same time National Socialist conceptions of female roles were unabashedly reactionary. In a telling essay on "Woman and Public Health," Arthur Gütt, architect of the Nazi sterilization laws, railed against the Weimar "age of individualism," the old bugbear that had already been used to criticize the women's movement decades earlier:

> Everything was subordinated under the goal of benefiting the individual … things went so far that every woman was pitied who was condemned to give life to a child. People extolled life as an individual, they encouraged and favored unmarried life, they preached cohabitation and the right of a woman over her own body. People deferred to the desire of men to follow an unrestricted, free lifestyle, and ignore the consequences of their relationships with women. They left it up to each woman to undertake the murder of her own child in her womb. They wrecked the health of German women with drugs, alcohol, nicotine, excessive sport, overexertion at work etc. All this happened under Jewish leadership, covered with the mantle of Christian love of one's neighbor, and with the connivance of Christian parties. Yet people talked and talked of public health, of the rights of women, of the emancipation of women. In reality they made the German woman a slave of her job, they took advantage of her dilemma, they drove her onto the streets, made her a "lady-friend," destroyed the German family and the sense of family.[15]

Except for the blatant anti-Semitism, echoes of this diatribe continue to reververate in current debates: the irresponsibility of the individual, the

14. James Woycke, *Birth Control in Germany, 1871-1933* (New York, 1988), 148. See also Grossmann, *Reforming Sex*, 83-87.

15. Arthur Gütt, "Frau und Volksgesundheit," in Ellen Semmelroth and Renate von Stieda, eds., *N.S. Frauenbuch* (München, 1934), 129-30.

destruction of the family, the necessity of intervention by the benevolent state, the obligation of the woman toward the state to maintain her health for child-bearing duties, and so on.

The Nazis not only reintroduced harsher penalties for abortion, but lost no opportunity to turn their prejudices into government action. Nazi policy was simple and straightforward, and it moved ever further forward to translate this into fact: on the one hand as many babies as possible from healthy Aryans, and on the other hand sterilization for the physically and especially racially unfit. One contemporary health manual went so far as to assert that childbearing was positively beneficial: "Motherhood is the surest protection against numerous physical disorders." Reciting a common view of "natural" roles, it continued by claiming that whereas the man's role in marriage, "from the purely biological standpoint of nature," was fulfilled simply by the sex act, the woman was not really a whole woman unless she became a mother.[16]

After 1945 only some elements of the Nazi legacy were repudiated while others persisted into the Federal Republic. In her nuanced analysis of some of the points of continuity that span the first half of this century, Atina Grossmann stresses that in sex reform and social hygiene, there was "a profound and irrevocable break in 1933 that could not and would not be reversed after 1945." In terms of the personalities involved, "the left-wing, mostly Jewish, reformers who advocated abortion reform and birth control and sex counseling" were simply no longer around. Those who had survived the Third Reich in exile usually chose not to return.[17] After the defeat of the Nazi regime in 1945, the Allies themselves saw no reason to throw out Paragraph 218 of the Imperial Code, though its enforcement was relaxed in light of the countless thousands of rapes in the early days of victory, especially by soldiers of the Red Army.[18]

After the tremendous loss of life in the Second World War, many countries pursued a pro-natalist policy in order to generate the manpower for going on and rebuilding. In spite of competing ideologies, this was also the case in both Germanys during the 1950s. In the West, campaigns in 1946 and 1948 to ease the rules had little success, although the penalties of hard labor and death were formally stricken from sentencing rules in 1953. More typical of the prevailing spirit, the Federal Republic's first Family Minister, Franz-Josef Wuermeling, declared it a duty of "every at all fertile marriage" to produce three children merely in order

16. Section on "Hygiene der Ehe und Schwangerschaft" in Hermann Brechmann, ed., *Neuer Hausschatz der Heilkunde* (Leipzig, n.d.), 819.

17. Grossman, *Reforming Sex*, 212.

18. Lisa Heineman, "The Hour of the Woman: Memories of Germany's 'Crisis Years' and West German National Identity," *American Historical Review*, 101 (1996): 354-395.

to reach the population levels of the parents' generation. Reinvoking older arguments the Federal Family Minister solemnly intoned that "millions of inwardly healthy families with decently brought-up children are at least as important *as all the measures of military security* as a bulwark against the populous peoples of the East" [emphasis added].[19]

Abortion was also outlawed in the German Democratic Republic, although it had been permitted in some states in the immediate postwar years even on grounds of social distress, in addition to medical expediency. As the standard East German women's encyclopedia explained rather fantastically as early as 1960: "The so-called social grounds for the termination of pregnancy are no longer valid; for society in the workers' and peasants' state enjoys a sufficient number of social facilities and a sufficiently high general standard of living that 'social distress' no longer exists."[20] For the moment East German pro-natalists restored the ban on abortion (Paragraph 11 of the Law for the Protection of Mothers and Children of 1954). The only exceptions were when the life or health of the expectant mother would be seriously endangered by carrying the pregnancy to its full term; or secondly when one of the parents suffered from a serious hereditary illness.

A recent study of East German women in the 1950s concluded that "the real content (of women's policies) was the instrumentalization of women for economic and reproductive purposes …. The declining willingness of women for reproduction was a warning signal to which [the government] reacted with material incentives to stimulate births (birth subsidies, children's allowances, later interest-free marriage loans that could be paid off with children [*abgekindert*])."[21] After the construction of the wall had stopped the constant manpower drain, in 1972 the SED leadership, in a display of apparent support for women's rights, permitted a new law legalizing abortion in the GDR during the first twelve weeks after conception *(Fristenlösung)*. Actually this measure had as much to do with maximizing the availability of young women for the labor force and it was accompanied by a wide array of pro-natalist provisions to encourage childbearing so as to minimize its demographic effects.

Only during the cultural revolution of the 1960s did West German sexual practices liberalize and a renewed debate set in about changing legal norms as well. "Sexual intercourse began/In nineteen sixty-three …

19. Hans-Georg Stümke, *Homosexuelle in Deutschland: Eine politische Geschichte* (Munich, 1989), 140.

20. Irene Uhlmann, ed., *Kleine Enzyklopädie: Die Frau* (Leipzig, 1960), 122.

21. Ina Merkel, … *und Du, Frau an der Werkbank: die DDR in den 50er Jahren* (Berlin, 1990), 174.

/Between the end of the Chatterley ban/And the Beatles' first LP," wrote Philip Larkin in his marvelous poem, "Annus Mirabilis."[22] As a result of the new sexual freedom, challenges multiplied to the restrictions concerning gender relations and women's role in the family and society. In West Germany *de jure* penal sentences had been reduced or suspended for abortions performed on the basis of the specified "indicators" by 1969. But even within this reform climate, it was difficult to change abortion law, since this could be described as a taboo within a taboo.

A country-wide program for sex education and family planning under SPD-Minister Käte Strobel re-opened the door for legalization in the FRG after 1970. The Bundestag's social-liberal majority adopted trimester legislation in April 1974, which the conservative Bundesrat majority immediately sought to block. Bolstered by strong Church opposition to reform, five CDU/CSU state governments joined 193 conservatives (only 10 of whom were women) in taking the case to the *Bundesverfassungsgericht* (also BVerfG). In its 5-to-2 decision (with one abstention) of February 25, 1975, the Constitutional Court's first chamber upheld the state's obligation to see pregnancy carried to full term. It compelled the Bundestag to promulgate a new law in May 1975, exempting women from criminal prosecution only when the need for abortions, requiring doctor certification, fell under one of four indicators based on medical, eugenic, criminal, and "social hardship" factors *(Indikationslösung)*. The law applied to resident foreigners as well as to citizens who might seek abortions outside FRG borders.

The Wall's collapse triggered new public discussions of abortion, centering on the principle of women's rights to self-determination. Conditioned by the constraints and opportunities afforded by two ideologically opposed systems after 1945, the personal *qua* social identities of eastern and western women had diverged considerably by 1989. The roles and rights of GDR women were framed by their *simultaneous* functions as mothers and wage-earners. West German women fell into three distinctive categories: those who defined their primary roles in terms of children and household; those who pursued the two roles sequentially; and those who identified themselves as career women (as evidenced by negative population growth). The political challenge was, therefore, to reconcile the different legal traditions as well as living experiences of eastern and western women.

During the collapse of the GDR the number of abortions in the East rose dramatically in response to the insecurity of women's futures. As moribund state industries shed female workers in order to survive capi-

22. Philip Larkin, *Collected Poems* (London, 1988), 167.

talist competition and the bankruptcy of the SED social system threatened to reduce the safety net, women increasingly terminated unwanted pregnancies. Doctors estimated that as many as 250,000 abortions were performed in 1990. Yet the courts exercised restraint about such emotionally charged cases: there were precisely seven convictions for illegal abortion in 1990 among an overall total of 700,000 criminal convictions.[23] To left wingers that was a sign that there was now little point in having this law on the books, yet most CDU/CSU supporters still felt that the amended law was too liberal.

Since irreconcilable differences on abortion might slam the fleeting window of opportunity for unification shut, the government deliberately shelved the issue until after the passage of the Unification Treaty in the fall of 1990. Because the problem was so prominent, complete silence was not an option, so that paragraph 31 (4) of the treaty, as a pragmatic interim solution, upheld the status quo in both parts of the country, while promising a standardization of abortion law by the end of 1992. For the moment, then, eastern German women could continue to have legal abortions, while western Germans could only do so with constraints, unless they traveled to the East. As a result of this *Tatortprinzip*, the place where the abortion was performed would decide its legality during the interim period. In the event, many Westerners snubbed their noses at eastern clinics (where they could have received a legal abortion only by agreeing to a hospital stay) and continued to travel over the Dutch border for fast (but expensive, and under German law, illegal) outpatient surgery there.

In many ways, this provision of the Unity Treaty itself planted the seeds of the ensuing controversy. Positing a semi-modern construct of female identity, it obliged legislators to recognize "the different legal and institutional starting conditions in the employment of mothers and fathers … to be shaped from the point of view of *the ability to combine career and family*" [emphasis added]. On the one hand, the new law was to guarantee "the protection of pre-born life"; on the other hand, it insisted on a reform guaranteeing, "in conformity with the constitution, the mastery of conflict situations arising from the legally secured claims of women, especially in relation to counseling and social assistance." Both goals were to be met "in a way that is better than [had been] the case in both parts of Germany." [Art. 31/4 UT]

On June 25, 1992, the Bundestag debated the problem of how to reconcile the different East and West German ideas as well as practices of abortion. This discussion took place in a parliament that was dominated

23. *Plenarprotokoll*, 8260.

by Chancellor Helmut Kohl's center-right majority, composed of his own moderate CDU, its more conservative Bavarian ally CSU, and the neo-liberal partner FDP. The opposition contained the large left-of-center SPD as well as the smaller and more radical Greens and the East German regional party PDS. Appealing to widely differing sectional, class, and religious constituencies, these parties invoked the pro-choice and pro-life viewpoints on the abortion questions that had been elaborated during the past century in a setting that was complicated by the traumatic disregard for life, experienced in the Third Reich.

2. Reading the Post-Unity Abortion Debate

This analysis of the 1992 Bundestag debate on abortion draws upon the framework developed in Mary Poovey's book, *Uneven Developments: The Ideological Work of Gender in Mid-Victorian England.*[24] Poovey's conceptualization of *ideology* stems from Althusser, who defined it as the "imaginary relationship of individuals to their real conditions of existence." Though ideology is construed as coherent, authentic, and complete, it is actually artificial, internally unstable, and "fissured by competing emphases and interests." Poovey examines several different ideological debates in which the artificiality of Victorian notions of gender becomes particularly clear: concerning the use of anesthesia in childbirth, divorce and married women's property rights, the social status of the "man of letters," the governess, and the modern nurse.

Two types of *ideological work* take place in most debates. First one must consider *the work of ideology*, meaning that representations of gender at mid-century were part of a system of interdependent images in which various ideologies became accessible to individual men and women. In another sense, however, there is *the work of making ideology*: representations of gender constitute one of the sites on which ideological systems have been simultaneously constructed and contested. As such, the German representations of gender debated in 1992 were themselves contested images, the sites at which struggles for authority occurred, as well as the locus of assumptions used to underwrite the very authority that legitimized those struggles.

The language of the 1990 Unity Treaty bore the discursive imprint of the 1975 Constitutional Court ruling, which had declared the fetus a human life worthy of state protection against all who might threaten it,

---

24. Mary Poovey, *Uneven Developments: The Ideological Work of Gender in Mid-Victorian England* (Chicago, 1988).

including its mother.[25] The Basic Law of 1949 which now serves as the all-German constitution defines the legal status of its citizens in Articles 2 and 3, emphasizing the "free development of the personality," "the right to life," and the "inviolability of person."[26] The desire to portray their own positions as reconcilable with the *Grundgesetz* influenced the formulations of Bundestag Members (MdBs) across the political spectrum, all of whom declared their commitment to the defense of life before laying out their own views. The Treaty's charge that the Bundestag protect "life" thus defined profoundly limited the parameters of their legislative effort.[27] Established fifteen years prior to unification, the postulate that the "free development" and "inviolability" of the woman may be directly challenged and overridden by "life in the process of becoming" augured badly for the preservation of rights women had achieved in the GDR.

Even the titles of the seven legislative proposals submitted for deliberation suggested a fundamental neglect of women's interests during the initial phase of policy-formulation. Only the names of draft-laws submitted by Bündnis '90/Die Grünen *(Entwurf eines Gesetzes zur Sicherung der Entscheidungsfreiheit von Frauen beim Umgang mit ungewollten Schwangerschaften)* and the PDS/Linke Liste *(Entwurf eines Gesetzes zur Legalisierung des Schwangerschaftsabbruchs und zur Sicherung von Mindeststandards für Frauen zum Schwangerschaftsabbruch)* contained an explicit reference to women. The FDP and SPD undermined the precept of women's self-determination through an emphasis on *Familien- und Schwangerenhilfe*; the majority and minority CDU drafts stressed the "protection of unborn life" and even that of "unborn children." The ungainly title of the tri-partisan compromise "Group Resolution" that stood the best chance of being adopted by the Bundestag promised to protect prenatal life, promote a child-friendly society, provide assistance

25. Douglas G. Morris, "Abortion and Liberalism: A Comparison Between the Abortion Decisions of the Supreme Court of the United States and the Constitutional Court of West Germany," *Hastings International and Comparative Law Review* 11 (1988): 164-65.

26. On the transformation of the fetus into "life" see Celeste Michelle Condit, *Decoding Abortion Rhetoric: Communicating Social Change* (Urbana, 1990); Barbara Duden, *Disembodying Women: Perspectives on Pregnancy and the Unborn*, trans. Lee Hoinacki (Cambridge, 1993); Sarah Franklin, "Fetal Fascinations: New Dimensions to the Medical Scientific Construction of Fetal Personhood," in Sarah Franklin, Celia Lury, and Jackie Stacey, eds., *Off-Centre: Feminism and Cultural Studies* (London, 1991), 190-205; Rosalind Pollack Petchesky, *Abortion and Woman's Choice: The State, Sexuality, and Reproductive Freedom*, rev. ed. (Boston, 1990); and Rickie Solinger, "'A Complete Disaster': Abortion and the Politics of Hospital Abortion Committees, 1950-1970," *Feminist Studies* 19 (1993): 241-268.

27. Monika Frommel, "Zur aktuellen Diskussion des Paragraph 218," *Unter anderen Umständen: Zur Geschichte der Abtreibung* (Berlin, 1993), 118.

in conflicts about pregnancy, and regulate the termination of pregnancy, but made no reference to "women" at all. As Angelika Merkel, East German turned CDU/CSU Minister for Women and Youth, observed in the course of the debates: "There were stretches in the argumentation where the woman didn't appear at all anymore." (8244)

Though the legislative drafts spanned the full range of positions on abortion, the debate itself was waged on more restricted ground. Both proponents and opponents of decriminalization couched their arguments in similar assumptions about womanhood. Having already yielded for legal reasons some of the ground on which they needed to situate their counter-arguments, the defenders of women's rights deprived themselves of the ammunition necessary to mount an ideological counter-offensive. The initial proposals of the PDS/Linke Liste and Bündnis '90/Die Grünen had offered language defending women's unrestricted right to abortion, with the PDS also proposing a constitutional amendment to protect abortion rights. Yet neither party mounted a particularly vigorous defense of its positions during the fourteen-hour exchange ending on June 26, 1992. Instead, the entire legislative debate was framed by a *maternalist discourse* that conceives the essence of womanhood (or women's defining characteristic) to lie in women's reproductive capacities.[28]

At the most obvious level, the 1992 debate constituted an ideological struggle pitting women's right to self-determination against the state's right to regulate and control reproduction. As Marlies Deneke, Coordinating Council member of the PDS's Women's Task Force, put it:

> The confrontation over the new regulation of Paragraph 218 as mandated by the Unity Treaty is therefore more than just a fight over a single law. The struggle for the elimination without substitution of this seemingly medieval paragraph of shame is for me a crystallization point in the struggle for rights to self-determination for the women of East and West.[29]

The fetus figures in the German debate not merely as a person, as American right-to-lifers argue, but is elided with life *tout court,* against whose claims any woman's desire for autonomy stands little chance. At best, a

28. Poovey argues that the controversy over the right to abortion is even more fundamentally a debate about the meaning of masculinity and femininity: "If the normative woman is a mother, then the mother-nature of woman is one of the linchpins of sexed identity and therefore, by the oppositional logic of gender, one ground of the intelligible masculinity of men." Mary Poovey, "The Abortion Question and the Death of Man" in Judith Butler and Joan W. Scott, eds., *Feminists Theorize the Political* (New York, 1992), 243.

29. Marlies Deneke, "Das Selbstbestimmungsrecht ist unteilbar: Der Standpunkt der PDS zum Paragraph 218," 152.

woman is viewed as a guardian or custodian of "life"; as expressly decreed by the High Court, her needs are secondary to those of the "life" she bears for the duration of the pregnancy. At worst, women are represented as potentially hostile not just to their own fetuses but to all other forms of life. Ultra-conservative delegates could thus paint women not merely as too weak and defenseless to be allowed to decide on abortion by themselves, but also (and paradoxically) as too powerful and dangerous: women's freedom to choose pitted menacing murderesses against "life."

In the first speech of the debate, Irmgard Karwatzki declared for the CDU/CSU:

> It is only when we succeed in showing pregnant women what chances they have for making their lives with children easier, ways in which they will be able to nurture and educate them according to their own preconceptualizations, in which they will be able to reconcile family and career and receive support, counseling, and help in view of their life circumstances, only then will there be any prospect that many women who are not pregnant by choice will comprehend life with a child as a worth-while and positive opportunity, and say yes to life. [8226-27]

Inge Wettig-Danielmeier, the first SPD speaker and one of the architects of the Group Resolution, made virtually the same point in more liberal diction: "Only when a woman is finally equal, has equal rights and privileges, [and] can trust the fact that her life will not be solely at the disposition of her partner and children every day, will she be able to decide to have children with a real sense of joy and complete inner acceptance." [8228] "For you know," Wettig-Danielmeier added delicately, "that women usually do not want to do the things that they see themselves forced to do by circumstances." [8229]

Among the dissenters to the maternalist discourse, the Eastern women were the most vocal. Petra Bläss (PDS/Linke Liste) staunchly defended women's right to decide against motherhood, posing the key question: "Will a woman finally be able to determine for herself what she does with her body and her life, or will she continue to be criminalized and have conditions imposed upon her?" [8238] To support this minority position, she presented the Bundestag with the signatures of 33,000 East Germans opposed to Paragraph 218.

The opposite pole of this debate was occupied by Herbert Werner, author of the minority CDU/CSU draft, who wished to eliminate entirely women's right to regulate their reproduction. In a typical rhetorical outburst, he demanded "finally to say good-bye to the ideology of having children 'only if one wants them'." [8256] Advocates of women's choice had little room to maneuver in a body where one delegate from the FDP (the party that claimed to uphold the liberal ideal of "individual freedom") decried them as the "the blinded proponents of the so-called 'my-belly-belongs-to-me' movement," [8285] and another from the SPD (the party Brandt had urged to "dare more democracy") declared, "We cannot promulgate any regulation, by means of which we promote the conviction that 'I can do whatever I want with my body.'" [8332]

The draft-bill submitted by Bündnis '90/Die Grünen and authored by Christina Schenk, member of the East German Independent Women's Union, made short shrift of the fiction that the fetus is an independent person. Yet during the debate itself Schenk proposed only in the most cautious of terms that *some* women might find an unexpected pregnancy an unwanted nuisance:

> The spectrum of possible definitions regarding her own situation is a very broad one for the pregnant woman. I state that here with all due clarity. The embryo may be construed by her as a child, as a human being from the very beginning, loved from the first moment onwards, because she wanted and longingly waited for it. It can also be for her – I know what I am saying – a parasitic pile of cells, (interruption by the CDU/CSU: Shameful!) which has the potential of destroying her life-long plans, and which therefore has to be removed as quickly as possible. [8300]

Another Eastern feminist, PDS delegate Barbara Höll, swiftly disassociated herself from that position: "A woman ... does not make a decision over a little bit of cell-tissue, but rather over her own flesh and blood and over the picture of the cute little baby that she could perhaps acquire." [8318] When even supporters of the unconditional right to abortion pay homage to such maternalist assumptions about women's nature, and embellish their remarks with elaborate maternalist flourishes, they erode the rhetorical ground from which a counter-argument could be launched supporting women's right to decide *not* to be mothers.

But the maternalist discourse was also riven and fissured by contradictions that emerged over the course of the debate. Abortion itself is an obvious problem to adherents of maternalism: if maternity is every woman's natural calling, why do countless women nonetheless decide to terminate their pregnancies? Parliamentarians insisting that women are incapable of (or should be prevented from) making this particular decision also confront an ideological double-bind: to embrace their *calling* as mothers, women must freely decide to carry their pregnancies to term and care for their children after birth, voluntarily choosing to subordinate their individual needs to those of their families. Conservative legislators walk an ideological tightrope between their declaration that women cannot or will not decide responsibly when abortion is at issue, and their insistence that women are responsible decision-making agents when they choose to mother. Therefore Edith Niehuis (SPD) asked indignantly:

> How can one explain the fact that the same people who want to impose on women the responsibility [of caring] day and night for a child – as helpless as it may be – no longer trust women with the responsibility of making a decision regarding the termination of a pregnancy? That is a contradiction which can only make women suffer. [8270]

Efforts to make the physician bear the ultimate responsibility for a decision to terminate a pregnancy, as mandated in hard-line conservative resolutions, reflect a belief that women lack the capacity for moral judgment by virtue of their sex alone. That reasoning did not keep a few of them from considering themselves moral enough, as CDU/CSU parliamentarians, to impose their ethical standards on others. At the same time women are expected to resume their "natural" roles, one of which has always been to assume primary responsibility for the moral education of their children. How can mothers be expected to transfer moral capabilities and national virtues they do not possess? Is it conceivable that whatever lessons women impart at home will be internalized by their sons but not their daughters?

In order to retain a notion of women as moral agents who *in most cases* willingly and responsibly assume their maternal duties, the language of the Group Resolution presumed abortions to take place only in "exceptional situations." It is "a necessary evil born out of desperate circumstances," as Rosalind Pollack Petchesky put it in a formulation that marks a concession to anti-abortion and anti-feminist rhetoric.[30] Her comment mirrors the logic of the Constitutional Court which held in 1975 that the decision to interrupt pregnancy was made in "a conflictual setting which generally does not permit a clear moral judgment and in which the decision to abort a pregnancy can acquire the status of a commendable decision based on personal conscience."[31]

The deep spiritual crisis into which women are purportedly thrust can be adduced as proof that women who abort are virtuous and moral even if they are not mothers. During the Bundestag debate many delegates elaborated upon the features of that crisis. Irmgard Karwatzki, the CDU/CSU's first speaker, proclaimed abortion to be "ethically defensible … only in cases entailing very grave need or conflict." [8227] Sigrid Semper (FDP) insisted: "I don't know one single affected woman, who has or would make a frivolous, irresponsible or some such decision with regard to a conflict situation involving pregnancy." [8325]

30. Petchesky, *Abortion*, 390.
31. Günther Pursch, ed., *Paragraph 218: Die Entscheidung* (Frankfurt, 1992), 425.

The overwhelmingly maternalist tenor of the debate forced proponents of a woman's right not to choose motherhood onto the defensive, often leading them to frame their own arguments in the terms it offered. Barbara Höll defended her party against Karwatzki's claim that the PDS's proposal was premised upon the "the woman's right of self-determination," insisting that it also acknowledged women's "ethical conflict-situation." [8318] From within the confines of the maternalist discourse, the failure of GDR legislation to recognize the decision to abort as fraught with conflict was interpolated as proof of its inadequacy, an affront to women's moral sensibilities that the new legislation would need to redress. The Bündnis '90/Grünen proposal underlined the admission that abortion had also carried a certain stigma in the GDR, despite its ease of access:

> The overall atmosphere and the framework conditions under which pregnancy terminations were carried out in the former GDR were nonetheless grounds for dissatisfaction. The topic of abortion remained taboo for the public, which gave rise to the impression that abortion was something that was indeed permitted but at the same time also something that was morally tainted.[32]

The claim that ethical conflict always accompanies a decision to terminate pregnancy allowed proponents of stricter regulation to portray women as potentially so incapacitated by their spiritual crisis that they needed help from others such as the community and the state. Legislators favoring decriminalization joined opponents of choice in basing their arguments on the premise of "help instead of punishment." Women under duress could thus be represented as weak and helpless creatures incapable of standing on their own, needful of the assistance that proper legislation would assure them. Defending the majority CDU/CSU proposal, Hannelore Rönsch, CDU/CSU Minister for Family and the Elderly, presented women's vulnerability as the rationale for requiring mandatory abortion counseling, which would relieve distraught pregnant women of the burden of deciding for themselves: "A pregnant woman [can] be so pressured and trapped by her situation of need that she feels overpowered or overtaxed by the necessity of making such an irrevocable existential decision all by herself."[33] This argument was likewise incorporated into the more "liberal" Group Resolution, in hopes of wooing CDU politicians: "Counseling should contribute to the mastering of existing need and conflict situations, which coincide with the

---

32. Pursch, *Entscheidung*, 395.
33. Hannelore Rönsch, "Der bessere Schutz ungeborener Kinder im vereinten Deutschland – Chance und Verantwortung der CDU," 123.

pregnancy. It should place the pregnant woman in a position enabling her to reach her own consciously responsible decision." [8276]

Supporters of self-determination decried this erosion of women's autonomy, arguing that "forced counseling" denies women's capacity for responsible action. [8334] Freedom of choice advocates declared themselves "humiliated and deprived of worth" by the impuation that women must be instilled with a sense of responsibility they do not presently possess. They pointedly contrasted the conception of womanhood on which the compromise bill was premised with the treatment that real women had received in the GDR. It was Easterner Angelika Barbe who countered much later in the debate that pro-natalist policies had actually protected "life" in the GDR despite free access to abortion: "Because at the time there was a major social benefits package attached to it. We in the East are the ones who had a birth surplus – not you in the West" [8316]. The insight that mandatory counseling *might prevent* women from making the wrong decision, while an array of social welfare measures *would encourage* them to make the right one, impelled all parties to call for generous social benefits in order to provide "the framework conditions for a decision to have a child" [8322].

Like anti-abortionists internationally, German *Lebensschützer* (prolifers) argued that abortion was a "slippery slope" which, once entered upon, might ultimately legitimate other forms of "murder." Bavarian Minister Mathilde Berghofer-Weichner predicted that legalized abortion would constitute "the start of a disastrous development in the wrong direction, which would perhaps end several years later with the grandmother in need of special care" [8268]. Such cynical comparisons, Waltraud Schoppe, Minister from Niedersachsen, charged, allowed German anti-abortion forces to portray "aborting women" as "the real danger that a system so devoid of respect for human life would return." The present debate, she continued, deployed a "myth of the aborting woman" represented as "the real threat to the survival of the human species .... Exercising control over intentions to terminate a pregnancy is thus considered as exorcizing the danger of a recurrence of human extermination." [8266]

The most extreme argument in this exchange was an attempt to equate abortion with the genocidal practices of the Nazis. This exaggerated and misapplied analogy threatened to relativize Hitler's crimes in a manner reminiscent of the 1986-87 *Historikerstreit*.[34] Claus Jäger (CDU/CSU) characterized "the 1.2 to 1.5 million" abortions performed

---

34. Charles S. Maier, *The Unmasterable Past: History, Holocaust, and German National Identity* (Cambridge, 1988).

since unification as "holocaust numbers which in view of German history, will lie as heavily as lead on the consciences of politicians if we do not stop this avalanche of death." [8283] His insistence that the Catholic Church had fought against Nazi euthanasia in the 1930s (and his implication that abortion reform in the 1990s would lead to the murder of the elderly) ignored the fact that the Vatican's accords with German and Italian fascists cut off resistance to those regimes, subjecting millions of non-Aryan women to "scientific experiments" and death. [8283]

Waltraud Schoppe was the only Westerner to challenge the 1975 Constitutional Court decision itself by presenting the 1974 legislation as a justified attempt to "work through" the abuses of fascism with regard to sterilization and abortion. Women were neither the perpetrators of that regime, intent on exterminating whole peoples, nor would their individual decisions to terminate a pregnancy augur a return to totalitarianism. Though only a small minority of legislators resorted to such extremist assaults on women, their formulations forced defenders of choice into the maternalist trap of reaffirming women's connectedness to life. Hence a delegate from the PDS/Linke Liste could aver, to the applause of his own party and that of Bündnis '90/Die Grünen, the SPD, and delegates from the FDP: "I am deeply convinced that women are the genuine protectors of life ...." [8251]

Members of the Bundestag acknowledged that there was no "absolute protection for life in the process of becoming," [8273] that no society had ever been able to prevent all women from terminating their pregnancies. As one supporter of the Group Resolution put it, "In all of the conversations I have had with women, I have learned one thing: that an effective protection of life can not be realized against [the wishes] of the woman but only in conjunction with her." [8271] For many legislators, the way out of this contradiction lay in the assertion that unfavorable social conditions were the main cause of the situations of conflict in which women decide on abortion: women *wished* to be mothers, but, to borrow a phrase from Brecht's *Threepenny Opera*, "The conditions, they just aren't so." An adequate range of pro-natalist incentives could resolve this dilemma, making it possible for women to say *Ja zum Kind.*

Given these currents, abortion debate participants did indeed engage in *ideological work* in Poovey's sense: the Bundestag became a site of struggle as legislators constructed a definition of woman's place in the New Germany. One can read the parliamentary exchanges as an ideological effort to bring all parts of the reconstituted nation into line with West German notions of "protecting motherhood," to borrow from

Robert Moeller's study of post-1945 gender relations in the FRG.[35] The discursive parameters of the debate forced lawmakers favoring an alternative, self-determined image of women onto the defensive; they resorted to arguing on ideological terrain already occupied by conservatives, with the result that they could not effectively contest the *a priori* argument that all women should be(come) mothers and that such women need the protection of men, the community, and the state – despite evidence to the contrary drawn from the lives of real existing German women. The Group Resolution compromise should not be seen merely as a legal/administrative attempt to discover a "third way," that is, one seeking to preserve the best features of FRG and GDR abortion policy prior to unity; it must also be understood as an ideological effort to roll back GDR notions of gender equality while retaining its pro-natalist emphases.

3. The Constitutional Court Verdict and the Legislative Response

The FRG's elevation of *unborn life* to a constitutionally protected category fifteen years prior to unification preordained that the struggle for "the free development" of women's personalities in the New Germany would be difficult. The legislative underrepresentation of women further complicated the task of parliamentary consideration of choice. In the crucial debate of 1992 all Bundestag parties sought to intrumentalize "their" female members; the first six speakers, all women, covered the partisan spectrum. Among the first thirty to address the issue, 18 were women and 12 were men, including one male and five female ministers; 23 speakers hailed from the West, seven from the East. Only two eastern delegates dared to address the parliamentary gender imbalance, recommending that women alone be allowed to vote on the draft laws.

The 1992 compromise bill was the product of a multi-party Select Committee on the "Protection of Unborn Life," constituted after it became clear that none of the six legislative proposals before the Bundestag could muster the requisite votes for passage. Though this proposal offered "a broad [albeit underfunded] pallet" of pro-natalist social assistance measures, intended to compensate for the loss of multiple "socialist achievements" which had underwritten motherhood, its provisions represented an essential, even existential defeat for East German women.

35. Robert Moeller, *Protecting Motherhood: Women and the Family in the Politics of Postwar West Germany* (Berkeley, 1993).

On June 25, the Bundestag nonetheless approved the tri-partisan Group Resolution, combining the "trimester solution" with mandatory counseling, by a vote of 357 to 283 (527 men and 135 women voted in 1992, compared to 468 men and 28 women in 1974). Of the 32 renegade votes cast by conservatives, 19 hailed from the East. Surveys taken at the time found that 76 percent of the public supported the new law.[36]

The euphoria following the vote quickly faded into a veritable repeat of 1974: at once 248 conservative deputies (215 of whom were male) appealed to Karlsruhe to block implementation of the new statute. The second chamber of the Constitutional Court imposed a temporary injunction on August 4, 1992, prohibiting full-scale implementation; provisions involving mandatory counseling and a three-day waiting period nonetheless became operative immediately.

Announcement of the verdict was postponed through December, owing to mounting tensions among the judicial ranks. Of the eight justices in the second senate, four of the men were practicing Catholics: one had served as an active member of the Lawyers' Association for the Right to Life until 1990; another had helped to file the conservative case against the 1974 reform. The two "expert opinions" commissioned by the Court were penned by known anti-abortion activists.[37] Twice postponed, the verdict was finally announced during a live press conference on May 28, 1993. The verdict was six to two against the reform bill; the majority consisted of one woman and five men.

Declaring abortion "illegal but free from punishment," the Court insisted that the nation's lawmakers had no power under the existing constitution to render abortion a general "right" of women; in short, women's constitutional rights are secondary to those of the *nasciturus* as of conception, especially in relation to Article 4/1 (freedom of belief, conscience, and religion). It nonetheless conceded that the "carrot" of obligatory counseling could replace the "stick" of criminal punishment during the first twelve weeks of pregnancy, provided such counseling took place at a "recognized" center, both organizationally and financially separate from medical personnel performing the abortions, at least three days prior to a termination; its specific purpose was to "encourage" all women to continue their pregnancies. Each counselor is henceforth required to provide the doctor with a detailed, written protocol of the discussion, though actual certification is to remain anonymous, if expressly desired.

36. "Die Konterkapitäne von Karlsruhe," *Der Spiegel,* 50, (December 7, 1992): 80-85.
37. The Catholics were Böckenförde, Kirchhof, Kruis and Winter. The assignment of particular cases to each senate has become more or less arbitrary, and it seems likely that the first chamber would have decided 7 to 1 in favor of the 1992 law. Hanno Kühnert, "Wenig Hoffnung auf Karlsruhe," *Die Zeit,* December 11, 1992.

The "illegal" standing of abortion, the Court continued, means that costs incurred outside the medical, criminal, and embryopathic indications need not be borne by health insurance *(Krankenkasse)*. Women themselves are to pay the full price of their decisions to end a pregnancy (ranging from DM 300 to 1400); in cases of extraordinary financial need, costs may be covered by social assistance payments (which requires sacrificing anonymity).[38] Buried deep within the long list of pre-/proscriptions was nonetheless a recognition of the "trimester" principle as well as an acceptance of the woman's ultimate right to choose.

The SPD-dominated Bundesrat rejected a revised law pushed through by the CDU-FDP majority in July 1994, leading to a third legislative round in the spring of 1995. On June 29, 1995, the Bundestag once again approved amendments to Paragraphs 218, 219, 240, and 170 of the State Criminal Code by way of a *Schwangeren- und Familienhilfeänderungsgesetz* tailored to the Constitutional Court verdict of 1993. Also known as the "Pregnancy Conflict Law," the new regulations took effect throughout Germany on October 1, 1995. Only two indicators – medical and criminal – have been preserved out of the old Paragraph 218, meaning that the new law differentiates between *legally exempt* terminations and *illegal but unpunishable* ones in terms of payment requirements, a distinction characterized by one observer as a form of "morality with a financial framework."[39] Lawmakers eliminated the embryopathological indicator in the hopes of preventing future discrimination against persons with disabilities (prior to 1994, 98 percent of all pregnancies involving Downs-Syndrome diagnoses were terminated). It is assumed that the medical indicator will cover whatever mental or physical health problems might ensue for the woman with fetal complications (the 22-week deadline has been dropped); the general 12-week deadline is to be enforced in cases of rape and incest. Section 5 of the new law grants women a right to sex education and counseling with regard to family planning. Abortions performed on the basis of medical and criminal indicators will be covered by public insurance, despite reservations expressed in the 1993 High Court ruling.

Specifics concerning payment in other cases are outlined in the "Law on Assistance for Women seeking Abortions in Special Cases," which took effect on January 1, 1996. Although "universally" applicable in the-

38. The director of the Hartmannbund, Hans-Jürgen Thomas, who estimated that striking abortion from the list of payable expenses could save the health system DM 15 billion, "since all those things that have to do with pregnancy ... are not illnesses anyway." Ursula Ott, "K(l)assenfrage," *Die Woche*, June 3, 1993. Further, "Legal, illegal, teuer: Abtreibung in drei Klassen," *die tageszeitung*, May 29, 1993.
39. "Gefährliche Lücken," *Focus*, 27 (June 1995): 45-47.

ory, this law continues in practice to divide German women along territorial lines (admitting to the disproportionate hardships imposed on eastern women through unification). Women with monthly incomes of less than DM 1700 (West) or DM 1500 (East) can apply to have the cost covered by their respective medical insurance plan; the income threshold rises if a woman can show that she is primarily responsible for the upkeep of children (DM 400 per western child, DM 370 per eastern child), or if her rent exceeds DM 500 (West) or DM 400 (East). Likewise exempt from payment are the recipients of state welfare aid, unemployment benefits, job-training grants, as well as students and certain groups of foreign women. All other women are required to pay the full cost of the procedure based on a "service contract" to be signed with the operating physician. Each state has to provide hospital as well as out-patient facilities. A woman's salary is guaranteed for days of work missed due to the procedure itself or as a result of subsequent complications; medical costs linked to ensuing complications will be financed by the *Krankenkasse*.

Details regarding the obligatory counseling requirement are contained in yet another law, the text of which entails a verbatim incorporation of key passages from the 1993 Constitutional Court verdict.[40] Women must submit to counseling at least three days prior to undergoing the procedure, and each woman is to be "made aware that the unborn has its own right to life *vis-à-vis* hers during every stage of the pregnancy."[41] Thus the revised Paragraph 219 formally codifies an autonomous right-to-life for the unborn, although the outcome of such counseling is to remain "open." Counseling centers must submit to accreditation proceedings once every four years, while individual counselors (including physicians) must spend a specified number of certified hours in formal training (at least 40 hours for non-medical personnel). Doctors are required to "encourage" women to reveal their grounds for seeking to terminate a pregnancy but the latter cannot be forced to do so.[42]

As more recent developments reveal, however, the abortion debate is far from over. In June 1996, the Bavarian state legislature introduced a "supplementary" law that would compel women to reveal their names as well as their reasons for seeking to terminate a pregnancy. At that time

40. "Die Lizenz zum Abbruch ist für die Frau eine Lizenz zum Leben," *die tageszeitung*, October 10, 1995.

41. *Richtlinie des Ministeriums für Arbeit, Soziales, Gesundheit und Frauen über die Anerkennung von Schwangerschaftskonfliktberatungsstellen* (Internal document, Brandenburg, December 1, 1994).

42. When in 1995 the federal Frauenministerin, Claudia Nolte, ordered the production of 1 million car-bumper stickers with the slogan, "Fetus on Board" / "A heart for fetuses," she was forced to withdraw them under protest from the Springer Press and babyfood manufacturers who had initiated the earlier pro-baby campaign!

23 of the 35 accredited counseling centers in Bavaria were Catholic, six Protestant, and six non-denominational. Abortion activists feared that the introduction of such new requirements could lead to a replay of the 1991 "Memmingen Witch Trials."[43] State law would further prohibit doctors and clinics from securing more than 25 percent of their incomes through abortion services – a move intended to eliminate out-patient clinics from Bavaria's pastoral landscape (in both the agricultural and Catholic sense).

In response the SPD has threatened to return to Karlsruhe to test the "constitutionality" of the Bavarian approach – a risky strategy, even though the Court is now headed by Jutta Limbach, a pro-choice Social Democrat. In addition to making a rather unprecedented effort to assert the supremacy of "states' rights" over federal law (despite Article 31 GG), Bavarian officials may be pushing for an even more restrictive judicial interpretation of the new law "through the back door," according to outspoken choice-proponents. While proponents of choice hope that the Constitutional Court will at the very least uphold the current compromise, opponents hope that the weight of the restrictive legal tradition will serve to limit abortion rights further. At the time of this writing (summer 1996), the fate of the Bavarian initiative remains unresolved.

4. Systemic Ramifications of the Abortion Debate

The delegitimization of GDR abortion policies took place within the context of a general discrediting of East German social policies. The debate of 1992 and the subsequent judicial as well as legislative struggles also highlighted differences between the FRG and the GDR regarding policies on sex education, contraception and health care. Western women asserted that little progress has been made in the old Länder since Minister Strobel first broke the taboo on sex education in 1969. The role of German men in initiating unwanted pregnancies was conspicuously ignored by all but a few pro-choice advocates. Women from the PDS/LL were the sharpest critics of an implicit acceptance of men who impreg-

43. "Kritiker uneins über den Gang nach Karlsruhe," *Süddeutsche Zeitung*, June 12, 1996. The Memmingen trial grew out of the Bavarian government's decision to expropriate a doctor's private records containing the files of 500 women who had terminated pregnancies over a period of two decades. Their names were published (many were practicing Catholics), all were investigated, and 200 were retroactively convicted based on the judge's refusal to accept their "hardship" certification, duly signed by an accredited physician. See "Magdalena wehrt sich, Memminger Hexenjagd geht weiter," *Emma*, 7 (July 1990): 4-5; and "BGH bestätigt Memminger Urteil gegen Frauenarzt weitestgehend," *Der Tagesspiegel*, December 4, 1991.

nate women through unprotected intercourse, demanding that males submit to obligatory counseling "before each unprotected sex act, every one." [Dr. Barbara Höll, 8319]

In spite of the GDR's practice of providing free contraception of all types to women of all ages, GDR fertility rates had consistently exceeded those in the West (90 percent to 60 percent) prior to 1990.[44] The Bundestag's post-unity decision to provide only the Pill and the IUD free of charge to females under 20 implies that women alone bear responsibility for contraception, while the vote to subsidize only the most intrusive contraceptive devices (as opposed to barrier methods, including condoms) mirrors a curious disregard for potential health risks to younger women.[45]

As a result of economic uncertainty in the wake of unification, East German birth-rates suffered a veritable collapse: 42,547 fewer children were born in the new states during the first seven months of 1991 than in 1990. Indeed, the total number of live births registered on East German territory plunged from 198,922 in 1989 to 80,532 by 1993. Birth-rates in Mecklenburg-Vorpommern, for example, declined by nearly 59 percent, matched by comparable "free-falls" in the other new Länder; the "free state" of Saxony registered only 23,502 births in 1993, compared to 31,376 in 1991. In contrast, the western birth-rate has risen slightly since unification (from 681,537 in 1989 to 717,915 in 1993), perhaps because the biological clock has reached "five minutes before twelve" for the tail-end of the old FRG Baby Boom.[46]

The imposition of a common legal framework has resulted in a decreasing number of abortions, especially in the East. Initially, pregnancy terminations among women aged 18-24 increased following unification (by 28.1 percent in Magdeburg), in addition to a dramatic rise in the number of sterilizations (400 percent in East Berlin). But eventually, the number of officially registered abortions for Germany dropped to 111,236 in 1993. In Saxony the total decreased from 14,719 in 1991 to 9,559 in 1993; Leipzig witnessed a decline from 2,432 in 1991 to 933 in 1994, while in Dresden, the figure fell from over 10,500 in 1994 to roughly 6,200 in 1995. According to a 1996 inquiry conducted by the Saxonian Landtag, 49 percent of the women who gave reasons in 1995

44. Comparative figures from Gunnar Winkler, ed., *Frauen-report '90* (Berlin, 1990).

45. Conservatives who supported this earlier bill either failed to grasp how an IUD works, or they did not recognize the symmetry between Paragraph 219 StGB and the uses of RU-486. Smoking is on the rise among young women, a condition at odds with the Pill; the IUD is also unsuitable for women with multiple sexual partners due to possible cervical/pelvic infections.

46. "Frauen im Osten verweigern das Kinderkriegen," *Berliner Zeitung*, November 12, 1993.

cited financial problems, 38 percent "completion of their families," and 37 percent loss of their jobs; 20 percent stressed their age, 16 percent personal health, and 14 percent lack of housing (many offered multiple reasons).[47] In Thuringia, the number of abortions per 1,000 women dropped from 21.9 in 1989 to 11.1 in 1993.

In personal discussions, eastern German women voice considerable resentment about the deterioration of their freedom of choice. Interviews suggest that they view the new stipulations as yet another arduous obstacle against procuring state services in united Germany as opposed to the centralized administrative practices of old. They perceive the new code as an extraordinary imposition, since they are already depressed over their involuntary unemployment, loss of day-care facilities, and increasingly unaffordable rents; they now face the added burden of being charged with having engaged in a criminal act, should they resort to abortion in an effort to assert some control over their thus fragmented lives. Due to the deterioriation of child-care support, they hardly construe it as an act of clemency on the part of society that they will not be subject to criminal prosecution if they have an abortion.

The debate over abortion is clearly connected to women's identity in matters of economic self-determination within the context of a larger systemic shift. The Kohl Government's efforts to redefine the enlarged FRG's national economic priorities for the sake of competitiveness are increasingly at odds with the tradition of the welfare state. Discounting the argument that women in a country "as rich as Germany" often cite financial reasons for rejecting a life-long maternal responsibility (62 percent of eastern women are involuntarily jobless at present), post-unity conditions have pushed many formerly self-supporting women into a qualitatively different dependency upon the liberal-patriarchal state, as opposed to their former reliance on state paternalism.[48] For instance, officials in Thuringia have thus far failed to live up to their legal obligation to cover the abortion costs of economically disadvantaged women in several hundred cases.[49]

In economic terms, unification has made it more difficult to support children in eastern Germany. Since the forms of assistance emphasized

---

47. Federal totals are taken from the *Statistisches Jahrbuch 1995*, compiled by the Statistisches Bundesamt (Wiesbaden, 1995). Länder figures were graciously provided by Ute Maier, Referat für Gleichstellung von Frau und Mann in Leipzig, as well as by Frau Gruner, Referentin for the Gleichstellungsbeauftragte in Erfurt.

48. On state paternalism, see Irene Dölling, "Between Hope and Helplessness: Women in the GDR after the Turning Point," *Feminist Review* 39 (Winter 1991): 10.

49. "Frauen werden im Stich gelassen: Land zahlt die Abtreibung nicht," *Thüringer Landeszeitung*, May 21, 1996.

during counseling are only temporary (e.g., DM 1000 at the time of birth to cover "baby equipment"), the problem of having children is hardly a matter of attitude alone. If women feel they are not able to support more children at the time of birth, it is not clear how they can be expected to do this in the long run, given the highly gendered impact of unemployment and cutbacks in social services (including ABM programs), added to capital investment burdens at the communal level. Brandenburg's feisty Minister for Social Affairs, Regine Hildebrandt, reported in December 1994 that the average cost of raising a child "from cradle to career" now stands at DM 400,000.

In order not to jeopardize conservative support for the 1992 Group Resolution, SPD and FDP parliamentarians had agreed to postpone "family-friendly" investments. For the sake of saving public expenditure, warranting a legal right to daycare places for children over the age of 3 would only begin in 1999; thus females impregnated since unification have not had access to the infrastructural supports GDR women took for granted as of the early 1970s. Current plans to delay long-planned increases in child subsidies *(Kindergeld)*, announced in conjunction with the 1996 Savings Package, angered even the actively Catholic, anti-choice Frauenminister, Claudia Nolte. "Saving" the federal budget an estimated DM 21 billion in direct costs for 1996 alone, the gradual phasing-in of full-scale provisions for public child-care is creating considerable hardship for those who do want to have children.

The fact that 80 percent of all abortions certified in the western Länder through the 1980s were based on the "social hardship indicator" suggests that the welfare state may have failed some of its women.[50] Gender-based rights are simultaneously rooted in class (and race) cleavages, given women's restricted access to full-time jobs (owing to a dearth of "all-day" schools); lower wages and fewer benefits increase their reliance on smaller state pensions, despite the fact that women live longer and thus face higher costs over time; the age for drawing a full pension is now expected to be raised to age 65 for women (effective as of 2000), despite a previous Constitutional Court ruling stating that retirement at age 60 with full benefits does not violate the equality clause of the Basic Law, in view of women's doubly burdened work life. The DM 600 per month paid to women utilizing the *Erziehungsjahr* (extended maternity leave) provisions stands in stark contrast to average monthly earnings of DM 4,000 among German men.

50. For a broader discussion, see Fiona Williams, "Race/Ethnicity, Gender, and Class in Welfare States: A Framework for Comparative Analysis," *Social Politics*, (Summer 1995): 127-159.

By creating a "backlash" against the gains of western feminists, the struggle over abortion helped drive a wedge between the "step-sisters" of East and West. The much-maligned "socialist achievements," intended to foster women's participation in the paid labor force, were denounced as the "legacy of communism", despite their pro-natalist character.[51] Attempts to (re)secure those benefits are discredited, because women who now insist on their rights to day-care, maternity leave, abortion, etc., are attacked as socialist apologists, if not real "communists" – though their share of seats at the highest levels of the SED Party was smaller than those in successive FRG Cabinets. For Angelika Barbe (SPD-East) it seemed more than ironic "that women in Germany only counted as adults during the period of communist dictatorship."[8317]

As result of abortion conflict, Eastern and Western feminists were denied a chance to re-consolidate the political identity of their respective movements, grounded in divergent notions of equal opportunity. Surprisingly, neither women in general nor feminist organizations in particular saw fit to engage in sustained protest following the 1993 Constitutional Court verdict or the June 1995 vote. The general reaction was one of relief, coupled with resignation, over the fact that this highly contentious issue had been "resolved" – until Bavaria fired another unexpected salvo. Yet many related conflicts concerning broader questions of women's identity in United Germany continue to smolder. Instead of providing common ground for future campaigns bearing on gender equality, the post-unity debate over abortion has, in some respects, intensified perceptions of *difference* between the women of East and West.

Since women in the old and new Länder have had little control over the course of national policy since unity was attained, they suffered from a *democratic deficit*. (The sole exception of an influential power-broker was Treuhand-Director Birgit Breuel, 1993-1995). Elected in 1990, the Twelfth Bundestag consisted of 526 men, 136 women; the ratio of Westerners to Easterners stood at roughly four to one (256 electoral districts versus 72 districts). Regarding the question of representative strength, *the West is to the East as man is to woman* – though women in both the old and new states comprise a demographic and thus an electoral majority. For that reason, in the legislative decision-making both western and male views prevailed over Eastern and female positions. One modestly positive outcome stemming from government efforts to strike unfettered choice and related "woman-friendly" GDR social policies has

---

51. Conservatives frequently interrupted eastern MdBs during the debate with such derogatory comments, especially Christina Schenk (Bündnis '90/Greens), Petra Bläss (PDS/LL), and Gregor Gysi (PDS/LL).

nonetheless been a gradual increase in the number of women elected to serve as state legislators since 1993, especially in the five new Länder.[52]

German opponents of legal abortion posit the state's ability to legislate morality under the motto, "criminal law creates legal consciousness" and, by implication, conscience. By contrast, MdBs supporting decriminalization contend that restrictions on legal access have failed to prevent women from terminating unwanted pregnancies. Historically, women of economic means go elsewhere, but women without means resort to life-threatening methods. Renegade voter Horst Eylmann (CDU-West) stressed that only seven out of nearly 700,000 nationally registered criminal convictions in 1990 entailed Paragraph 218 violations (1993: 3 out of 695,118). While 1990 saw 200,000-250,000 legal abortions performed in the old states, doctors registered only 78,000 procedures (despite an official reporting requirement), though they were compensated for 88,000 cases by the *Krankenkasse*. [8260]

A final systemic dimension of the abortion struggle has been the religious undercurrent of the debate. Only the eastern deputies Schenk and Gysi dared to argue that it was not the constitution which prohibited abortion but rather the justices' interpretation of Article 1, rooted in their personal "Christian belief structure." Unification has brought millions of self-professed atheists, along with millions of potential Protestants, into the FRG. Grounded in the Reformation, the Evangelical-Lutheran Church allows for individual interpretations of the Bible, hence, for *self-determination* of "right and wrong." It is also worth noting that dissident Catholics who favor decriminalization derive their support from groups, born of the anti-nuclear movement, known as the "Church from Below." Legislators repeatedly stress their own need to exercise freedom of conscience with respect to abortion votes, yet many deny the same rights of conscience to women by asserting the morally absolute quality of fetal rights.

The balance between the two religious communities has turned heavily toward Protestant believers, western secularists, and eastern agnostics, tipping the scales in favor of decriminalization and moral self-determination. To restore their political advantage, religious anti-choice elements, e.g., in Bavaria, must resort to the judiciary in order to check the power of the legislative branch of government – something they did not hesitate to do in 1975 and 1993.[53] Denying the label "Christian" to all

52. Younger women have also displayed an increasing tendency to vote for the PDS – based, in part, on its programmatic demand that Paragraph 218 be deleted from the Criminal Code without substitution.

53. This strategy misfired when the Court in August 1995 negated the constitutionality of a Bavarian law requiring all state schools to display a crucifix in every classroom. Hans Schueler, "Die Kirche bleibt im Dorf," *Die Zeit*, 25, August 1995.

who dare oppose the most restrictive abortion code, western representatives of the C-Parties assume the role of surrogate Church leaders. The CDU/CSU permits its largely Bavarian-based minority to invoke directly the teachings of the Catholic Church; the majority remains conciliatory, reluctant to antagonize further the not-so-unified German population along the lines drawn by the Thirty Years' War. These are but a few of the areas in which the debate over women's reproductive roles – as distinguishable from productive roles of men – are tied to questions of institutional and ideological realignment in the New Germany.[54]

5. Political Implications of Gender Ideology

The ideological abortion struggle over gender roles in the new Germany was, unfortunately, lost by proponents of choice and perhaps women in general. Despite efforts by some officials to defend women's "self-reliance," their "freedom to decide," as well as their "dignity and self-determination," the compromise promulgated by the Bundestag, reluctantly embraced by many proponents of female self-determination, portrays women as too weak (or, as conservatives argue, too dangerous) to stand on their own. Yet they are inevitably defined as mothers. Western feminist Alice Schwarzer, attacking Easterner Petra Bläss in an *Emma* editorial, argued pragmatically that as far as the making of policy was concerned, something was better than nothing. [55]

In contrast, eastern feminists understood that the construction of women's nature embodied by the bill is profoundly opposed to feminist interests as regards *the making of ideology*. In Barbara Höll's words, the proposal adopted by the majority amounted to the "permanent inscription of a reactionary, outdated image of women, cloaked in accompanying societal measures that once again are only binding for women." [8319] Christina Schenk was even more scathing:

> There is nothing else at issue here but a patriarchal exercise of power against women. The reproach of murder, the forced [self-]justification, the obligatory counseling and the threat of punishment serve the single and sole purpose of transporting the partriarchally determined image of women in West German society [eastwards], according to which women are ignorant, clueless and, in essence, juvenile beings, whose sex renders them fundamentally devoid of any capacity for culture. [8300]

54. For the "re-gendering of democracy" as a result of the pressures of competitiveness see Hortense Hörberger, *Europas Frauen fordern mehr. Die soziale Dimension des EG-Binnenmarktes am Beispiel der spezifischen Auswirkungen auf Frauen* (Marburg, 1990).

55. Alice Schwarzer, "Wird der Paragraph 218 verschärft?" in Andrea Hauner and Elke Reichart, eds., *Paragraph 218: Zur aktuellen Diskussion* (Munich, 1992), 223-227.

Few German parliamentarians would dare to reimpose motherhood as the sole role of Everywoman, yet many view her temporary or partial redomestication as an antidote to a myriad of unresolved social problems. Another eastern feminist, Kirsten Thietz, stressed the broader economic implications of the abortion debate:

> In contrast to the ineffective economy of the GDR, [the one] in the Federal Republic has no need for women, yet all of the magnificent politicians and the minor and major guards of the economy need a woman who will keep the house in order and wipe the noses of their kids. The female industrial reserve army is being demobilized for the present and will be parked in a place where it can't take a job away from any man – in the well cared-for home.[56]

Fewer women seeking paid employment will reduce the pressures of a saturated labor market, though maternity and full-time housework are unlikely to alleviate juvenile delinquency, crime in the streets, the mass influx of refugees, etc.

In theory, the German Unity Treaty mandated the legislation of a common legal framework by December 1992 to ensure the women of East and West "equal protection before the law." Yet the new abortion rules as promulgated (and revised by the Court in 1993) are inherently unequal in their consequences. As analyzed by Andrea Lederer (PDS/LL), the "reform" of Paragraph 218 StGB offers an immediate improvement for women in the South, and it affords a liberalization, with minor disadvantages, for women of the North. For women of the East, however, it entails a re-criminalization of abortion, fraught with major disadvantages of cost and access, thus violating the Unity Treaty's promise to improve conditions for all. [8295] Having stepped "through the looking glass" of unification, eastern German women discover that the ostensibly democratic forces of the western *Rechtsstaat* – a state of law, rooted in popular consent – can easily lead to a reassertion of *Staatsrecht* – a rule by the state superseding the rights of the individual. The ties that bind women of the New Germany are those which divide them from German men.

As the conundrum of constitutional rights implies, abortion reform in Germany is also intertwined with other efforts to *re-form the concept of citizenship*. The acquisition of citizenship is erroneously perceived as a discrete act, not as a *process* of inclusion, be it national, regional, or supranational in character.[57] As the Paragraph 218 deliberations attest, the political identity of women does not automatically flow from an

---

56. Kirsten Thietz, "Zwischen Bevölkerungspolitik, Lebensschutz und Selbstbestimmungsrecht – Das Dilemma der Abtreibungsdebatte," *Ende der Selbstverständlichkeit? Die Abschaffung des Paragraph 218* (Berlin, 1994), 15.

57. Judith Shklar, *American Citizenship: The Quest for Inclusion* (Cambridge, 1991).

extensive catalogue of rights associated with the paradigm of liberal democracy. In contrast to liberalism's focus on the uniqueness of the individual, exemptions under the new law codify women's rights in terms of their *group status:* individual needs, circumstances, and degrees of *Zumutbarkeit* linked to involuntary pregnancy are deemed "exceptional." To critics women's rights therefore seem neither equal, "inalienable," nor tied directly to formal membership in the polity. Their constitutional rights must be "earned," contingent upon the discharge of externally (or "naturally") imposed duties, and they are secondary to those of the fetus as of the moment of conception. Male rights, by comparison, appear to be inherent and inviolable.

At issue are also the limits of Euro-citizenship and identity crises ensuing from a "Europe without borders." Foreign women in Germany remain subordinate to FRG restrictions on abortion, despite more liberal provisions prevailing at the EU-level with respect to abortion law. Critics charge that women's legal identity is defined in terms of *territorial* belonging *(jus soli)*, a violation of the Basic Law's general principle of descent *(jus sanguinis)*. Just as the 1975 Court decision against liberalization failed to stem the flow of women seeking "illegal" terminations in the Netherlands, the 1993 verdict proved impracticable due to "abortion tourism," though the "ability to pay" has created a barrier for some. Active enforcement would require authorities to subject every German woman of child-bearing age, crossing the border into the Netherlands, to a gynecological examination (such as in the case of Katrin K.).[58] Such police-state methods clearly violate the "free movement of people" foreseen by the SEA, and fundamental freedoms underlined by the Maastricht Treaty and the EU Charter on Fundamental Social Rights. Eventual community-wide use of RU-486 will pose equally intractable problems of implementation and control.

References to the FRG's "Christian" foundation also raise troubling questions as to what kinds of "life" and "morality" are actually valued within Germany's borders. Linked to a reconfiguration of public and private spheres in the New Länder is a debate concerning the future relationship between ideology, theology and values in postmodern and post-communist society. The secularization of FRG society had served to "delegitimize" the inordinate power of institutionalized religion in the conduct of public affairs by the 1970s. After unification the Church in the East also lost its moral authority, based upon opposing godless com-

---

58. In 1990, a 22-year old married mother was searched and arrested on suspicion of abortion while crossing the border between Holland and the FRG. The young woman was subjected to a forced vaginal exam, becoming a *cause célèbre* when it was revealed that she had fled to the West from Jena in 1988, where the procedure was still considered legal.

munism. Nonetheless, self-anointed spokespersons for organized religion portray themselves as the only authorities moral enough to fill the
socio-ethical vacuum in both parts of the country, thereby blurring the
line between public and private values. As noted by eastern theologian
turned politician Wolfgang Ullman, "Christianity is being misused to
stabilize authoritarian, hierarchical, patriarchal social systems." [8282]

Last but not least, the abortion struggle reveals the gender dimension
of *national identity* as a strategy for defending national sovereignty. CDU
Finance Minister Waigel enunciated the theme of national strength
when declaring, "we need the protection of unborn life and the help that
goes with it, and we need the defense of our sovereignty and the freedom
of Germany." [8272] Latent regional and intra-national tensions, aggressive forms of economic competition, and self-centered notions of ethnic
superiority were subsumed for four decades under the bloc-based struggle against "the enemy without." But with the end of the Cold War the
question of German reproduction and immigration has come to the
forefront. Some political leaders fearfully insist that the Germans are
dying out – in part as a result of women's demands for self-actualization
and the materialistic orientations of unified youths.

The abortion issue is therefore also becoming caught up in natalist
concerns that focus on the future of social security. Some xenophobic
politicians seek to root out the enemy "from within," foreigners in their
midst who generate more children than the "natives." Ironically, these
alarmists overlook that Turkish offspring are steeped in the kind of "strict
family values" of which the indigenous population has lamentably lost
sight. The same authorities argue vehemently that the "boat is full" when
the debate shifts to asylum and immigration policies. Strength defined in
terms of demographics bears little relationship to the "erosion" (one
could say "pooling") of national sovereignty seen within the European
Union since 1957. Multicultural antagonisms are a reflection of new turf
wars over the redistribution of state power, the right to define policy priorities, and the power to dictate the dominant code of "national" values
for the decades ahead.

In conclusion, the abortion issue is perhaps the most contentious
aspect of the remapping of gender identities in united Germany. The
unification crisis has, with its massive deindustrialization and unemployment, already fundamentally rearranged work-patterns and life-
expectations for eastern women in the enlarged Federal Republic. The
new rights they have gained as citizens of a parliamentary democracy and
as consumers in an affluent mass culture are at the same time being
restricted through the reimposition of more traditional social roles. The
political parties ranging from the conservative CSU through the neo-lib-

eral FDP, the welfare-oriented SPD, the ecological Greens to the post-communist PDS offer fundamentally different prescriptions for coping with the traumatic changes. How individual women will reconfigure their personal identities in order to navigate this transition is still somewhat unclear. It may, however, be expected that both genders in eastern and western Germany will experience an ambiguous, even conflicted relation to femininity thus being redefined, as well as in regard to other ideological debates rending the new Germany.

Chapter V

GERMANY AND EUROPE

Finding an International Role

Volker Berghahn, Gregory Flynn, and
Paul Michael Lützeler

𝔍n a book published in 1987, the well known Humboldt University
historian Hartmut Kaelble advanced the argument that the nations
of western Europe have, since the late nineteenth century and notwith-
standing the political upheavals and periods of intense nationalism that
the continent experienced, found themselves on the "Path toward a
European Society."[1] To buttress his hypothesis, he marshaled a variety of
data on mobility, family, and the economy. If Kaelble's analysis is correct,
then Germans, too, have grown more and more like their European
neighbors. More than that, if daily lives and structures have become
more similar, such developments are bound to have implications for the
self-image of the Germans and their perceptions of others.

This chapter is designed to test Kaelble's arguments from an interdisciplinary perspective. It represents the joint effort of a historian of
popular attitudes, a political scientist, and a literary historian to see if,
regardless of their divergent methods and tools of analysis, there is common ground between them when they explore the relationship between
the national identity of the Germans and what Kaelble would define as
an emergent European identity.

---

1. Hartmut Kaelble, *Auf dem Weg zu einer europäischen Gesellschaft* (Munich, 1987).
See also Stefan Immerfall, *Einführung in den Europäischen Gesellschaftsvergleich* (Passau,
1994), 53ff.; Michael Wintle, *Culture and Identity in Europe* (Aldershot, 1996).

A social historian approaches this problem from the perspective of deep structures of mentality in the population at large. Viewing the issue of identity from the grass roots properly introduces an analysis of the broader historical forces shaping popular attitudes through a succession of experiences with various political regimes. While the elite groups try to influence discussions among the population at large, popular opinions, shaped by tradition and deep-seated feelings, clearly also exert an influence "from below" upon elite groups and decision-makers, determining the limits within which elites must operate. Such an approach can therefore present evidence on the curious relationship between the political fragmentation of German identities in the nineteenth century and the disastrous consequences of forcing national homogeneity in the twentieth century. The postwar learning processes, triggered by the traumatic legacy of nationalism, may go a long way toward legitimating alternative orientations in the present.

For the political scientist, what is at issue in exploring this topic is structures of political communication and policy legitimacy. National identity is intimately related to values and norms, as well as interests, that populations required to be represented in their countries' policies. Political elites, whether elected or bureaucratic, are confronted on a daily basis with the questions of Germany's relationship with the outside world and most frequently with its neighbors, and how this is best represented in order not only to protect national interests, but also to maintain public support. Part of Germany's Europeanness comes from the experience of working with its partners to build and manage the institutions of the European Union, and from deciding when and how the European framework is best used for pursuing Germany's interests. The political scientist is interested in whether this experience is changing patterns of action and preferences on the part of political elites; and how such changes may have affected a key ingredient of governing, namely the ability to mobilize and maintain support for policies at home.

Finally, the literary and intellectual historian examines ongoing public debates, in this case discourses about identity, among writers, artists, journalists, and philosophers. The problem to be pursued is: how have these people – who, like the political and economic elites, are also involved in societal processes of interpreting the country's past, present, and future – grappled with the question of Germany and Europe? In assessing the fluid debate about the possibility of a multicultural identity within Germany or the wider European context, the literary commentary on the emotional question of the war in Bosnia offers a particularly instructive case study.

This three-pronged approach to the question of Germany's identity within contemporary Europe is inconclusive in the sense that none of the co-authors knows the future. It is also intriguing because it reveals a large "philosophical" issue that is underlying all debates of this problem. While an author's stand on this question may be related to personal values and autobiographical or temperamental factors, it is not conceived in a vacuum. Instead, these factors mirror a more fundamental polarity between the "Euro-optimists" and the "Euro-skeptics" around which much of contemporary public discussion seems to be revolving. The former find evidence that identification with the traditional nation-state is on the wane and thus take a more confident view of the prospect that Europe will evolve as postulated by Kaelble. The latter take a more pessimistic view: even if they might wish Kaelble's arguments to be true, their response is that whatever gains may have been made up to the 1980s have been seriously eroded by the strong resurgence of nationalism and ethnocentrism throughout Europe after the fall of communism.

1. Region, Class, and German Identities in Europe

For the scholar taking a long-term look at the history of German society since the first unification in 1871, the debate on the future of Europe raises two questions. The first of these issues revolves around the proper lessons of the catastrophic German past. Well before unification, Jürgen Habermas, the Frankfurt philosopher, who is advocating a "European constitutional patriotism" today, pleaded for a "West German constitutional patriotism." He did so in response to the *Historikerstreit* in which Ernst Nolte's hypotheses concerning the dialectic between bolshevism and fascism and the alleged origins of the Nazi "Final Solution of the Jewish Question" unleashed a major controversy.[2] When vigorously refuting with powerful historical documentation Ernst Nolte's peculiar interpretations of modern German history, Habermas never lost sight of the immediate political context in which the whole debate had to be seen.

The opposite position was most forcefully articulated by the Erlangen historian Michael Stürmer who, in a series of articles, had raised the question of a larger cultural identity that, he believed, continued to unite all Germans and hence transcended the country's political division.[3] To

2. The best book-length studies in English on this controversy are: Charles S. Maier, *The Unmasterable Past* (Cambridge, 1988); Richard J. Evans, *In Hitler's Shadow* (New York, 1989); Peter Baldwin, ed., *Reworking the Past* (Cambridge, 1990). Translations of the most important articles by German scholars involved in the debate are to be found in *Forever in the Shadow of Hitler: Original Documents on the Historikerstreit* (Atlantic Highlands, 1993).

3. See Volker R. Berghahn, "Geschichtswissenschaft und Grosse Politik," in *Aus Politik und Zeitgeschichte*, March 13, 1987, 25-37.

be sure, the political unification of the two Germanies was then at best a distant dream even to Bonn's neo-conservatives; still, Stürmer was not the only one to talk about the continued existence of the *Kulturnation* and to argue that this larger German identity was defined by a common language, culture, and history – albeit a history that was at the same time being cleaned by these neo-conservatives of its Nazi horror-chamber aspects. It was against the background of these trends that Stürmer asked the key question: "To Whom Does German History Belong?", adding that whoever determines the interpretation of the past also commands the present and future of a particular society.

Worried about the renewed attempts to "normalize" German history and to relativize the Holocaust, Habermas countered the notion of an overarching *Kulturnation* to which all Germans owed their loyalty with his concept of "constitutional patriotism."[4] He believed that rather than chasing the dangerous chimera of a pan-German nationalism the political and social order the 65 million West Germans should identify with that of the Federal Republic and its Basic Law. In his view enough was left to do in the Federal Republic to align the realities of politics and political culture more closely with the spirit of the Basic Law and its first 21 articles; he urged his fellow countrymen to work to give more substance to the ideas of a modern civic society enshrined in the Bonn Constitution. After Auschwitz, he wrote, this, rather than Stürmer's, was the only "patriotism" the citizens of the Federal Republic might adhere to; these were the lessons to be drawn from the Nazi experience. There was no need to direct attention further east to national tasks beyond West Germany's borders.

This contemporary debate about the correct way to deal with the troubled past raises a second, more substantive question: whether the identity of the Germans was as strongly determined by the nation-state as has been assumed. To be sure, through the ages intellectuals and politicians, especially on the right, worked hard to generate this identification. However, looking back at the experience of the Germans since the first unification of 1871 one might well ask if their efforts were really ever that successful and lasting. Were there other loyalties that continued to cut across the Germans' identification with "their" nation-state and in fact proved more powerful in the long run?

It is not easy to visualize today just how fragmented Central Europe was at the time of Germany's first unification. There were many reasons for this. To some extent it was a function of an underdeveloped communications

---

4. Jürgen Habermas, "A Kind of Settlement of Damages: The Apologetic Tendencies in German History Writing," in *Forever*, 34-44, (note 2 above).

system. But there was also the impact of politics. Thus the *Kulturkampf* against Germany's Catholics in the 1870s may have acted as a temporary glue to bring the liberal Protestant bourgeoisie into the fold of the Kaiserreich; but it deeply alienated some 40 percent of the population – Catholics from all walks of life, most of whom lived on the southern and western periphery of the new country, reinforcing existing regional consciousness.[5]

Improved communications subsequently helped to hook these peripheries up with the rest of Germany, and the struggle against the Catholics was abandoned in the later 1870s. Regional traditions and loyalties also weakened when millions of people migrated from the agrarian regions to the emerging urban centers in middle Germany and Rhineland-Westphalia. True, more work needs to be done before we fully understand to what extent these migrants took their original cultural identities with them and why these proved quite durable in their new environment. This is particularly striking in the case of the so-called *Ruhrpolen*. Perhaps it was precisely the frantic quest of the government and its intellectual aides to destroy cultural diversity to Germanize everyone and to harass those who refused that played a major role in this persistence.[6] Whatever the causes, the decisive point is that regional and local identities survived and continued to undermine efforts at the center to promote patriotism.[7]

Nor was it possible to overcome, with the help of nationalist propaganda, the class divisions that grew more acute toward 1914. This particular development is most tangible with respect to those industrial workers who, as former agricultural laborers, first arrived in the cities displaying little class consciousness, but soon joined Social Democratic labour unions and the SPD. While historians have intermittently debated the degree of working-class patriotism, it is clear that the rank-and-file members saw class, as defined and theorized by the party, increasingly as their primary point of orientation. They all dreamed of (and some actively worked for) a Germany that would be organized not along nationalist lines, but along those of an international socialism.[8]

If the creation of a German national identity was stalled not only by regionalism but also, and increasingly so, by the evolution of the Wilhelmine class state, the marked polarization of politics into a socialist and

---

5. See e.g., Helmut W. Smith, *German Nationalism and Religious Conflict* (Princeton, 1995), and Paul Nolte, "Hanging Together, Falling Apart: Self-Understandings of German Society from 1800 to the Present," *Working Paper* #51, Center for European Studies (Cambridge, 1994).

6. See, e.g., Christoph Kleßmann, *Polnische Bergarbeiter im Ruhrgebiet, 1870-1945* (Göttingen, 1978). On the treatment of minorities before 1914 more generally see Volker R. Berghahn, *Imperial Germany, 1871-1914* (Oxford and Providence, RI, 1994), 96ff.

7. See e.g., Celia Applegate, *A Nation of Provincials* (Berkeley, 1990).

8. Vernon Lidtke, *The Alternative Culture* (Oxford, 1985).

an anti-socialist camp became the concrete manifestation of this trend. All this indicates that the success of shaping a popular identification with the existing constitutional order was at best patchy. Even if they conceded that these were the domestic conditions under which Germany entered the July Crisis of 1914, most historians have argued that the emergency situation of foreign war resulted in a broadly based identification with the Reich. They confirmed the Kaiser's dictum that there were supposedly "no more parties [and, by implication regions], only Germans."

Recent research has shown that historians may have been copying from their predecessors for all too long when writing about popular feeling in 1914. Fritz Fischer was among the first to query the orthodoxy, when he discovered that demonstrations had taken place in the major cities of the Reich on July 25 and 26 to warn the government in Vienna, Germany's ally, against an escalation of the Balkan crisis.[9] Volker Ullrich and others then came along to show in local studies that even in the hour of mobilization for an allegedly defensive war against the Russian "steamroller" war enthusiasm and nationalistic fervor was far from unanimous and that there were many doubters.[10]

This evidence would seem to confirm the older argument that the much-vaunted *Burgfriede* of 1914, if viewed from the perspective of popular history, was a facade from the start.[11] The story of the subsequent total collapse of this truce and of the downfall of the Hohenzollern monarchy as a result of a "military strike" by the front soldiers and disillusionment at home is by now well-documented. In 1918-19 the idea of what it meant to be German had become more elusive than at any time since 1871. This state of affairs barely improved throughout the 1920s. The dwindling number of confirmed Republicans proclaimed "Weimar" to be their Germany. The extreme Left remained wedded to a communist internationalism and a strengthening, not of the Weimar Republic, but of the Soviet "Fatherland." Right-wing nationalists maneuvered either to integrate themselves, or to collaborate, with the most successful right-radical movement of the early 1930s, the Nazis whose militant Germanism had always had a flipside: the exclusion of political opponents as well as of Jews and other "inferior" ethnic minorities from the peculiar national community of the Third Reich.[12]

Even if the "Hitler Myth"[13] proved a strong integrating force in the "New Germany" and class differences subsided, not least because they

---

9. Fritz Fischer, *War of Illusions* (London, 1973), ch. 22.
10. Volker Ullrich, *Kriegsalltag* (Cologne, 1982).
11. Jürgen Kocka, *Facing Total War* (Leamington Spa, 1984).
12. See Detlev Peukert, *Inside the Third Reich* (New Haven, 1987).
13. Ian Kershaw, *The Hitler Myth* (Oxford, 1987).

were not allowed to articulate themselves, regional identities that the tensions of Weimar politics had done much to reinforce persisted. In the history of the Third Reich there appears to have been only one point when most Germans identified with the Nazi *Volksgemeinschaft*: swept off their feet in 1940/41 by the "fantastic" victories of the *Wehrmacht*, the nation seemed more united than ever before. However, again the reverse side of this celebration of unity was the simultaneous removal from their midst and subsequent murder of fellow citizens who had been publicly stigmatized as "un-German."[14]

The exuberant mood of 1940-41 disappeared after the summer of 1941 when the campaign in the East ground to a halt and the specter of defeat appeared on the wall. The total defeat and social collapse of 1945, then, left the Germans with little to identify with, except for their families and local communities. With the restoration of federalism, this untarnished regional identity provided an escape from the burden of nationalism and this was once again sanctioned by the authority of the Basic Law. Nothing would seem to demonstrate the continued force of regionalism more impressively than its capacity to absorb some eleven million refugees who arrived at the end of World War II in the western zones and were resettled from Schleswig-Holstein in the north to Bavaria in the south. While their arrival initially created many tensions, in the long run they were integrated not only economically and politically, but also culturally. The descendants of these refugees now living in, say, Rosenheim near Munich no longer distinguish themselves from their native Bavarian neighbors by more than their Slavic-sounding names.

Others began to look toward Europe as a greater, less problematic "fatherland." A Pan-European movement, it is true, had existed during the Weimar years; but its numerical weakness and insignificance as a historical force in its time is probably the best indirect proof of the strength of other identifications during the 1920s. No doubt German Europeanism and the desire to overcome the nation-state was genuinely felt by its advocates.[15] But what strengthened European enthusiasm in the 1950s was the realization that it also offered a chance for the Federal Republic to regain a place in the Western community of nations. With the prospect of reunification receding once the Cold War and the "division of the world"[16] intensified, European unity and the creation of a *West* German identity became not only buzzwords among politicians

14. See e.g., Robert Hertzstein, *When Nazi Dreams Come True* (London, 1982).
15. See e.g., Clemens Wurm, ed., *Western Europe and Germany: The Beginnings of European Integration, 1945-1960* (Oxford, 1995).
16. Wilfried Loth, *The Division of the World* (New York, 1988).

and intellectuals, but also appealed to millions of inhabitants of the newly established Federal Republic as a worthy and attractive goal.

The historical legacies that affect German feelings about themselves and Europe are therefore considerably more complex than often assumed. First, the tradition of political fragmentation, religious strife, and class division runs deep in Central Europe, and its force was only rarely buffered by the wider horizons of European relationships. Second, in its initial motivation nationalism justified itself as a modernizing effort to overcome particularism, but its imperialist and racist turn, manifested in the two world wars, largely served to discredit the nation as an emotional and practical reference point. Third, in the postwar period, due to the division of their country, Germans fell to some degree back onto their pre-national habits, but in a more constructive response also reached out for a wider European economic, political, and psychological framework so as to avoid the danger of a possible return of nationalism. After reunification, Germany therefore confronts a broad ensemble of possible choices, all of which have some support in prior experiences, and the question is whether the identity given through the postwar domestic and international context will find sufficient reinforcement in the emerging order.

2. Politics, Institutions, Germany and Europe

There can be little doubt that postwar West Germany was deeply influenced by its rehabilitation as a democracy embedded in a Western framework of institutions. This framework both nourished new governing instincts domestically and provided the Federal Republic a sense of collective destiny with its partners. German notions of sovereignty and security were shaped in critical ways by the country's experience in the European Community and the Atlantic Alliance – in ways that indeed seem to have become anchored in Germany's sense of self. With the dramatic changes internationally since 1989, it is now important to ask how context-specific this transformation of German values may have been, and how easily they may be modified once again because of the new European context.

This section argues that the behavior of German policy makers – the policies they pursue and the language they use – provides evidence that European institutions remain central to the way German political elites conceive of the country's national interest and to the ways in which Germans conceive of themselves. Since 1989, German leaders have continued to sustain the symbols and myths surrounding the postwar external sources of German identity. Indeed, in the debate over German policy and the future of European order, no political leader has yet been willing to attempt a serious modification of the symbols that have been a source of German identity. In part this is clearly because the institutional embodiment of that postwar identity is considered to be a viable formula to foster order in the new Europe. But it is also an attempt to revalidate the postwar structure of political communication, symbols, and political legitimation within a new context.

There can be no doubt that German leaders, Helmut Kohl in particular, see continuity in Germany's new postwar identity as important for both Germany and Europe. At the same time, this German self-conception will be doubly challenged: by a popular demand for proof that Germany's interests can indeed continue to be best guaranteed by a European framework that often requires short-term sacrifices in the name of longer term collective gains; and by a new Europe that will bring German national interests more frequently into conflict with those of its partners, requiring some difficult adjustments on the part of both Germany and its partners, including certain elements that have become a part of German identity from its postwar experience.

In order to explore this new dynamic, it is useful to focus on two interrelated areas that embody strong elements of German identity and which are challenged by the new European situation: the future shape of the European Union and the future of Eastern Europe.

In the face of the momentous changes that have occurred in Europe since 1989, Germany has been remarkably consistent in its policy toward European integration. This has been a public declaration, for both internal and external consumption, that the new Germany is fundamentally the same as the postwar Federal Republic. Three key elements of postwar German identity have been responsible for this stance.

The first is a profound commitment among the overwhelming majority of Germans that Germany should never again become a source of instability in Europe. As the Soviet empire collapsed and Germany was reunified, the German government's primary concern outside its borders was to reassure its neighbors, particularly France. This meant more European integration of the traditional kind. Further integration would symbolize the inextricable bond between Germany and the West, while at the same time, it would also provide a stabilizing core in the face of the emerging disorder to the East, and would prevent a renationalization of perspectives and policies at least in the western half of the continent. Although there was little that integration would bring in and of itself that was time-sensitive, the German government argued that European integration remained the best means of pursuing Germany's national interests. Indeed, for the government, it was the only conceivable way Germany could possibly achieve all of its objectives in the new Europe, shaping its own destiny without fundamentally threatening its neighbors.

The second has to do with Germany's basic conception of sovereignty. Germans have less trouble than most of their partners with the concept of shared sovereignty. This outlook surely has much to do with the country's postwar experience of limited sovereignty and a divided nation. It also has a great deal to do with the political institutions of the Bonn republic. The Federal Republic's experience with a federal system has left deep marks on German attitudes toward governance and political power; Germans are comfortable with the ideas of shared powers and multiple layers of authority. Indeed, federalism as a form of government today has become a very important element in what it means to be German today. As a society, Germans have learned to pursue their interests at many levels, through vehicles both below and beyond the nation-state. Thus in an important way, Germany as a nation is comfortable with the reality of a contemporary Europe of pooled sovereignties, and the idea that nations cannot accomplish alone certain basic elements of their respective social contracts. This comfort level is best represented by the fact that Germany committed itself in the Maastricht Treaty to sharing new levels of sovereignty precisely at the moment it was regaining its sovereignty.

The third element has to do with collectivity. If one needs an illustration of German commitment to collectivity, it lies in the negotiations over Maastricht. In the name of collective progress, the German government accepted a vision of the European Union in the Maastricht Treaty that differed from its preferred vision of Europe. Bonn would have preferred a stronger political force at the center of the new Union than that mandated in Maastricht. This was particularly true when it came to the creation of a political authority with sufficient legitimacy to arbitrate the political, social, and above all distributional conflicts that occur in any society and would be indispensable to the functioning of any eventual monetary union. Indeed, German leaders have repeatedly said that Germany cannot be expected to sacrifice the Deutsche Mark to a common currency unless and until such a political authority exists. But progress at Maastricht, momentum for a core source of Germany's sense of self, was deemed more important than the specifics of the model. The "bicycle theory" of integration prevailed, and core questions were postponed in the hope that time would help sort these out.

The debate about Maastricht in Germany was more controversial than many had predicted. With hindsight, that should not be so surprising. As in much of Western Europe, there has been a real democratic deficit in Germany stemming from the fact that integration has always been pursued from the top down. The public in Germany has actually never been consulted on European integration and there is no real public experience in debating the tricky issues surrounding the concept of sovereignty. Indeed, during the postwar period, Germany never had the luxury of debating the concept because of its division.

During and since the Maastricht debates, the public in Germany has clearly indicated that it expects to be consulted and have its say as European integration proceeds – as the boundaries between which objectives and policies are approached nationally, locally, or at the European level undergo redefinition. However, this desire should also not be misunderstood, especially when Germany is compared to many of its partners. During the postwar period, because of its special situation, Germany's debate about identity focused on the nation and the pursuit of unity, not sovereignty. As a result, German identity is less bound up with traditional visions of sovereignty and the state than many of its partners. In Germany, therefore, unlike France, the debate over Maastricht actually seems to have been on alternative visions of Europe rather than alternative visions of the nation. Thus, while the German public is no longer as passive as it once was when it comes to the specifics of the European integration process, the concept of the nation and its relationship to that process is considerably more flexible than in many other member states of the Union. The popular demand is for consultation, but is not motivated in the first instance by a rejection of the European framework. The public wants to participate in the future definition of that framework, especially those portions that affect peoples' daily lives. Yet, given the overall comfort with the multiple layers of authorities seemingly shared by most Germans, this should not be seen as a devaluation of the framework that has been so central to German self-definition.

None of this is to argue that the German commitment to European integration and collectivity is unequivocal or that Germany is prepared to sacrifice sovereignty easily or completely. Even Germany may have difficulty at some point with the integration process, although it is virtually certain that Germany's partners will have more difficulties with the process on the grounds of identity. For Germany, however, the concerns with European integration will only be identity bound insofar as they are functional: that is, that vital German interests continue to be served by the integration process. If Germans blow the whistle on the integration process, it will be because the Union no longer performs certain functions that have been crucial to Germany's identity. And the only function that would seem to be of this level of importance, as discussed below, is extending security and stability eastward.

It is highly unlikely that a slowing down of integration, or specific visions of the nature of the Union, would cause identity problems for Germany, given its comfort level with shared sovereignty. The issue for German leaders is not the speed of European integration or any specific amount of integration at any given moment; these are not identity-bound. Nor are short-term reversals of the process an issue. Rather, the issue is keeping the long-term trajectory of European integration on target, and keeping the system responsive enough to new needs as these arise. Whether these fuzzy criteria are met will determine whether Germans have a serious identity crisis because of the changes in Europe. The problem for German political leaders will be learning how to use their power to mold the integration process in a way that meets the nation's identity needs while not threatening its neighbors, and while keeping the public in tow.

German political elites are clearly attempting to keep key elements from postwar German identity valid in the new European context. Two specific recent actions speak forcefully to the durability of this commitment. In the process of reunification, Germany took the unprecedented step of amending Article 23 of its Basic Law to include commitments to develop the European Union and to realize a united Europe, thus anchoring the link between German national and European interests in the constitution.[17] The second is the decision of the German Constitutional Court on the Treaty of Maastricht, which had much to say about the democratic deficit of the envisaged Union, but which found the emergence of the Union as envisaged totally compatible with national interests because the Treaty took cognizance of the "national identities of its member states."[18] The future of European integration and Germany are formally and intimately linked, at least until Germany discovers that its commitment to integration has become dysfunctional.

In many ways, the German political elites' attachment to making the Western framework remain functional in the new Europe is a proclamation of faith that the identity Germany has acquired during the postwar period will remain viable under all foreseeable conditions.[19] In a sense, there is no allowance for failure in the German calculation. To contemplate it would be to admit that Germany once again would have to accept the possibility of redefining who it is.

17. For a discussion of this and other related issues, see Hans-Peter Schwarz, "Germany's National and European Interests," *Daedalus*, 123 (1994): 81-106.
18. See "Ein Bundesstaat Europa ist möglich," *Frankfurter Allgemeine Zeitung*, November 24, 1993, 5.
19. See Christoph Bertram, "Visions of Leadership: Germany," in Steven Muller and Gebhard Schweigler, eds., *From Occupation to Cooperation* (New York, 1992), 48-69.

The German concept of order for the new Europe is an encompassing one. Germany is committed to helping not only Germany but Europe to grow together again. On the one hand, this is a question of core values, indeed of another central element in Germany's postwar identity: the German commitment to reconciliation. While reconciliation is a concrete policy with regard to Poland, and a strong factor influencing policy toward Russia, it is also a more general philosophy about dealing with post-Wall Europe, given that the division of Europe resulted from a war that Germany brought about. Because of the differences between East and West in Europe, wholeness will for the foreseeable future be largely symbolic. But those symbols will be important both for setting long-term objectives and giving short-term hope.

On the other hand, this is also a question of interests: many Germans see danger, particularly for themselves, if the new Europe is divided once again, but this time between the haves and have-nots. Germany is closer to Eastern Europe than any of its Western allies and sees itself as more affected by conditions there. While German security has been enhanced by the retreat of Soviet and Russian power and the emergence of a *cordon sanitaire*, the region is as likely to be a source of German insecurity as it will be a source of security. Indeed, many German politicians and policy-makers feel that Germany "has moved from the front-line to the front-line," and the new Eastern Europe is seen as posing a threat that is far more difficult to deal with than before. Given the strong German penchant for stability, particularly on its borders, Germany simply will not be comfortable with Eastern Europe in turmoil. In security terms, the region to Germany's east will not be able to perform its role as a buffer zone unless it is stable. Germany's leaders will seek to produce that stability as a major dimension of their security policy.

German political elites thus have a strong stake in the success of the transformation underway in Eastern Europe. This stake is much stronger than for any of Germany's Western partners. They also perceive Germany incapable of dealing with the task alone, both for historically grounded political reasons and for reasons of feeling overstretched by the simultaneous demands of unity and conversion in the East.[20] The problem is thus not that Germans will voluntarily go into Eastern Europe by themselves and set up a comfortable sphere of influence that will be perceived by others as a threat. Rather, the dilemma is that German leaders feel that the problems in the region must be dealt with, will be seeking partners to that end, and others may not follow.

20. See Daniel Hamilton, "A More European Germany, A More German Europe," *Journal of International Affairs* (Summer 1991): 127-149.

While several institutions will be involved in meeting the needs of Eastern Europe during the coming period, there seems to be a broad consensus among German political elites that the European Union must be the core of long-term integration on the continent. Nobody expects the European Union to bear the entire burden of coping with Eastern Europe's problems of transformation and security. Both NATO and the OSCE will have to play a significant role in reaching out eastward and building a network of institutionalized relationships across the continent. There is, however, a clear belief that the Union will also have to play an increasingly key role in this network, that the Union's short-term policies will embody the most important symbols about long-term possibilities for Eastern Europe, and that formal membership may not be put off indefinitely for at least some of the Northern Tier countries.

The importance of this issue and its potential for causing problems between Germany and its partners was highlighted in the by now famous CDU paper on European Union issued in September 1994. As the authors write:

> If [West] European integration were not to progress, Germany might be called upon, or be tempted by its own security constraints, to try to effect stabilization of Eastern Europe on its own and in the traditional way .... However, this would far exceed its capacities and, at the same time, erode the cohesion of the European Union .... Only if the new system set up after 1945 to regulate conflicts, to effect a balancing of interests, to promote mutual development and to ensure Europe's self-assertion in its external relations can be further developed and expanded to take in Germany's neighbors in Central and Eastern Europe, will Germany have a chance of becoming a center of stability in the heart of Europe.[21]

This statement demonstrates two explicit links between finding a solution for Central and Eastern Europe and German identity over and beyond the belief that Germany has a special responsibility for helping to make sure that Europe does not remain divided: the need for Germany to be a source of stability in Europe; and the need for collectivity. Both have become central elements of German identity if the earlier analysis is correct; that is, they constrain the alternatives available to Germany in adapting to the new context. The very fact that the reflection about "going it alone" was ever made in print surely signifies German elites' fear of a disjunct between their perception of what needs to be done and the perceptions of their partners, and the desire to worry out loud about what that would portend (whether this should be interpreted as a threat is in the eye

21. "Reflections on European policy," *CDU/CSU Fraktion des Deutschen Bundestages*, September 1, 1994, 3-4.

of the beholder). In reality, it would take a great deal to provoke Germans even to debate a national approach to the problems of transition to its East, in part because the task (as noted) is simply too big for a single country and in part because it would mean having to redefine completely how Germans think about themselves. Nonetheless, the transformation of Central and Eastern Europe is powerful in a way that few other issues are insofar as it forces Germans to confront whether the collectivity will continue to provide a security guarantee for Germany.

Collectivity thus has two significant meanings: it is a sense of self; and it is a source of security. The two almost certainly were developed together and are probably inextricable. It is thus quite literally impossible to know what would happen if Germany's sense of self came into conflict with its perception of its security needs over Eastern Europe. What we can say is that Germany during the postwar period has grown extraordinarily attached to the idea that security can only be achieved collectively. This is not only an anchor of Germany's identification with the Western framework, but also an anchor of the entire Western framework itself. If the collective framework could not deal with a German perception of threat to security, then Germany would have to force the framework to deal with its needs, or learn to live with the insecurity. If it could do neither, then it would be forced to accept that the framework was no longer valid in the new context, and undergo a rather profound identity crisis in the process. This is precisely why the realist school of international relations theory has predicted a breakdown of postwar integrative institutions and the ultimate need for Germany to acquire nuclear weapons.[22]

Certainly this perspective is exaggerated in the short-term, but Germany will nonetheless be placing major demands on its partners in the meantime. It is certain that Germany will attempt to use the framework of Western institutions and most especially the European Union to deal with its new security needs, and that Germany does not see a basic incompatibility between these new security requirements and the maintenance of the Western collective framework. Germany knows that its ability to deal with problems in the East is a function of the viability of Germany's western links. The core of long-term security is the western integration process. Collective western engagement in Eastern Europe and an extension of integration eastward are the means to deal with problems of both regional security and conversion. Deepening and widening are not only judged compatible but both are seen as indispensable to

22. The most frequently cited article making the realist argument about post-Cold War Europe and Germany is John Mearsheimer, "Back to the Future: Instability in Europe after the Cold War," *International Security*, 15 (Summer 1990): 5-56.

German security requirements. Deepening without widening will create a serious security problem on Germany's eastern border. Widening without deepening will undermine the credibility of the framework that has provided Germany with a surrogate fatherland.

3. German Writers and the War in Bosnia

One of the most serious challenges by the new Europe to Germany and its partners has come in the Balkans. The war in Bosnia has confronted political elites with the profound gaps between their policy aspirations and the tools available to affect outcomes, and between international objectives and what can be sustained domestically. Bosnia has not only been a cause of considerable dispute among Germany and its partners about both ends and means, but it has also been a source of considerable debate in Germany about moral responsibilities as well as the appropriate German role in dealing with such crises. As such it provides fertile ground for analyzing the literary-philosophical dimension of contemporary identity formation in Germany and Europe.

It is not the writer's job to make political decisions, nor to declare or end wars. But writers have traditionally contributed decisively to the formation of public opinion in Europe. In the past, they have influenced the political consciousness of the European population with their positions on the Reformation, the French Revolution, the politics of Napoleon, the Revolution of 1848, the Cold War, and the events of 1989. The influence exerted by writers in the history of the European mentality must not be underestimated. More freely than pragmatic politicians, literary figures can think about the future and argue about the moral implications of certain courses of actions.

After the collapse of communism, Jürgen Habermas forcefully made the liberal case for strengthening European integration as an antidote to the revival of nationalism in the East. In his Essay on *Staatsbürgerschaft und nationale Identität. Überlegungen zur europäischen Zukunft*, Habermas points out that Europe needs "a new political self-confidence that corresponds to its role in the world of the twenty-first Century," and he adds that Europe will not be able to implement its new opportunity as a world power in the old nineteenth century fashion of "power politics" but only "under the changed premise of a non-imperial understanding and of a learning from other cultures."[23]

23. Jürgen Habermas, *Staatsbürgerschaft und nationale Identität. Überlegungen zur europäischen Zukunft* (St. Gallen, 1991), 25, 24, 19, 23f.

Habermas was the first German philosopher who – even before Daniel Cohn-Bendit and Thomas Schmid published *Heimat Babylon* – envisioned the European Union as a multicultural society. Habermas pleads for working toward a "European constitutional patriotism." While he acknowledges that a "European public opinion" does not exist yet, he is optimistic that a European public sphere with a multicultural basis is in the making. He foresees that "the single European market will be the beginning of a more extended horizontal mobility" and that it will lead "to a proliferation of contacts among members of different nations." Furthermore, Habermas is certain that the "immigration from Eastern Europe and from the poor regions of the Third World will intensify the multicultural diversity in the European Community." And finally, he believes that international social movements (like those for peace, for the environment, and for women's emancipation) will demonstrate that their problems cannot be solved nationally but only at a European level.

"In the future," Habermas predicts, "the diverse national cultures could merge into one common political culture." While the political culture would gradually become more European, other cultural forms (like the arts, literature, historiography, and philosophy) would continue to be national for quite some time. Habermas distinguishes between "political culture" and the "culture of a specific way of life." In order to prevent chaos in the future European multicultural society, the political and legal culture of a democracy based on universal human rights could not be compromised. Everybody in the future European Union (including the immigrants from non-Western countries) would have to accept the democratic political culture with its legal system while, at the same time, each citizen should be able to adhere to religions and follow traditions of his or her own choice, as long as these do not contradict the democratic principles of the community. Habermas cites the United States of America and Switzerland as examples of countries where this relation between the political/legal and the practical/traditional culture is the guarantee of a peaceful coexistence and cooperation among diverse ethnic, religious, and national groups.

According to Habermas, a multicultural European society is not an end in itself but a necessary step in the direction of the "status of world citizenship." This status is already "taking shape in the form of global political communications,"[24] he states. Immanuel Kant, Habermas writes, envisioned a "global public sphere," and now "this communication of world citizens can become a political reality." "World citizenship," he continues, "is no longer a mere phantom, even if we still have a long way to go"; it is a phenomenon of which "we can at least recog-

24. Ibid., 33f.

nize its contours." Two years later Habermas repeated this thesis in his discussion with Charles Taylor on the problems of multicultural societies. Here he pleaded for a continuous dialogue between the cultures of the majorities and the minorities, a mutual recognition, and a willingness to enter new symbioses. Such a dialogue would avoid the error of the ethnocentrists, who are working with a model of an exclusive, often essentially racist, collective identity.

Coming at a time when conservative intellectuals called for Germany to return to a more national outlook, the war in Bosnia shook this progressive self-confidence to its very foundations. In contrast to Habermas' transnational vision, some writers such as the playwright Botho Strauss in a programmatic essay advocated a more skeptical, irrational worldview and tried to revive certain national traditions. Confronted with unspeakable atrocities on their own continent that they thought had long been left behind, German writers were also deeply divided in their assessment of what is at stake in the former Yugoslavia. The shock of the incredible bloodshed broadcast by the news media has reinforced currents of pessimism, although other commentators also use the Balkan war as an argument to call for even tighter integration. The most important of the writers who have focused on the war in Yugoslavia are Peter Schneider, Richard Wagner, Herta Mueller, Hans Magnus Enzensberger, and Peter Sloterdijk.

Wagner, Schneider and Mueller all have a decidedly pessimistic view of the situation in the former Yugoslavia and its implications. In *Der Balkan gegen Ende des Jahrhunderts,* Wagner states that the Balkans' "multicultural face" has turned into a "multibarbarian grimace," that Bosnia has become "an expandable death model."[25] He is convinced that if the European community does not find a way to stop the war, it will eventually spread into other parts of Europe.[26] Wagner notes that nothing good can come of nationalistic solutions in Eastern Europe. The "alienation of the minorities" there, he writes, began with the "imposition of the nation-state." The drawing of national boundaries after 1918 resulted in "relocation, deportation, and expulsion." The consequence of the Paris treaties ending World War I was the "tearing apart of the regions."[27] For the "minorities in Eastern Europe" Wagner can see only "supranational solutions" in the form of a "European legal framework."[28]

25. Richard Wagner, "Der Balkan gegen Ende des Jahrhunderts," in *Mythendämmerung. Entwürfe eines Mitteleuropäers* (Berlin, 1993), 69.
26. Ibid., 72.
27. Richard Wagner, "Der nationale Wanderstiefel. Minderheiten in Osteuropa," *Kursbuch*, 107 (1992): 134.
28. Ibid., 141.

Peter Schneider also reflects on the reports from Bosnia: "These images of war are even more horrific than those that sent millions of Europeans into the street 25 years ago. Whatever the language, whatever the ideology in those days, the slogan was simple: 'Stop the war in Vietnam!' These days, the outrage is limited to a low sigh in front of the TV screen."[29] Schneider went to Sarajevo to see for himself, and his report tells the story of the victims, of the people of besieged Sarajevo. In their opinion, "Europe has demonstrated that [Bosnia] does not belong to Europe," and they are desperate about "Europe's inactivity and cynicism."[30] Herta Mueller's position is basically identical with that of Wagner and Schneider. In two newspaper articles (reprinted in her essay *Hunger und Seide*), she came to the conclusion that this war is not going to end without a massive military intervention from the outside. All three authors see Serbian nationalism as the cause of the war, and all three of them blame the West for its passivity.

It is interesting to observe that the Hungarian Gyorgy Konrad, one of the most prominent Europe essayists, sees things similarly: "Europe is on the verge of insanity," he commented in reference to the war in the former Yugoslavia. Like the three German authors, he is attempting to drive home the point that Western Europe cannot remain untouched by the war in the Balkans. "Eastern Europe continues to need confederative solutions," Konrad states;[31] he also feels it is absurd that "nationality reigns supreme" in the Balkans.[32] Europe should approach the problem step by step:[33] first a "central European equilibrium" must be created, following which, after a "middle step, total European integration" could ensue.[34]

In contrast to these attitudes, it is interesting to analyze the writings of Hans Magnus Enzensberger. In years past Enzensberger prided himself on his stance as a European intellectual who sang the praises of Europe's cultural diversity. He wanted to protect this plurality from the European Community's bureaucracy in Brussels, which he saw as the great equalizer and even destroyer of Europe's culture. But now, when multiculturalism is about to be extinguished in one part of Europe, Enzensberger has taken refuge behind a nationalistic position. This is all the more surprising, since in his essay *Die Grosse Wanderung* he had

29. Peter Schneider, "Bosnien oder Die Lehren der Geschichte," in *Vom Ende der Gewissheit* (Berlin, 1994), 57.

30. Peter Schneider, "Sarajevo oder Der kurze Weg in die Barbarei," in *Ende der Gewißheit*, 72.

31. Gyorgy Konrad, "An Europas Horizont kichert der Wahnsinn," in *Europa im Krieg. Die Debatte über den Krieg im ehemaligen Jugoslawien* (Frankfurt/Main, 1992), 24.

32. Ibid., 21.

33. Ibid., 23.

34. Ibid., 24.

questioned the validity of thinking in national categories when one confronts the global issues of our time. During a visit to Uganda – where civil war had raged for years – an African author suggested to him: "Only one thing will end a civil war, and that is total exhaustion .... Leave it alone!" And Enzensberger "didn't feel like contradicting him."[35] The same perspective is reflected in his contribution to the Suhrkamp volume *Europa im Krieg*.

Enzensberger provides a detailed explanation of his resigned attitude in his essay *Aussichten auf den Bürgerkrieg*. He bases his comments on the thesis that the civil wars of the present lack legitimacy, ideological foundation, and conviction.[36] Conflicts of nationalities, like the one currently being waged in Yugoslavia, provide only "fragments of the historical ragbag," only "ideological garbage." According to Enzensberger, the "nationalists from the past" have sunk to the level of destructive "gang members." The Serbian president and the "most ignorant Rambo," he writes, have one thing in common: "a radical loss of self" and "a cynical or bored indifference." Enzensberger perceives no qualitative difference between what he calls the "molecular civil war" in the cities of Western Europe and the political-ethnic civil war in Bosnia. In his opinion "any subway train can turn into a Bosnia *en miniature.*" He sees the present political violence as a raging "death wish." Enzensberger is convinced that neither a global organization such as the United Nations nor the European Union will be able to prevent the "increasingly common civil wars," since any sort of mediation would presuppose the desire and the ability of those leading the civil wars to make peace. But since the warring factions seem to prefer to continue the war until they themselves are destroyed, a political, diplomatic solution would be a useless enterprise.

The war in Yugoslavia demonstrates, according to Enzensberger, that the Europeans are neither willing nor able to enforce peace. Here the author includes himself in the count, since he is one of those Europeans neither willing nor able to envision a peaceful solution to the Balkans' problem. He reasons that, while universal solidarity would be a noble aim, it would be impossible to end all the world's civil wars. He pleads for a "gradual delegation of responsibilities," a "setting of priorities." In setting these priorities, Enzensberger dismisses all global and, along with these, all European concerns. What interests him is solely the civil war in his own country, the socalled "molecular civil war" in German towns like "Hoyerswerda and Rostock, Mölln and Solingen." Germany, Enzens-

35. Hans Magnus Enzensberger, *Die grosse Wanderung. 33 Markierungen* (Frankfurt/Main, 1992), 90.

36. Hans Magnus Enzensberger, *Aussichten auf den Bürgerkrieg* (Frankfurt/Main, 1992), 20ff.; also for the following.

berger argues, is kept busy fighting this war; he considers all other measures – to interfere with the fighting Bosnians, for example – extreme, unfitting, adventurous, and inadvisable (so much for Enzensberger's European engagement after 1989).

Authors such as Konrad, Schneider, and Wagner would tell him that the civil war in Bosnia will not simply "dry up"; they would point out the threat that an escalation of the war in the Balkans would eventually have an impact on the rest of Europe. Enzensberger seems to miss the obvious difference between Mölln and Sarajevo. While the events in Mölln represent individual civil rights violations, Sarajevo is the casualty of a war that was initiated and legitimized by a state government. Such a war is not a matter for the civil court, but must be adjudicated by the international community. "We have enough to do in dealing with our own civil war. Let the Germans deal with their skinheads and the Bosnians with their Serbs," Enzensberger seems to believe. But equating "molecular" civil war with "militaristic" civil war is untenable; the "molecular civil war" that Enzensberger perceives in Germany is not a civil war at all. Enzensberger uses his theory of the molecular war as a means to make excuses for Western Europe's passivity in crisis situations after 1989.

In the recent discussion on Europe, Peter Sloterdijk opposes Enzensberger's position without mentioning his name. Sloterdijk's essay *Falls Europa erwacht* appeared in 1994, one year after Enzensberger's *Aussichten auf den Bürgerkrieg*.[37] In 1989, shortly before the iron curtain was lifted, Sloterdijk had published his book *Eurotaoismus*, in which he viewed European culture in a defensive position: Europe should stop its aimless mobility, should regain strength by reflecting on its own values. In his new book, Sloterdijk tries to formulate both these old values and Europe's new goals in the post-1989 situation. He attacks the passivity of the European Community with respect to the "Yugoslav crisis," and he criticizes its "wavering between indifference and helpless indignation" at "Bosnia's dismemberment." Europe's "Bosnian disgrace" is revealed by the fact that the EC is doing nothing except "sending observers and stretchers" to the former Yugoslavia. According to Sloterdijk, these are the "obscene results" of a European politics that started in 1945, a politics of "emptiness," of "illusion and laziness."[38]

Enzensberger's and Sloterdijk's ideas about Europe's future are diametrically opposed to each other. Ever since the publication of his essay collection *Achtung Europa* in 1987, Enzensberger has been raving about

---

37. Peter Sloterdijk, *Falls Europa erwacht. Gedanken zum Programm einer Weltmacht am Ende des Zeitalters ihrer politischen Absence* (Frankfurt/Main, 1994).

38. Ibid., 44.

the eccentric regions at Europe's peripheries, acclaiming the sometimes poor but always idyllic or strange places in Italy, Portugal, Sweden, and Poland. As is typical for him, the leading industrialized European nations like France, England, and Germany were not even dealt with in this book. In a postscript to *Achtung Europa*, he situates the narrator in the year 2006, looking back at the past twenty years; he imagines a continent where the EU has been dissolved and, instead of European unity, one is confronted with a chaotic disarray of anarchistic small nations. Tiny and hidden, nearly invisible, neat, unassuming, but at the same time making the lives of the superpowers difficult – this is Enzensberger's vision of Europe. In such a quiet corner of the world, civil wars cannot really occur. But if they do exist, one ignores them and is sure that this accident of history will somehow correct itself.

In contrast to Enzensberger, Sloterdijk's new vision of Europe is that of an extraordinarily active, attentive, and ambitious world power. He is convinced that Europe after 1989 is destined for greatness. The Europeans, he argues, must take their fate into their own hands. The postwar period has ended, Europe is no longer the object of American and Soviet politics; the time of European "absence" is over. Europe, Sloterdijk writes, is no longer a "cramped zone" between the two big nuclear powers.[39] Not the small, minimal, unambitious, agnostic, torn, decentered world of Enzensberger, but the "ensemble of maximal demands," greatness, big plans, and "the principle of world power" are the essential elements of European identity if one subscribes to Valery and Nietzsche, as he does. The neat and the hidden, the modest and the inconspicuous are characteristic of the ideology of the "vacuum," a world-view that was typical of the period of European "absence," i.e., of the Yalta period of European division between 1945 and 1989. According to Sloterdijk, a Europe awakened from the sleep of "absence" has to reconsider and to rediscover those forces of European culture that have defined its identity from the beginning. For Sloterdijk the most characteristic element of European history is the *translatio imperii*, the transfer of the idea of the empire as it occurred in post-Roman times from the Roman emperors to the popes, from the popes to the medieval emperors, from these rulers to the kings of the European nations. Sloterdijk defines this transfer as "the mythomotoric beginning of all cultural, political, and psychosocial processes" in European history. He is neither fantasizing about the reincarnation of the Carolingian empire nor picturing a continuation of the national-imperialist powers whose time ended in 1945. What he envisions is the "transfer of the imperial idea to a Greater European Federation of continental

39. Ibid., 13ff.; also for the following.

states," a federation that would leave behind the EC as "the crutch of the dream period" and "the construct of the age of absence."

In his essay *Brüssel oder Europa*, Enzensberger saw the EC as a frightening imperialistic Goliath that would have to be defeated by the small future Europe made up of small regions. Sloterdijk, in contrast to Enzensberger, sees the EU as a toy with which one can only simulate power, and he believes that it needs to be replaced by an organization with real power and impact. Sloterdijk envisions a "Greater European Federation" that groups around a "new axis," Berlin-Brussels-Paris.[40] Words like "awakening," "great," "empire," "Reich," and "axis" remind one in an extremely disturbing way of the megalomaniac language of the National Socialists. But time and again, Sloterdijk makes the point that he is among the decidedly anti-fascist thinkers. Europe, he asserts, will have the difficult task of being responsible for her own destiny, and it will have to leave behind those national tendencies that led to the two world wars. According to Sloterdijk, Europe will have to overcome not only all national-imperialist tendencies but also all continental imperialistic ambitions. He understands the Greater European Federation as a bastion of "human rights," as a "source of revolt against human misery." Human rights, Sloterdijk says, are the result of "Europe's most profound thoughts" and figure at the center of a future European identity. Fascism, on the other hand, stands for "cynicism" and "contempt;" it is defined as an "activism of contempt." The future Europe should be able to "transform the empire into a non-empire," into a "federation of federations."

The author does not go into detail when he refers to the European "multi-national federation" of the future. Yet it is evident that he believes in a Europe that will not repeat the mistakes made during the time of European imperialism. Rather, the imagined European construction of the future will have to "break up the imperialism of a superpower," will have to "think beyond imperialist limits." In this fashion the future Greater European Federation could "become a trans-imperial or post-imperial political entity of vast dimensions," and the "future European political philosophy" would be one of "post-imperialism."

Sloterdijk sees three major ideas as the basis of European identity: the idea of maximal ambitions, of the transfer of empire *(translatio imperii)*, and of human rights. This is an original combination, not to be found in other essays on Europe. Sloterdijk accepts Valery's 1922 catalog of maximal ambition without any restriction or criticism, and without reservation he proclaims Valery's ideal of "maximal interference in nature."[41] This does not

40. Ibid., 54ff.; also for the following.
41. Ibid., 27.

sound convincing in an age of environmental disasters. Nevertheless, Sloterdijk tries to formulate a vision for an independent, post-colonial, and post-imperial Europe with human rights as its spiritual center. In this connection it should also be mentioned that he sees "the problems of the Third World" as "part of Europe's responsibility."[42] The deficiency of Sloterdijk's essay is not confined to his ignorance with regard to ecological problems, but is equally obvious in the lack of discussion of multicultural realities and tendencies characteristic of present-day Europe. In general, the issue of multiculturalism has been neglected within the discourse on Europe.

The ink on the Dayton Agreement had hardly dried when in January of 1996 a new kind of Balkan war broke out, a literary war among authors on the topic of the fights in former Yugoslavia. The Austrian poet Peter Handke is habitually among the quietest writers and the politically most disinterested intellectuals. Unexpectedly, he ignited a bombshell in the German daily *Süddeutsche Zeitung* by writing a diatribe against those few authors and those countless journalists of the *Nouvelle Observateur, Time* magazine, the *New York Times,* and the *Frankfurter Allgemeine Zeitung* who had sided with the Bosnians in dehumanizing the Serbs and glorifying the Muslims.[43] After the appearance of Handke's lengthy article, there was hardly a German or European newspaper that did not react. Most of them accused Handke of falsifying history, particularly Peter Schneider, whom Handke had attacked as one of the blind, uninformed, and biased authors who had accused the Serbs of being the aggressors. Schneider – in his answer in *Der Spiegel* – could easily show that Handke was not able to produce a single new fact capable of changing world opinion on what happened during the war in Bosnia.[44]

Yet Handke's essay is not merely a frontal attack, a kind of one-man world war against international journalism, but also a travel report on Serbia in the post-Dayton era. Schneider concedes that this other part of Handke's article has the potential of furthering the cause of peace between the former warring factions. On the one hand there is this aggressive, militant, and unjust voice in Handke's contribution, a voice that makes unfounded accusations; on the other hand there is a thoughtful considerate voice that questions its own position, that is, reconciliation. The literary intertext in this part of Handke's essay is Ivo Andric's 1945 novel, *The*

42. Ibid., 18.
43. Peter Handke, "Gerechtigkeit für Serbien. Eine winterliche Reise zu den Flüssen Donau, Save, Morawa und Drina," *Süddeutsche Zeitung,* January 5-6 and January 13-14, 1996. The essay appeared in book format under the title *Eine winterliche Reise zu den Flüssen Donau, Save, Morawa und Drina oder Gerechtigkeit für Serbien* (Frankfurt/Main, 1996).
44. Peter Schneider, "Der Ritt über den Balkan," *Der Spiegel* 3 (1996).

Bridge over the Drina. This masterpiece, which won Andric the Nobel Prize in literature, is a poetic chronicle of the famous Visegrad bridge that for centuries connected the Ottoman Empire with the Occident. The bridge, which was beleaguered and even destroyed time and again, symbolized the difficult yet on the whole successfully functioning multiculture of this particular region. Handke believes that the bridges between the various cultures of the Balkans can be rebuilt, and he tries to encourage his readers to begin anew. Toward the end of his essay he writes: "To something else, and this something is the 'art of vital diversion'" *(Kunst der wesentlichen Ablenkung).* What he means is that the former opponents need to concentrate on the common heritage of their everyday culture, to remember what they have in common. Handke describes the life in the marketplace, the special foods he encounters in Serbia, the different types of landscapes. By doing this he tries to give an example of the "art of vital diversion." His reason for doing so is not to advocate the repression of feelings, for he knows that the traumas and wounds of the war cannot be overcome simply through concentrating on the simple pleasure of living. But for the time being, during the transition from war to peace, during a period when feelings of revenge still dominate, Handke's strategy and technique deserves to be given serious consideration.

The above debate, heightened by Peter Handke's recent intervention, indicates that the broader lessons to be learned from the civil war in the former Yugoslav republic are still very much in dispute. The compelling arguments of these various writers can be adduced to serve the cause of both European pessimists and optimists. In considering the creation of united Europe improbable, the former can cite the bloody break-up of Yugoslavia as the inevitable consequence of a super-ethnic state that does not rest on the loyalty of its citizens. The latter can employ the terrible circumstances of partition as a cautionary tale of the consequences of falling back into unrestrained nationalism. Moreover, it is not clear which version resonates more in the population and which specific policies will be linked to them. Though the process of dealing with the aftermath of this most recent European catastrophe has barely begun, the debate about the Yugoslav case will probably continue to drive home the dangers of ethnic hatred to the German population and thereby may ultimately serve to strengthen the sense of European solidarity.

4. Reconciling German with European Loyalties

The most common path for exploring the relationship between Europe and German (or any other European) national identity is through the theory of multiple identities. By now it is widely accepted that identities are not exclusive, that it is possible for an individual to have multiple identities – multiple objects of loyalty – each of which can claim priority depending on the circumstances. It is clear in a country like Germany, for example, that many individuals have strong regional identities. It is equally clear that these same individuals will feel German rather than French. At the same time, many Germans may also have a well-developed sense of a European identity.[45] The key to resolving this apparent contradiction is to understand which identity will dominate at which moment, and on which issues.

One customary way to approach this question is to attempt to measure how strong the European dimension of the Germans' identity is and whether this has changed over time. This is usually done by looking at public opinion data on how European Germans feel and there are large numbers of polls over the years that have data, for example, on the strength of German support for European integration or institutions. The difficulty with such survey material, however, is that it is devilishly hard to predict behavior from the measurement of attitudes. If one wishes to determine whether German behavior has been fundamentally changed because German identity has been changed by the country's postwar experience, and whether the new European context is likely to provoke a new change in identity and/or behavior, public opinion data can offer hints by revealing trends in attitudes, but ultimately it cannot help much with a specific understanding of cause and effect. Specifically, knowing whether the German population feels more or less European at a given moment does not help in determining whether collectivity will remain synonymous with German national interests in the new Europe.

Part of the challenge facing Germany today derives from the almost perfect fit between the content of German identity created in response to the external context during the postwar period and the adjustments that were necessary to Germany's sense of self in the wake of the experience with Nazism and the Second World War. The implanting of certain German national functions into a collective European and Atlantic framework was not only an adjustment to constraints imposed by the

---

45. This identity is, it seems, also being fostered from another direction by the continued "American challenge." This means that, while American mass leisure and consumer culture, as it is coming across the Atlantic, is partly being absorbed and integrated into the societies of Western Europe, it also appears to make the Europeans more aware of their own commonality as they face the products of Hollywood, Disney, and Columbia Records. This ambivalence is interestingly reflected in recent scholarly debates on "Americanization." See e.g., Rainer Pommerin, ed., *The American Impact on Postwar West Germany* (Oxford, 1994).

international system, but was also a central factor in Germany's success in coming to grips with its past. This content was also in complete harmony with the attempts to bring about a fundamental change in the essence of German identity through the internal transformation of Germany's political and social structures.

In regard to the remapping of what it is to be "German" Hartmut Kaelble, who was mentioned in the beginning, may have a point, even if there is less of a structural dimension to his *Path toward a European Society* than a subjective (and hence also more precariously balanced) one than he makes out. Certainly, looking back over the social and cultural *experience* of the Germans during the past century, it seems that German self-definitions have reached a peculiar state of affairs in the 1990s. While class-consciousness as a major ingredient of identity formation has waned and no longer possesses the force it had assumed in the Wilhelmine and Weimar periods, regional identities, together with traditional denominational ones that had always overlapped with them, have remained powerful.

If the German's sense of self has become less national than feeling among neighboring peoples, this finding spells both hopes and dangers. The danger is that it might promote the "Balkanization" of Europe and the eruption of regional ethnic conflicts, the harbingers of which some intellectuals, discussed in this article, see in former Yugoslavia. On the other hand, there is the hope that regions will strengthen existing peaceful ties across national boundaries, for example between Baden-Württemberg, northern Switzerland, and Alsace-Lorraine, and that they will do so in cooperation with, and with the explicit support of, the European Union, thereby eroding pressures to identify with the new, but traditional German nation-state that reemerged in 1990.[46] Seen from this perspective, there may be considerable promise in the more optimistic scenario mentioned in the beginning of this article that highlighted the federal institutional structure of Europe and its compatibility with Bonn/Berlin's federated regionalism that has such deep roots in German history.

46. See e.g., the discussion of a "Europa der Regionen" in Urs Leimbacher, "Westeuropäische Integration und gesamteuropäische Kooperation," in *Aus Politik und Zeitgeschichte*, November 1991, 45ff. Cf. also from a global perspective Kenichi Ohmae, *The End of the Nation State. The Rise of Regional Economies* (New York, 1995).

CREATIVE CHAOS

A Methodological Postscript on Interdisciplinary Cooperation

Andreas Pickel

$\mathscr{T}$he present volume discusses changing identities in post-unification Germany from a variety of historical, political, and literary perspectives. To some, the great diversity in the ways in which the concept of identity is employed may appear as a sign of confusion on the part of its authors. Others may see a lack of coherence and integration in the volume as a whole, while still others may find only further proof that this concept will obfuscate any debate in which it is allowed to play a central role. None of them would be completely mistaken. But the absence of greater uniformity, coherence, and commensurability is only to a very limited extent due to the authors or the editor. The project's objective was to treat the problem of changing identities in post-unification Germany in an interdisciplinary fashion. It is sometimes assumed that different disciplines, approaches, schools, and traditions can be made to work together harmoniously, if only a corresponding effort at collaboration is made. But this assumption is more often than not unwarranted and naive. On the contrary, it may be precisely the difference, divergence, incompatibility and seeming incommensurability in the way different approaches construct, conceptualize, analyze and discuss the "same" object – and not their harmony or uniformity – that makes interdisciplinary endeavors such as this intellectually exciting and potentially fruitful.

The purpose of this methodological postscript is to explain why any discussion of German identity today is bound to be particularly contentious and contested, more so at any rate than most other questions one might ask about unified Germany. Four methodological points about identity will be made, relating to (1) the nature of the social fact itself; (2) the essentially contested nature of the concept; (3) the methods used in different disciplines to study identities; and (4) their highly political and politicized context. Against this background, the chapter concludes by considering the relative success of the interdisciplinary project presented in this volume.

1. What Kind of Social Fact?

In the humanities and social sciences, our objects of study are people – as individuals, groups, or societies – their activities (behavior) and their products (material goods, art, ideas, values, institutions). What is peculiar about these objects of study, say compared to the study of rocks or cells or genetic codes, is that they are reflexive. A good part of what the social sciences and humanities are interested in is bound up with people's capacity to think, reflect, choose, conceptualize, believe, decide. The social facts we study may be "hard" facts, such as election outcomes, economic statistics, or survey results, about and with which we develop theories and explanations. Social scientists with a particularly strong "scientific" orientation will insist that "hard" facts of this sort are the *conditio sine qua non* of serious analysis. However, there are also "soft" social facts, such as values, cognitive frames, and symbolic universes which are much more resistant to being turned into "hard" data. These "soft" facts are the very stuff of which people's reflexive capacity is made. They are more or less articulated "theories" about the environment – we live in (reality), about what is right and wrong (morality), and about who we are (identity).[1]

"Soft" social facts are no less real, no less objective, and no more constructed than "hard" social facts. Two scholars who agree on a set of

1. The distinction between "hard" facts and "soft" facts made in this section would probably be unsatisfactory to both major camps in the contemporary debate. "Positivists" would argue that it is only "hard" facts that can serve as the empirical foundation for theorizing, while "soft" facts, if their existence is recognized at all, would be dismissed as irrelevant for science.

"Relativists," on the other hand, would argue that the distinction between "hard" and soft" facts is spurious since all facts are produced by interpretations, and thus "soft." (For the somewhat simplistic but at the same time useful distinction between positivists and relativists as the two main positions in the debate, see Ernest Gellner, *Postmodernism, Reason and Religion* (London, 1992). The reason for my making the distinction between "hard" and "soft" facts is to underscore the importance of reflexivity in the social and human sciences without endorsing one of the two basic positions in the debate.

"hard" data will nevertheless often disagree on how to interpret these data, and they may draw fundamentally different, even contradictory, theoretical conclusions from them. The situation is further complicated when we are dealing with "soft" facts. Scholars dealing with the "same" set of "soft" facts will tend to construct and conceptualize them in different ways. So rather than simply disagreeing about the proper interpretation of a "given" (i.e., agreed upon) set of facts, those dealing with "soft" facts routinely disagree precisely about what the "given" facts are. This is because, in contrast to us theorizing about some statistical or empirical artifact (the "hard" fact), we theorize about "theories" other people hold ("soft" facts). Theorizing about German identities of course tends to fall for the most part in the latter category.

2. What Kind of Concept?

Many of the central concepts used in the human sciences are essentially contested.[2] While they are referred to all the time, they are often used in fundamentally different ways. Justice, democracy, equality, and liberty, for example, represent standard concepts for the usage and interpretation of which there are at least two (usually more) competing contexts and traditions. From Plato's exploration of justice to Marx's repudiation of liberal bourgeois conceptions of equality and liberty, challenging a concept that embodies a widely held ideal and reconceptualizing it in a more "adequate" manner has been a standard practice in Western social and political thought. Nowadays, it is usual to underscore and be sensitive to the plurality of contexts and traditions that give meaning to basic concepts such as democracy, equality, or indeed identity.

The concept of identity is essentially contested since it plays rather different roles depending on the particular context and tradition in which it appears. One long-standing – and politically by far the most successful – conception is that of a national collective identity, based on assumptions of the nation as a natural and homogeneous whole with essential and unchanging characteristics, a common past and a common future. A second, more "social scientific" conception of identity views it as a set of measurable individual attitudes and value orientations. A third, more "postmodern" understanding of identity refers to a great diversity of constantly changing meaning structures embodied in and mediated by discourse practices and codified in a variety of texts. In contrast to Plato and Marx, most of us today feel much less confident about pronouncing

2. W.B. Gallie, *Philosophy and the Historical Understanding*, 2nd ed. (New York, 1968), Chap. 8.

any one particular conception of identity evidently and demonstrably false. While we may have made a strong commitment to one view, we remain acutely aware that the ground we stand on is too shaky to simply dismiss those who have decided in favor of adopting another.

3. What Kind of Method?

Where the social facts are "soft" and the concept itself is essentially contested, there is unlikely to be one most adequate or appropriate method of analysis. Moreover, typical methodological differences between disciplines tend to assert themselves with particular force. For where the terrain to be surveyed is so complex and still quite unknown, we have to rely for orientation on the conceptual tools and "measuring instruments" provided by our discipline or by a specific tradition within it. In fact, answers to the two questions posed above – What kind of social fact? and What kind of concept? – are usually contained in a specific methodological approach. In this sense, the reality that emerges in the course of analysis is to a considerable extent shaped by the methodological tools that are being applied. This is what makes the interdisciplinary effort in this volume of particular interest.

The groups in charge of writing the individual chapters were composed of three authors, in most cases from three different disciplines; history, political science, and literary theory. While each group worked on a common theme, each member of a group had a distinct approach to that theme, depending in part on his or her methodological orientation. What are the distinct methods that have been used? To what extent were they complementary, to what extent were they in conflict with each other? How and how successfully did the authors bridge those gaps? We will return to these questions at the end of this chapter.

When the social sciences passed through their "behavioralist revolution" in the 1950s and 1960s, objectivity, value-free inquiry, high-level generalization, and rigorous empirical methods were considered crucial in moving these disciplines closer to becoming "true sciences." In the face of often sterile work that resulted from this research program and in the light of fundamental criticisms, much of that revolutionary ambition has waned. Indeed, an anti-behaviorist counter-revolution has swept the social sciences since the 1970s, stressing the importance, desirability, or unavoidability of subjectivity, normative commitment, and a plurality of methods. Similarly, the postmodern turn in the humanities has revolutionized the way in which many literary theorists define their work. While perhaps more resistant than the other humanities, historians have also not been immune to challenges of postmodern critiques.[3] This is the "disciplinary politics" that is reflected in the approaches taken in the present volume. But there is considerably more politics in the study of German identities than the "normal" competition between old and new approaches.

4. What are the Politics?

The highly political and politicized character of redefining German identities after 1989 is reflected in popular terminology that, somewhat ironically, is reminiscent of what in other contexts is discussed under the heading of ethnic politics. Widely known even among an international audience is the relatively harmless and good-natured distinction between *Wessi* (West German) and *Ossi* (East German). Perhaps less well-known but a staple of popular German discourse are the more acerbic and confrontational stereotypes of the *Jammer-Ossi* (the East German passive complainer) and *Besser-Wessi* (the West German arrogant know-it-all), as well as the cultural cross-over, the *Wossi* (the West German who has settled in the East and "gone native"). While a primary line of division remains that between East and West, the contributions in the present volume show why and where there are a variety of other salient divisions and sources of identity – past and present, women and men, natives and foreigners.

The process of identity contestation and reconfiguration is still far from settled, and it is difficult for any observer to maintain complete detachment from the different actors, positions, and views in the debate. This is of course particularly true for Germans themselves for whom, scholars or not, this cannot possibly be a purely academic matter. But the situation is not fundamentally different for professional observers of Germany in North America whose geographical distance might be expected to facilitate a somewhat higher degree of intellectual detachment. The very act of investigating and interpreting an ongoing and open-ended political process makes it by definition and in principle impossible to assume and maintain a value-free and apolitical posture. Anyone who is familiar with and works on aspects of German culture cannot help but feel some sympathy for or antipathy toward one or the other group of actors, their values, goals, and struggles. The authors in this volume differ as to what constitutes a proper response to this situa-

3. For the effect on German studies, see for example, Michael Geyer and Konrad H. Jarausch, "Great Men and Postmodern Ruptures: Overcoming the 'Belatedness' of German Historiography," *German Studies Review*, 18 (1995): 753-773.

tion. While some gladly and even enthusiastically embrace partisanship and commitment, others uphold the ideal of objectivity and neutrality as a regulative principle.

Part and parcel of this more or less desirable or unavoidable politicization of identity studies is the intrusion of the observer's own particular intellectual and political background. Whether to be welcomed as a fresh perspective or to be derided as ethnocentrism and unprofessional bias, it is an inherent condition of the outside observer to arrive on the scene with preconceptions, questions, sensibilities, and prejudices that are at least in part rooted in the "politics" of his or her own society. This applies with special force to identity politics and the North American observer. How relevant and applicable are the debates, standards, and values that have developed around ethnicity, gender, and citizenship in the United States and Canada for Germany and most other European countries where contexts, problems, and perceptions differ, often in fundamental ways? The North American commentator is here confronted with the basic tension between universalism – in this case, an affirmation of the universal validity of North American values of multiculturalism – and relativism – that is, an acceptance of different, ethno-culturally based conceptions of citizenship, all of which of course adds only further complexity to the "politics" of identity studies.

5. How Successful an Interdisciplinary Effort?

The merits of this interdisciplinary collection of identity studies will be decided by its readers. The preceding comments have hopefully underlined just how philosophically, conceptually, methodologically, and politically charged and controversial is the problem of changing identities. This postscript does not attempt to provide tools for rationalizing what, in addition to its obvious strengths, may well be significant weaknesses in the current volume. But the reader should be alert to the particular challenges presented by an interdisciplinary study of changing German identities and judge the results contained in this book in their light. My concluding remarks, coming as they do from a participant in the project, are intended above all as a series of suggestions about what questions to ask and what standards to apply in evaluating the current effort.

The discussions among the authors very quickly established a considerable area of agreement on identity as a social fact (see Section 1 above), restated in one form or another in each of the chapters. As opposed to essentialist, singular, and static conceptions of identity, the participants felt that (a) individuals have multiple identities, (b) societies contain competing collective identities, (c) identities are not fixed in structure and time but are composed of contradictory and variable elements that (d) are subject to constant redefinition and reconfiguration in a political process and cultural discourse in which (e) scholarly studies such as those assembled in this volume are bound up. This common view on identity as a social fact entails of necessity a high degree of tolerance with respect to how the important issues are to be framed, what methods are to be applied, and what degree of political commitment or detachment is called for. Obviously, the danger of such openness and pluralism is a highly fragmented, perhaps even incoherent series of interdisciplinary analyses that create little of the intellectual synergy that is the hoped for reward of such projects, causing instead consternation and confusion on the part of the reader.

The present project, which I believe has to a large extent avoided these pitfalls, required a patient effort on the part of its participants, in particular the leaders of each group and above all the editor, to develop and repeatedly revise individual contributions to the chapters in order to attain a degree of overall coherence and integration. Not surprisingly, this was easiest in those cases in which the team's members had common methodological and political positions. In the other cases, it turned out to be crucial to develop a common dominant theme or set of questions to draw together the authors' "naturally" disparate disciplinary and normative concerns. Logistically and politically, moreover, the fair but firm and intrusive hand of a "central authority" (the editor) and the committed services of "local administrators" (the group leaders) appear to be basic structural preconditions for keeping in check the anarchic impulses of an interdisciplinary state of nature. In any case, the present volume suggests that the coming together of different disciplines and approaches is most likely to meet with success if at least one of two conditions is met: (1) there is a dominant common theme or problem addressed by all members of the interdisciplinary team (this may be either the result of an analytical focusing effort or the "given" structure of the issue); (2) there is a common normative or political view of the situation. I will briefly illustrate this thesis with reference to the individual chapters.

"The Presence of the Past," written like the other chapters except one (chapter III) by a team consisting of a historian, a political scientist, and a literary theorist, perhaps most clearly shows how an analytical focus defining a common theme can tie together different approaches to produce an integrated and coherent whole. A national identity, understood as an open-ended contest for cultural hegemony, is always constructed historically, that is, with reference to a particular conception of the country's past. While the section by the literary historian traces the deeper symbolic traditions of German consciousness, the political scientist surveys the democratic transformation of public opinion and political behavior after World War II, together sketching the context for the historian's analysis of the current German debate over the proper appropriation of the past.

The chapters on "Natives and Strangers" and on "Women and Men" derive much of their interdisciplinary understanding from a common normative and political orientation. The former focuses on the problematic relationship between Germans and "others" residing in Germany, and in particular the unresolved problem of citizenship for the millions of foreigners living in Germany. In other words, it is the authors' critical view of the ethnic-cultural definition of what makes a German citizen, this conception's historical origins, and its manifestations today that bring their different methods and perspectives together into a coherent and persuasive case for cultural change and political as well as legal reform. Similarly, the chapter on "Women and Men" subjects the patriarchal discourse and practices prevalent in Germany to a feminist critique from historical, political, and literary perspectives. This chapter achieves an additional degree of integration by restricting its thematic focus to the issue of abortion, though obviously at the cost of not being able to systematically consider a broader range of gender issues.

Taking as their common point of departure the thesis of an emergent European identity, the authors of "Germany and Europe" bring to bear their clearly stated, distinct approaches on what the general debate on the future of European integration itself has defined as the fundamental cleavage, i.e., that between Euro-optimists and Euro-pessimists. While thematically, the authors of "East and West" pursue rather different aspects of the post-1989 unification process as they relate to changing identities, the opposing normative/political orientations, and judgments concerning successes, failures, and prospects that structure Germany's unification discourse at large – the positive/optimistic versus the critical/pessimistic view – are reflected in the individual authors' approaches and conclusions. In spite of the stylistic integration of these texts, the individual sections of both chapters remain methodologically at odds and somewhat disparate in the absence of one of the two conditions suggested earlier – a dominant common theme or a basic normative and political consensus. Yet we might ask at the same time to what extent such a relative lack of integration actually reduces the fruitfulness of the results. In other words, is the unresolved tension in those chapters necessarily an indication of interdisciplinary failure?

If there is one dominant recurring line of division between the contributors to this volume, it is that between proponents of a descriptive/analytical approach, on the one hand, and proponents of a committed/positional approach, on the other. This line tends to coincide with disciplinary boundaries, though not necessarily in each case. Historians and political scientists are usually found in the former camp, literary theorists in the latter. Those supporting a "subjectivist" approach point out that normative assumptions are implicit in any analysis, and they infer with some plausibility that an explicit normative/political commitment, i.e., positionality, is therefore preferable to denying the inevitable. Those supporting a more "objectivist" approach argue that specific analytical categories do not necessarily imply a particular normative commitment, i.e., they may be quite compatible with different political and ethical stances regardless of a scholar's politics in general and motivation behind her analysis in particular.

If the latter were true, this would create some room for types of analysis that, while not value-free, maintain a distance from substantive political positions and commitments. For one danger inherent in positionality, i.e., politically committed theorizing, seems to be a reductionism in the analysis of complex phenomena in the interest of validating and reinforcing a given political position – a danger that the attempt to maintain detachment and objectivity as regulative principles may guard against. Yet, assuming such distance can be maintained, is it desirable to maintain it, for example, when we are dealing with ethnic and cultural conceptions of citizenship that clash with liberal, universalistic values, or with abortion laws that curtail individual women's rights with reference to patriarchal conceptions of women's roles in family and society?

This volume suggests that positionality, while not unproblematic from a mainstream social science perspective, can in fact be intellectually quite fruitful, especially when it appears in the context and in conjunction with other approaches. Positionality, i.e., the explicit commitment in analysis to a specific set of political and social values, can in this way be relativized. In other words, it does not require our sharing these values in order to benefit from the analysis, nor does it compel us to endorse a particular "positional" analysis or the "positional" approach in general even if we do share the values and political commitments. Conversely, from the viewpoint of positionality problematic hidden political agendas and normative commitments implicit in "objectivist" analyses can be exposed and confronted in interdisciplinary projects such as this. In this sense, there is considerable value in an organized clash of methods and approaches.

It may seem to some readers that such a pluralistic conception of methods represents simply a euphemistic view of the Babylonian confusion and Kuhnian incommensurability that characterizes social and political theorizing today. What the present volume of interdisciplinary identity studies on the contrary shows, however, is that too much tends to be made of the gulf dividing practitioners of different approaches. Each of the chapters illustrates that scholars, with in some cases radically divergent methodological orientations and political commitments, cannot only speak to and understand each other; but by shedding light from their different positions and disciplinary vantage points on the same set of issues can produce rich and illuminating, and indeed coherent accounts of "their" particular aspect of changing German identities. It is perhaps the fundamental agreement among all contributors on the complexity of identity as a social fact – its multivalence, contradictoriness, and simultaneous fixity and mutability – that has made the present interdisciplinary effort a constructive clash of methods. For, in this light, differences in the conceptualization of identity, method, and political orientation and the disagreements and conflicts thus generated could be welcomed as necessary to the task. The framework provided by a common interest in Germany, a common set of themes revolving around changing identities, the requirement that three authors together write one chapter, and the dedication of one organizer and editor to pull it all together suggests that it may be above all such "formal" preconditions that determine whether and to what extent interdisciplinary endeavors will bear fruit. That they can bear fruit, and that more such plants should be cultivated, is the lesson this participant takes away from the project.

LIST OF CONTRIBUTORS

Mitchell Ash is a historian of science at the University of Vienna who is interested in German *Gestalt* psychology and the relationship between politics and science.

Volker Berghahn is a historian of Modern Germany at Brown University and has written on many topics, ranging from the imperial navy and militarism to postwar economics and culture.

David P. Conradt is a political scientist at Eastern Carolina University who is known for his overview of German politics and his exploration of public opinion.

Gregory Flynn is a political scientist Georgetown University who analyzes European politics and Western security issues from a comparative perspective.

Geoffrey Giles is a modern German historian at the University of Florida who has written on Nazi students, the history of alcohol and gender questions.

Konrad H. Jarausch is a German historian at the University of North Carolina who is interested in postwar history and has recently written on unification, GDR historiography and Americanization.

Christiane Lemke is a political scientist at Hanover University in Germany and has worked primarily on such topics as the dissolution of the GDR and the survival of socialism.

Sara Lennox is a specialist in comparative literature at the University of Massachusetts with particular interests in the reception of Nietzsche as well as in feminist theory.

Paul Michael Lützeler is a scholar of German literature at Washington University in St. Louis, many of whose works analyze the interplay between literature and politics.

Joyce Mushaben is a political scientist at the University of Missouri at St. Louis with special expertise in East German identity and gender questions.

Jeffrey Peck is a commentator on recent developments in German culture at at Georgetown University who focuses on methodological issues and Jewish life.

Andreas Pickel is a political economist at Western Ontario University in Canada who is interested in the transformation of the East German economy.

Dorothy Rosenberg is a German Studies specialist at Bowdoin College who has worked on women writers in East Germany, particularly from a cultural studies perspective.

Hinrich C. Seeba is a German literature scholar at the University of California at Berkeley whose work extends from eighteenth century drama and to current debates about national identity.

Helga A. Welsh is a political scientist with historical interests at Wake Forest University who has written on East German de-nazification and the problems of post-communist transition.

INDEX